Asia First

Asia First

China and the Making of Modern American Conservatism

JOYCE MAO

The University of Chicago Press

Chicago and London

Joyce Mao is assistant professor of US history at Middlebury College.

The University of Chicago Press, Chicago 60637
The University of Chicago Press, Ltd., London
© 2015 by The University of Chicago
All rights reserved. Published 2015.
Printed in the United States of America

24 23 22 21 20 19 18 17 16 15   1 2 3 4 5

ISBN-13: 978-0-226-25271-1 (cloth)
ISBN-13: 978-0-226-25285-8 (e-book)
DOI: 10.7208/chicago/9780226252858.001.0001

Library of Congress Cataloging-in-Publication Data

Mao, Joyce, author.
 Asia First : China and the making of modern American conservatism / Joyce Mao.
   pages cm
 Includes bibliographical references and index.
   ISBN 978-0-226-25271-1 (cloth : alkaline paper) — ISBN 978-0-226-25285-8 (e-book) —
 1. United States—Foreign economic relations—East Asia. 2. East Asia—Foreign
 economic relations—United States. 3. United States—Relations—China. 4. China—
 Relations—United States. 5. Conservatism—United States—History—20th century.
 I. Title.
   DS518.8.M265 2015
   320.520973—dc23

                    2014037014

♾ This paper meets the requirements of ANSI/NISO Z39.48-1992 (Permanence of
Paper).

Contents

Acknowledgments

Thanks are due to the many individuals and institutions that helped bring this work to fruition. The (very long) period I spent as a student at the University of California, Berkeley, shaped my research, as well as my firm belief in the importance of the public university. While there I had the pleasure of learning from and working with inspiring scholars and teachers. Kerwin Klein deserves special appreciation. His guidance, critique, and enthusiasm were instrumental at every stage. My work also benefitted greatly from the influence of David Hollinger, Colleen Lye, Kathleen Frydl, James Vernon, Mary Ryan, David Henkin, Robin Einhorn, Jennifer Burns, Jason Sokol, Dalia Muller, Camilo Trumper, Jocelyn Garovoy, and the late Jim Kettner.

Librarians and archivists around the country shared their expertise and their time. As usual, Theresa Salazar and Susan Snyder of Berkeley's Bancroft Library were enormously helpful. Staff at the Library of Congress, Hoover Institution Library and Archives, Arizona Historical Foundation, John Hay Library at Brown University, Harry S. Truman Library, Ethnic Studies Library at Berkeley, Huntington Library, and Sterling Library at Yale also provided skilled assistance.

At Middlebury College I have found an extraordinary community of colleagues and friends. The Department of History has provided an ideal home base from which to develop as both a scholar and teacher. I would also like to especially thank those who read early drafts of the project: Maggie Clinton, Rachael Joo, Febe Armanios, Alexis Peri, Max Ward, Sarah Stroup, Holly Allen, and Roberto Lint Sagarena. Ian Barrow, Kathy Morse, Paul Monod, Amy Morsman, Jacob Tropp, Eddie Vazquez, Sepi Alavi, Roger White, Renee Brown, Anna Harlan, Jamie McCallum, Erin Davis, and Amy Yuen each made vital contributions whether they knew it or not, and I am glad of this chance to express how much I continue to appreciate their generosity.

My family deserves a great deal of the credit for this book's existence. Words are not enough to thank my parents, Rosita and Ming, and my sister Grace for a lifetime of encouragement and support. The same holds true for my husband Ben Graves, whose love, patience, and humor have been constants throughout. He and our son Sinjin inspire me every day.

Introduction

Capitol Hill released a collective breath as 1954 drew to a close and marked the end of a particularly dramatic period. For the past four years, Sen. Joseph McCarthy's campaign to unearth communist subversion within the federal government had thrown Washington into an uproar. Now he lay physically as well as politically weakened, in the hospital because of an elbow injury and awaiting Senate censure thanks to the disastrous Army-McCarthy hearings.[1] The day before the vote, *Congressional Report* assessed what would come next for the Republican senator from Wisconsin and the movement he incited. If McCarthyism was to last beyond its namesake, its most important faction was a bellwether group of officials who used McCarthy to advance their interests against the more moderate Eisenhower wing of the GOP. *Congressional Report*'s list of agenda items that identified these "McCarthy senators" included curbing executive power, US withdrawal from the United Nations (UN), and immigration restriction. But at the very top was a shared belief "that America's destiny requires aggressive intervention in the Far Pacific." They were "Asia-firsters."[2]

Indeed, the Republican Party as a whole was historically well positioned to raise awareness of that region. It had a track record of commitment to the Pacific Rim, highlighted by the McKinley administration's declaration of war against Spain in the Philippines, the strategic annexation of Hawaii, and, of course, the notes regarding foreign trade in China penned by Secretary of State John Hay in 1899 and 1900. The idea of the "open door" took on particular cultural significance as Hay's requests became celebrated as firm policy that rescued Chinese sovereignty from further incursions by European and Japanese imperialism. They were nothing of the sort, but that version of events shaped a quasi-paternalistic view of China that lingered for much of the century.[3]

After World War II, GOP conservatives borrowed substantially from that partisan history as they revised their ideology and politics for a new political climate. Far from proving inadaptable, the Republican right staked a heavy investment in global affairs by advocating a foreign policy directly inspired by events in East Asia: It chose China. Insistence that the United States intervene in Asia quickly became a hallmark of conservatism's platform, and rather than contradicting what *Congressional Report* dubbed a "nationalist-isolationist" character, it was accepted as an extension of existing right-wing ideology.[4] Like many other political commentators, *Congressional Report* did not explain how such an interventionist impulse could also be an iteration of prewar isolationism.

This book seeks to unravel that paradox. It traces why postwar conservatives specifically made China a signature foreign policy issue during the early 1950s and how that strategy introduced a unique diplomatic ethos, as well as the imprint Asian affairs continued to make on the conservative crusade until the Reagan era. Simply put, China was an integral part of what made the "New Right" new. A reworking of the Open Door for the Cold War—in this case, promotion of Nationalist China as a particular kind of client state—facilitated the transition into internationalist modernity.

Within the realm of foreign policy, that development immediately added novel dimensions to conservatives' legislative proposals. The demands for unilateralism in foreign affairs, selective military intervention, and strident anticommunism all owed a great deal to overseas conflicts with Asian communism. At home, China inspired new forms of mobilization on the ground, helping to sustain rightwing growth within a changing electorate. Thus armed with an ability to address global challenges, the right could develop into the most enduring political movement of the twentieth century.

On an interpretive level, the story of American conservatism's evolution via the Pacific provides us important insight into US citizens' engagement with the wider world, namely, that internationalism does not always signal progressive politics. A turn to Asia and foreign policy allowed conservatism to claim it could effectively meet the challenges that accompanied the nation's new leadership status. By providing a topical common ground, it also impacted how politicians and activists of different stripes related to one another, resulting in the rightwing cohesion of the 1960s that Rick Perlstein describes as "an army that could lose a battle, suck it up, regroup, then live to fight a thousand battles more."[5]

Innovation of a specifically conservative vision of the United States' relationship with the world, including when and how the nation should intervene overseas, therefore helped make the New Right modern in terms of its makeup and tactics. At the same time, it allowed for a redoubling of emphasis on tenets such as constitutional originalism, small government, and unilateralism in foreign policy, even while the nation assumed unprecedented action abroad. That combination evidenced how internationalization could in many ways reinforce an ideological commitment to traditionalism.

Such an argument admittedly cuts against the established historiographical grain. Literature on the foundations of twentieth-century American internationalism largely concentrates on an explicitly liberal impulse toward overseas intervention: influential works on the transnational Progressive movement, studies of Wilsonian diplomacy, Franklin Roosevelt's victory over isolationism, and the formation of containment policy together demonstrate that predominant focus.[6] However, recent scholarship like Christopher McKnight Nichols's *Promise and Peril* proposes that the scope and variety of American internationalism was much broader; many individuals and groups dubbed retrograde "isolationists" at the time still formulated their beliefs with one eye on global contexts.[7] The project of rethinking what internationalism has historically meant in terms of politics and policy is a vital one, especially as the term continues to evolve in ever-shifting regional, economic, and technological frameworks.

Conservative internationalism's element of unexpectedness was certainly one of the reasons why its emergence represented such a shockwave during the early Cold War. Despite the GOP's earlier interventions in the Pacific, the years immediately preceding the Cold War gave little indication of the strong attachment the Republican right would come to forge with China. In 1937, the so-called special US-China relationship itself appeared in serious jeopardy. Japan's invasion of China imperiled a nation already riven by civil strife between the Nationalist Guomindang government and the Chinese Communist Party (CCP). Roosevelt's troubled second term as president also began that year. In between an ill-received Supreme Court–packing plan and a newly revitalized congressional opposition, the administration devoted scant attention to the Sino-Japanese War. What energy it dedicated to foreign policy proportionally prioritized events in Europe over those in Asia, a pattern that continued through World War II.[8]

Similarly, Republicans were focused more on domestic fights than on diplomatic affairs. Their economic and governmental philosophies faced severe challenges from Roosevelt's leadership of the New Deal. Old political identities were in flux as common understandings of liberalism shifted from laissez-faire governance to an interventionist welfare state. Suddenly, the par-

ty's traditionalist wing was saddled with the undesirable label of "conservative." "If we return to the true and honest meaning of the word liberal then
the Republican Party is and always has been the Liberal Party of the United
States," mourned one disconcerted observer.[9] Factional divisions widened
within the party. Moderates readily adapted and worked with Democrats on
legislation. Meanwhile, conservatives accused such "me-too" Republicans of
compromising what the party stood for; they struggled to control the party's
message and concede as little as possible to liberal consensus.[10] Overseas intervention, let alone in China, was far off the agenda.

Even as the Cold War began to crystallize, Republicans as a whole
struggled to identify weaknesses in a foreign policy dominated by Democrats.
The public generally gave Roosevelt credit for defeating the fascist enemy in
World War II, and he had worked assiduously to make that effort bipartisan.
The wartime coalition continued to dominate the framing of international
affairs well after 1945.[11] Pres. Harry Truman's deliberate inclusion of Sen.
Arthur Vandenberg (R-MI) in major diplomatic events preempted partisan
complaints. The involvement of Vandenberg, a nationally known conservative
and former isolationist, in the UN and the Senate Foreign Relations Committee gave the impression that politics stopped at the water's edge.[12]

Conservatives could count a few moments of success, though none of
them suggested future dominance. The 1946 elections retained key rightwing
officials and yielded the first GOP congressional majority since 1930.[13] Subsequent legislation, like the Taft-Hartley Act of 1947, showed the right could
wield influence over major national issues.[14] Still, growth was hardly ensured,
and liberal critics were quick to point out the imbalance that plagued conservative ideology. In *The Vital Center* (1949), Arthur Schlesinger Jr., scathingly
denounced conservatism's plutocratic tendencies and impulse to preserve the
free market at all costs. "Terrified of change, lacking confidence and resolution, subject to spasms of panic and hysteria," the right could not adapt to the
exigencies of modern American life, let alone "work steadily for the national
interest, *at home or abroad.*"[15] It did not help that figures like Col. Robert
McCormick, owner and publisher of the *Chicago Tribune*, still saw foreign
relations as a regional issue: "[T]he eastern internationalists really look upon
themselves as English Tories and are inflamed with an energy not understood
by an indifferent rest of the country."[16]

American conservatism's inability to respond to the demands of a new
global era was painfully obvious and a major liability. The urgency of the
Cold War required officials and grassroots leaders alike to permanently dis-
pel an isolationist reputation by making world affairs a cornerstone of their
agendas. "[W]e need to note that the war altered our whole attitude toward

foreign relations," said radio host George Sokolsky, "World War II made a complete change."[17] Their emphasis on traditional small government had to be tempered by a proactive foreign policy that addressed the global scope of the struggle against communism. Only then would conservatives be able to modernize their platform to the new postwar era and, in the process, regain an upper hand in the intraparty power struggle. Political survival depended on the development of an internationalist ethos that looked well beyond the spirit of the Monroe Doctrine. The Cold War demanded it. Voters expected it.

While the objective at hand was clear, the path toward achieving it was anything but. The presumption of bipartisan consensus in diplomatic affairs was maddening to those who felt they had little more than token input in Cold War strategy. The internationalist vision that underscored containment policy made them uneasy as it exponentially increased the number and variety of the nation's commitments overseas and created what conservatives deemed a gross expansion of federal bureaucracy.[18] "Liberal containment" granted the president unprecedented powers at home and abroad while infringing on the powers of the other branches—notably the Senate, where the GOP right held a stronghold. In a time when the boundaries of formal warfare were blurred, conservatives held fast to the belief that Congress remained duty-bound to protect the Constitution and its own prerogatives.[19]

Events in China at the end of the 1940s could not have come at a better time for leaders on the right who sought to create a conservative alternative to containment. Mao Zedong's victory and Chiang Kai-shek's exile to Taiwan were of course deeply concerning, but they also provided ammunition to critically assess liberal policies. Geography was a major factor, for the successes of the Marshall Plan and the Berlin airlift made disapproval of European construction daunting, not to mention politically hazardous. Truman had also been savvy with Japan. His appointment of Gen. Douglas MacArthur, one of the right's darlings, as head of Supreme Command of Allied Powers (SCAP) quashed grumblings about the direction and cost of the US-led occupation, or at least postponed them until later in the Cold War. China was the major exception to the rule of bipartisanship in foreign relations, thanks to Vandenberg's nonparticipation in East Asia policy. The GOP could accurately assert that it was not culpable for any missteps in China, which Vandenberg described in 1947 as a "vast and friendly republic, rich in wisdom, equally rich in democratic promises for tomorrow, and historically fixed in the orbit of our good will."[20] Just two years later he was looking for "any remote basis for salvaging Formosa [Taiwan]."[21]

Given such contexts, conservatives began to capitalize on criticism of

China policy that had steadily intensified since the Yalta conference, the Marshall Mission, and the release of the Wedemeyer Report. Their two-part argument offered intertwined contentions about domestic and international affairs. First, instead of actively opposing communism or rolling it back, containment actualized geopolitical fears of Soviet expansion. China was proof of the policy's ineffectualness. Second, liberalism itself was to blame, for unchecked federal growth meant a degenerative state apparatus that recommended faulty courses of action, such as a joint Guomindang-CCP government. The timing was therefore ripe for conservatives to make more extreme allegations about internal subversion, as Eric Goldman observed shortly after the political fallout.[22]

Beyond the immediacy of the communist revolution, China's cultural cache in the United States meant that it was a sustainable vehicle for conservative internationalism. Past perfect allegations that American mistakes had caused China's fall resonated with an existing sentiment that the latter was the United States' to "lose" in the first place—not in the colonial sense, but as a democratic and spiritual ally. Because it valorized the Open Door and ideas of American exceptionalism, a China receptive to Christianity and capitalism held wide appeal, and the immoveable existence of the People's Republic of China (PRC) ensured the issue would not quickly fade. By continuing to extoll the possibilities of a Free China aligned with the West, conservatives could show they had global concerns and simultaneously characterize opponents' Asia policy as an immoral betrayal of traditional ideals and interests.

The "Asia First" approach they developed during the 1950s was deceptively simple. Its proponents demanded that US foreign policy give the Pacific equal or more attention than the European Atlantic. Although their strategy appeared one-dimensional, its implications were potentially long lasting and expansive. On the diplomatic front, the spread of communism in Asia offered the Republican right a geopolitical issue to mark as its own, in contrast to liberal initiatives in European affairs. At home, conservative politicians' focus on the Pacific could better their fortunes among an electorate that was shifting due to the growth of Sunbelt states and the advent of the Cold War. Lisa McGirr's and Kurt Schuparra's respective studies of the Western conservative movement discuss how, in a reflection of this trend, a new wave of Republican officials from the Far West (among them Sen. William F. Knowland of California, Sen. Barry Goldwater of Arizona, and Gov. Ronald Reagan of California) became conservatism's rising stars.[23] The timing of Asia First's origins—after the conclusion of the civil war in China and just before a major election cycle—made a first impression that was difficult to shake. Detractors dismissed this new facet of conservatism as merely a ploy to inflict damage on Democratic policies.

Indeed, much has been written about the controversy that ensued after 1949. The "Who lost China?" melee was one of the most divisive episodes in twentieth-century American politics. The subsequent emergence of McCarthyism and the tragedy of the Foreign Service's China hands have received a great deal of scholarly attention, as has analysis of the implications for US Asia policy into the Vietnam War era.[24] However, the incendiary rhetoric used in conservatism's discussion of East Asia policy clouded analysis, both the analysis of people in the moment and historical analysis by later scholars, of what China actually meant for the right's political and ideological development. Historians have consequently acknowledged the connection between the Nationalist government and Cold War conservatives but tend to focus on the extremism of McCarthyism or other reactionary aspects of that bond.[25]

Although red-baiting was initially a significant element of Asia First, the China issue was more than just a red herring to critique the political opposition and containment. Throughout the 1950s, conservatives fought a two-fronted battle with moderate Republicans in addition to liberal Democrats. They needed to win control of their own party before they could claim a return to national prominence, let alone effectively challenge those on the other side of the aisle. Reframing the political story to include the GOP right's intraparty struggles—debates over constitutional balance of power and foreign policy during the Eisenhower administration, for example—accounts for the legislative impacts of the right's turn to the Pacific, as well as the long-term orientalism that colored conservative political culture.

One must also consider Asia First's longevity well past the Truman years. China engaged vital ideological and regional dimensions of the Cold War right, resulting in a durable internationalism that fundamentally reshaped the way conservatives viewed the United States' role in the world and how its government should respond to global threats. A series of conflicts through the 1950s, including the Korean War and multiple crises in the Taiwan Strait, fueled debates over fundamental issues such as executive power, growth of the defense state, and the efficacy of collective security. During that time, Congress was used as a base for a legislative approach to anticommunist internationalism while strife in the Pacific consistently provided popular incentive for foreign policy change. Those events provided Asia Firsters motivation and opportunity well after the ideal of a democratic Chinese mainland vanished and a Republican administration was in power, indicating their objectives ran deeper than partisanship alone.

It is also important to note that American conservatives' adoption of China as a foreign policy issue was never just about that one country, or even the Pacific as a whole. On the contrary, the Soviet Union was the ultimate target. However, the importance of anticommunism on mainland Asia also had to be recognized for its own sake. Sen. Knowland (R-CA) once complained that conservatives were unfairly accused of fixating only on China. Communism was "a global menace, and it would do no good to close the door in Europe and leave the door wide open in Asia." Therefore an Asia First position was not some shallow posture—it was a way to combat Moscow in a region where past US policy allegedly lacked vigor.[26]

A number of developments happening within the postwar right supported such a claim. Conservatives could draw upon a record of American opposition to the Soviet Union and socialism that extended back to the Bolshevik Revolution. Organic anticommunism was complemented by a renewal already underway in rightwing intellectual circles.[27] European émigrés who had experienced the aftereffects of totalitarianism were injecting new life into conservative thought. Austrian economists Ludwig von Mises and Friedrich Hayek, along with Russian-born novelist Ayn Rand, attracted legions of American admirers with their antisocialist, anti-Soviet teachings.[28] Additionally, thanks to the purging of the State Department's China experts, much of Washington inaccurately understood Mao as the Kremlin's puppet rather than its strategic ally. Although some policymakers had a better understanding of China's ideological and geopolitical autonomy, a public that saw only a "loss" to the Soviets prevented them from speaking out.[29] Conservatives subsequently interpreted active revision of US China policy as a way to fight the larger Cold War and liberal containment simultaneously.

Throughout these pages I use "Asia Firsters" to designate American conservatives who supported an anticommunist, "Free" China. The more commonly employed term "China Lobby" encompasses a wider body of figures, many of who were more moderate in their overall political inclinations.[30] Key Asia Firsters (i.e., William Knowland, Styles Bridges, and Kenneth Wherry) have previously been identified as members of the China Lobby, while others (Robert A. Taft, for instance) have had their associations with China gone virtually unrecognized. Their personal opinions about Chiang Kai-shek varied greatly, but they all looked to China as a way to drive conservatism forward—a motivation not universal among the usual China Lobby suspects. A diversity of private sector figures also comprised a major portion of Asia Firsters. These activists latched onto the GOP's right wing as the best hope for Free China and linked it to their search for a safeguard against an overbearing and wasteful government bureaucracy they believed infected by communism.[31] Institutional elites and grassroots leaders alike cherished hopes for

China, and the unity they forged there continued to inform conservatism's vitality and future development.

Because this book explores the history of an idea—the idea of China used by Cold War conservatives who sought to define the United States' global responsibilities—it necessarily draws from the pathbreaking text *Orientalism* (1978) by Edward Said. While his immediate subject was European colonialism in the Middle East during the nineteenth century, Said's theory of imperialism and cultural representation offers an interpretive model that transcends topographical and chronological boundaries. Because of his work, the idea of an orientalism specific to the United States has become increasingly familiar, and many scholars have recently used the framework of orientalism to analyze the American experience.[32]

As Said readily acknowledged, the United States' rendition of orientalism was distinct from imperial conceptions of the Middle East. Geographically it was "much more likely to be associated very differently with the Far East (China and Japan)."[33] Certainly, China had occupied the consciousness of a wide variety of Americans, from missionaries to labor leaders to politicians, for well over two hundred years by the time the Cold War began.[34]

There were fundamental ideological differences between European and American orientalisms as well. Both were similarly invested in power and capital, but the latter fashioned itself as an explicitly *anti*colonial project. As a result China was more often than not treated as a subjective reflection of the American condition itself: if the Middle Kingdom was doing well, it was due in large part to the intervention of a healthy, democratic US republic. "Most Americans may never have seen an Asian, much less visited Asia, but they had an image of Asia because they had an image of America," historian Akira Iriye explains.[35] Or as Kenneth Wherry, then mayor of Pawnee City, Nebraska, declared, "With God's help, we will lift Shanghai up and up, ever up, until it is just like Kansas City."[36]

The open door that supposedly enabled America to spread its benevolent influence at the dawn of the twentieth century was reimagined decades later as a way to halt Soviet expansion. Individuals and parties across the political spectrum invoked a special relationship with Asia in order to promote their respective plans for intervention. Robeson Taj P. Frazier has recently analyzed how African American activists sought to build bridges between the civil rights and black power movements and the PRC.[37] Christina Klein's *Cold War Orientalism* shows how mass culture's sentimental depiction of Asian countries helped US citizens to understand, and participate in, their own nation's identity as a progressive, anti-imperial power.[38] Similarly, in *China and the*

American Dream, Richard Madsen discusses liberals' idealizations of China during the Cultural Revolution. To those on the left, there were multiple versions of what China symbolized—from "troubled modernizer" to "revolutionary redeemer"—simply because there were so many different versions of America itself: "Like all the stories we use to understand our national identity and purpose, the central American story about China . . . was as much about America as about China; it construed American relations with China in terms of common understanding of the core values of American society."[39]

Those words could easily be used to describe the perspectives of individuals further on the right. Coverage by pro-Nationalist mass media outlets like Henry Luce's popular *Time* and *Life* magazines meant the Open Door retained a saliency that made its 1949 "loss" all the more acute.[40] Cold War conservatives likewise tapped into the long-standing and widely held idea of a relationship that cast China as an extension of American democratic empire and Chinese sovereignty as dependent on action by the United States and its citizens. Historical memory, however inaccurate, meant that Asia First gained traction among many who viewed the United States responsible for China's fate.

And yet traditionalism alone was not enough to facilitate conservatism's break from an isolationist reputation, let alone underwrite a serious foreign policy agenda. A large part of Asia First's efficacy stemmed from how it tempered the old with the new. By default, the doctrine demanded standing overseas action, which was in and of itself a new impulse for the right. While younger postwar conservatives were eager to shape diplomatic debates, a still-powerful old guard was less organically inclined (or less equipped) to do so. By drawing on the notion of the United States as guardian of China, Asia First cloaked a novel form of internationalism with the veneer of nostalgic tradition, making the reconciliation between permanent interventionism and existing conservative ideology an easier task. The right's dedication to saving China from communism appeared natural and justified by custom. Subsequently, politicians once deemed isolationist could become Cold Warriors, and Pacific intervention could be considered to be an extension of the right's platform. The combination of political need and nostalgia meant those developments would endure even after conservative internationalism failed to actually change US policy in East Asia.

Given that the changes Asia First wrought were primarily limited to the domestic sphere, it would be easy to pigeonhole the doctrine as a one-sided construction. However, the notion of Free China as a democratic counterpart was hardly an idealized abstraction created solely by the West. At least in its early phases, it was very much a joint product of the GOP right and the Guo-mindang. Both actively constructed an ideal of Chinese-American friendship; both used each other to propose policy change or retention, whichever would best promote their respective interests. Just as the timing of the Nationalist crisis kick-started the right's search for a foreign policy signature, Chiang hoped to find an audience that would translate into US aid and protection. The collaborative nature of Asia First's vision for China therefore challenges previous understandings about the parameters of American orientalism.

Given such contexts, the Guomindang's agency in that partnership bears thinking about. Chiang and his representatives, including his wife Soong Mei-ling, had a long history of seeking out American influencers (of any political persuasion) to strengthen the Nationalist claim to power via partnership with the United States. The results were decidedly mixed. During the war with Japan, Chiang outlined what would become a familiar refrain for his govern-ment: China was willing to fight its enemies alone; it needed only guns and money "to undertake single-handed the task of putting down this enemy of all who would dwell in peace on the shores of the Pacific." It was framed as the affordable option, an appeal for American ammunition and money, not American lives.[41] To battle their common enemy, he offered the US "all we are and all we have."[42] Roosevelt reciprocated with florid language and diplomatic gestures such as Chiang's inclusion at the Cairo Conference as a member of the "Big Four" and the symbolic repeal of the Chinese Exclusion Act in 1943.[43] However, the president proved less than willing to materially underwrite a regime dogged by reports of corruption and misappropriation.[44] Much to Chiang's disappointment and chagrin, China remained what War-ren I. Cohen has described as a "second-class" ally.[45]

Although resumption of civil war resulted in a disastrous outcome for the Guomindang in China, the Cold War in Asia stabilized US policy in its favor and dramatically improved Chiang's political fortunes among an American audience. His credentials as an ally against the Japanese and as an anticom-munist helped to alleviate lingering misgivings about a militaristic regime that bore scant resemblance to American-style democracy.[46] In 1953 John Fos-ter Dulles, then secretary of state, mused that Chiang was not a leader that the United States would support under normal conditions, "but in times like these, in the unrest of the world today . . . we know we cannot make a transi-tion without losing control of the whole situation."[47] The Taiwanese govern-ment was also quick to exploit the dearth of firsthand American knowledge about the PRC. Guomindang envoys eagerly offered to fill the epistemic void during state visits, in mass media, and via private meetings with the regime's supporters. They sought to secure aid for their government by crafting an image of Taiwan that balanced self-sufficiency with a reliance on American aid—a mix that resonated with cultural memory of the Open Door.

However, while the scope of Asia First was international, it was most impactful in kick-starting the *domestic* change that allowed its proponents increased opportunity to influence foreign relations and the defense state. That meant winning elections and policy battles. For example, the Guomindang's offer of "all they were" continued to appeal well after communist expansion replaced the threat of Japanese imperialism, but the Republican right could use it to critique "garrison" programs like Universal Military Training. The eagerness of the Nationalists to fight their own battle with Chinese Communism—albeit with American weapons and logistical help—dovetailed well with conservatives' concerns at home.[48] The repeated demand for Chiang to be "unleashed" to exercise his anticommunist expertise in military operations became a common refrain because Asia Firsters traded on the assumption that his plight continued to exemplify liberalism's supposed failings, not because all of them wholeheartedly trusted his ability.

The story of one political faction's relationship with a single foreign country may appear narrow at first glance, but as the following five chapters show, the case of American conservatism and China upends that assumption. Asia First dovetailed with major postwar events from westward migration to McCarthyism to the Vietnam War, and its iterations within the right alone were almost as numerous and varied.

Chapter 1, "Up from Isolationism," owes its title to *Up from Liberalism*, William F. Buckley Jr.'s 1959 critique of consensus politics. Liberalism and isolationism were two obstacles for conservatives to overcome, which were strongly connected given Democratic authority in foreign affairs. During a transition period from 1945 through the Korean War, leaders of the "old" right began to see the rapidly disintegrating situation in East Asia as a political opportunity. Both exemplified and led by Sen. Robert Taft, they were awakened to the possibilities of foreign policy by the events of 1949. However, the shift to internationalism, or even personal support of Chiang Kai-shek, was hardly straightforward. As conservative elites began to explore the benefits of an Asia First stance, private citizens and organizations were already rallying to aid the Guomindang however they could. Those efforts are the subject of chapter 2, which argues that the so-called China Lobby is best understood by the manner in which it turned nostalgic orientalism into a template for action that right-wing activists emulated well into the 1960s. Its strengths lay in an informality and ability to work outside of government to mobilize grassroots conservatism. These simultaneous intra- and extrastate developments illustrated Free China's wide political appeal, as well as the ways in which it drew together different types of conservatives who otherwise would have had more difficulty finding common ground.

The elections of 1952 ushered in a Republican White House and a GOP majority in the Senate thanks in large part to Asia First. A new generation of politicians, many from the West Coast and Sunbelt region, signaled conservatism's revitalization. Focusing on US-China-Taiwan relations during the early and mid-1950s, chapter 3 traces how conservative officials parlayed ongoing turmoil in the Pacific into practical legislative proposals. During Knowland's tenure as Senate Majority Leader, they addressed larger questions regarding executive overreach, collective peacekeeping, and preservation of constitutional principles vis-à-vis active global interventionism. Even if recovery of the mainland was impossible, those legislative firefights were proxy battles seeking to redress past foreign policy, and they extended China's political relevance well beyond the subject of Guomindang restoration. Outside Washington, Asia First activists also ensured China's longevity as a political issue; chapter 4 takes the John Birch Society (JBS) as a case study. Established in 1958, the JBS became one of the largest, and most controversial, grassroots groups in the nation. This section outlines the centrality of Asia to the organization's founding and anticommunist belief system, demonstrating the inherent internationalism its many members came to embrace. As an educational cautionary tale and emotional motivator, China was shorthand for how the politics of moderation had failed the United States.

Finally, chapter 5 turns to the immediate and long-term legacies of Asia First. One of the major triumphs of postwar conservatism was Sen. Barry Goldwater's capture of the 1964 GOP presidential nomination, a moment that could not have happened without the energy and right-wing unity that China helped to inspire. Goldwater's Vietnam policy distinctly recalled Asia First positions on military intervention, the UN, and defense state growth first cultivated during the Korean War. Goldwater was in fact a firm supporter of Chiang and Taiwan. However, after Richard Nixon announced his visit to Beijing in 1971, the senator and other conservative leaders arrived at their own surprising version of realpolitik. Asia First was a conservative principle, but it, like conservatism itself, allowed for flexibility and doctrinal change.

The mixture of institutional politicians and grassroots activists shows how internationalism, via China, impacted a wide range of conservatives at a critical moment in the early Cold War. Figures like Taft, Knowland, and Goldwater were party leaders who wielded lasting influence within the conservative movement and the GOP, while grassroots personages like Kohlberg and Welch were no less important as they led private-sector efforts that urged citizens to consider international affairs part of their everyday lives. A collective examination of these individuals and groups demonstrates how the challenge of communism in Asia helped to spur conservatism's development from the top down as well as the bottom up. By giving discrete factions common cause in a new era of international engagement, China contributed greatly to the postwar right's eventual transformation from political underdog into ideological and electoral powerhouse.

The global roles that citizens historically envision for their country tell us as much about domestic hopes and fears as they do foreign policy—perhaps even more. At a time when US superpower seemed less than absolutely certain, conservatives forged a relationship with China as a proactive response to communist expansion. Asia First literally and figuratively broadened conservatism's scope. With the Cold War political landscape thus reshaped, the stage was set for the emergence of a modern, thoroughly internationalized, American right.

Up from Isolationism: The Conservative Dilemma and the Chinese Solution

In the spring of 1946, as American wartime optimism began to turn into post-war anxiety, an unusual petition appeared in major newspapers and periodicals. The "Manchurian Manifesto" claimed the United States owed a special debt to China because the latter was "the victim both of our long appeasement of Japan and of our unpreparedness": The agreements reached at the Yalta conference the previous year—made "behind China's back"—granted USSR troops access to the province of Manchuria during the final weeks of the war. Now the Soviet army was giving Mao's Communists a vital advantage in the Chinese civil war and the United States should "insist on the strict observance of promises made to China." Defenders would say that Yalta negotiations took place before the certainty of the atomic bomb, and Franklin Roosevelt had sought to bring the Soviet Union into the war against Japan in the spirit of realpolitik diplomacy.[1] On the other hand, postwar critics charged that the Yalta agreement seriously compromised the moral leadership of the United States and imperiled the Open Door tradition of special friendship between the United States and China.

Drawn up by the American China Policy Association, the manifesto blamed Americans, not Joseph Stalin, for China's "betrayal" at Yalta. The corresponding argument that the United States was responsible for China's post-war destiny made it a classic example of American orientalism. Meanwhile, the far-reaching appeal of such paternalism was reflected by the variety of public figures endorsing the manifesto's claims. Numbering sixty-two in all, they ranged from *Time-Life* magnate Henry Luce and Congressman Walter Judd (R-MN) to the socialist Norman Thomas and American Federation of Labor president William Green to publisher Alfred A. Knopf and Mrs. Wendell Willkie. The names of well-known Chiang Kai-shek supporters, such as

Judd (a former medical missionary in China) and Luce (a son of China missionaries), were unsurprising, but the petition was not intended only for the eyes of the converted. It beseeched all Americans to rectify the wrong against a wartime ally: "Will the American people, at the strongest moment in their history, accept a Russian policy in Asia which we rejected in the case of Germany and Japan even when we were weak?" Anybody, whether a public figure or private citizen, had the power to change the course that had been set at Yalta.[2]

As the Manchurian Manifesto showed, disapproval of recent US China policy could be heard across the political spectrum. However, by 1950, the most vocal and organized critics came from the GOP right. Their efforts would pay off as "conservative foreign policy" ceased to be considered an oxymoron. Before World War II, few of them showed concern for global diplomacy, let alone a country with which the United States shared virtually no trade and a relatively slender ethnic heritage. The mainstream of American conservative ideology dictated that federal power should limit its concerns to national affairs.[3] Conservatives of the old guard recognized a fundamental shift had occurred after Pearl Harbor, but they had difficulty adjusting to the nation's new interventionism; as a result, a presumption that isolationism was a major tenet of rightwing thought lingered beyond the start of the Cold War.[4]

Sen. Robert A. Taft of Ohio, nicknamed "Mr. Republican," embodied that old guard. The son of former president William Howard Taft, he was a well-respected public figure even if he did not possess the most sparkling personality. H. L. Mencken once observed, "Taft is a pleasant enough fellow of very agreeable manners and gabbing with him was pleasant enough, but he certainly failed to inflame me with any conviction that he was a man of destiny."[5] What Mencken deemed to be a deficiency, many other Americans considered to be comforting and honest. Shortly after being elected to the US Senate in 1938, Taft gained a devoted national following, his supporters heralding him as the highest example of integrity and reason.[6] "I look at that man and I see everything which my father taught me to hold good," affirmed one Idaho matron.[7]

To supporters and critics alike, Taft's reputation rested with his positions on national issues like the New Deal and labor. Foreign policy was not his natural forte, and his negative positions on postwar issues like the North Atlantic Treaty Organization (NATO) solidified impressions that he was a strict isolationist. However, even before 1941, Taft did come to recognize that literal adherence to the Monroe Doctrine was hardly an appropriate, or practicable, response to the United States' growing place in the world.

The juxtaposition between widely held presumptions and a subtler, personal evolution has led to widely varying interpretations of Taft's place within the history of US foreign policy. Eric Goldman's sweeping narrative of the immediate postwar period, *The Crucial Decade* (1956), zeroed in on the senator as the unquestioned leader of the Republican right ("Taftites"), a faction that awkwardly grappled with foreign affairs at the beginning of the Cold War. In his account, Taft was a politician beset by circumstance, a man who had but little choice other than to change, however unwilling.[8] Conservative historian Russell Kirk and coauthor James McClellan painted a more proactive portrait in their 1967 biography. They credited Taft's desire to protect American institutions from actions taken in the name of "an amorphous international 'democracy'" and framed it within global contexts.[9] Their narrative ardently defended Taft against charges of irregularity on foreign policy, arguing that his shifting stances were no more inconsistent than those of Franklin Roosevelt, Harry Truman, or Dean Acheson. Change was not a symptom of an isolationist turned diplomatic dilettante, but, rather, a sign of flexible adaptability.[10]

More recently, scholars interested in alternative forms of internationalism have cited Taft as a significant example of how conservatives engaged with foreign policy as the nation stood on the brink of World War II. Christopher Nichols describes how during the 1930s, the senator adhered to a platform of "internationally engaged isolationist principles," including domestic reform, peaceful international engagement, and avoidance of foreign treaties and intervention in wars—a philosophy shared by public figures on both the right and the left. In his extensive study on Taft and foreign policy, Clarence Wunderlin traces how the senator's worldview attempted to balance domestic traditionalism with the demands of global circumstances: Taft had a "great reverence" for international law, a trait he inherited from his father. That respect led him to practice a conservative internationalism that supported certain forms of collective security and arbitration, even as it retained a distinct antistatism and was wielded as a political weapon.[11]

Taft has received a good amount of academic attention lately, but for much of the time he was the GOP right's standard-bearer, the finer points of early conservative internationalism were overlooked. Before Pearl Harbor, while Americans weighed the prospect of whether their government would openly abandon its neutrality, conservatives bore the label of outright isolationism since declaration of war was widely considered to be the only path to overseas engagement. Similarly, after 1945, Democrats' dominance of the diplomatic sphere meant liberal containment was the most obvious form of long-term intervention while challenges to its grand strategy were dismissed as neither grand nor strategic.

Outmanned and in the political minority as the Cold War took shape, conservatives could either play tightly defined roles in foreign policy (as Sen. Arthur Vandenberg did) or take exploratory steps on their own. Taft's outspoken criticism of the Nuremberg trials showed that his views complicated widely accepted definitions of isolationism. He argued that the trials were "instruments of government policy, determined months before" rather than instruments of justice; the United States' participation in what seemed a predetermined verdict via ex post facto laws was an affront to bedrock constitutional principles.[12] It was a highly unpopular view that made Taft a target of backlash from the press and colleagues. Nevertheless, the argument that the United States' tolerance for proceedings like Nuremberg was dangerous, especially in parallel with the nation's new leadership status, resonated within key circles. Corroboration from legal experts like Robert G. Neumann and Justice William O. Douglas later provided mitigating vindication, as did a laudatory portrait by John F. Kennedy in *Profiles in Courage* (1955).[13] While not enough to sway either public perception or a radical overhaul of conservative ideology, Taft's position as well as the support it received represented a small but important measure of early revision.

Profound change toward an original internationalism within the entire Republican right was bolstered when senior leaders like Taft adopted an Asia First position in the wake of the Chinese Communist Revolution. This chapter pursues a rather different portrayal than John Paton Davies's recollection of Taft as "an influential conservative who otherwise displayed slight interest in East Asia."[14] Using the senator as a vantage point, it examines conservatives' turn to China during the earliest years of the Cold War.

Because he ran for both the White House and the Senate after 1945, Taft's personal transition occurred in uniquely plain view. The press scrutinized his positions, and certainly he reflected important shifts within conservative thought. As *U.S. News & World Report* explained, "Some Republicans stand to his left. Quite a few are to his right. But, on most issues, the Ohio Senator is so close to the middle that when Republicans try to find a compromise they move into the position he has held all the time."[15] Neither on the cutting edge nor obstinately immoveable, he was a barometer, while his status and leadership in the GOP Congress (which also included high-ranking former isolationists like Sen. Styles Bridges of New Hampshire, Sen. Kenneth Wherry of Nebraska, Rep. Joseph Martin Jr. of Massachusetts, and Sen. Homer Capeheart of Indiana) helped legitimize conservatism's approach to foreign relations during the late 1940s.

Although that group of Republican conservatives may have been relative novices in the field of foreign policy, they did not consider their own brand of internationalism simply as a political tool. Their overarching goal was to project a specific vision of US superpower to the world, one that emphasized preservation of American unilateralism in international affairs, a strong military defense state, and a commitment to winning the conflict with global communism as quickly as possible. The story of how events in East Asia merged with postwar conservatism's foreign and domestic concerns was one of the most significant subtexts of postwar national politics. Conservative internationalism did not emerge easily, but its development was imperative as the pace of the Cold War accelerated.

A Quickening

The escalation of civil war in China meant a rapid deterioration of American interests in mainland Asia after 1945. Despite the country's Allied status and the Guomindang's openness toward the West, forging a course of action ranked among the most difficult of challenges facing US policymakers. The outcome of the Marshall Mission (1946), resumption of armed conflict between the Communists and the Nationalists (1946–47), and charges of pervasive corruption within Chiang's regime obfuscated any clear or speedy solution. At the same time, those events provided early opportunities for Republican conservatives to voice misgivings about the direction of America's Cold War policy.

George Marshall's mission to China was a case in point. Its purpose was to broker a working agreement between the Chinese Communist Party (CCP) and the Guomindang. Critics of the administration interpreted the secretary of state's objective as misguided at best; at worst, it tolerated communist expansion. In any case, the mission was virtually impossible to achieve given the circumstances, and Marshall failed to bring about a resolution.[16] Frustrated, he returned to the United States from Nanjing in January 1947, highlighting American ineffectualness in China. After the forcefulness of the Truman Doctrine and Marshall Plan later in the year, conservative hardliners could increasingly argue that Democrats prioritized Europe and the Mediterranean while neglecting mainland Asia. China was not even the first priority in East Asia, considering the weight thrown behind Japanese occupation. Criticism implicated the federal state as well: The goal of brokering peace between the Guomindang and the CCP led to allegations that a "Red cell" of China experts within the State Department had sabotaged US policy by advocating a coalition government in the first place.[17]

However, concerns regarding Chiang's efficacy lingered as rumors of his regime's oppressive tactics traveled across the Pacific, making mass aid to the

Guomindang a complicated option. One letter to Taft from Chinese nationals included an enclosure addressed to Chiang: "You must know that the country is paralyzed from your twenty years of political tutelage. You have trained many political slaves, whose political philosophy is dictatorship."[18] Contrary to the positive public image Chiang supporters promoted in the United States, even ex-isolationists were aware that the Guomindang regime was deeply flawed with questionable popularity among the Chinese. Some conservatives made statements about Chiang that echoed doubts long harbored by liberal internationalists.[19] One of Taft's close advisors even agreed with Owen Lattimore, describing the Guomindang as "feudalistic" and unable to understand American-style capitalism. As late as 1946, the senator himself characterized China as a "dictatorship."[20]

Once the Cold War crystallized, whether or not to support Chiang was a question answered in Manichean terms: Mao was a Communist, and Chiang was not. Therefore, Chiang should receive support from the United States. It was a message that met with general approval in the lead-up to the 1948 election. The lack of a definitive policy from the incumbent administration meant Truman faced harsh criticism on China from Republican opponents. Both GOP candidates—the conservative Taft and the moderate Gov. Thomas Dewey of New York—targeted Asia as a weak point.[21]

The Republican emphasis on China did not go unnoticed. In February, journalist Lowell Mellett classified criticism of China policy as a united, partisan attack. While he saw no real difference between Dewey's and Taft's motivations, he did note a significant change in the latter's position on overseas intervention: "Mr. Taft hasn't named his figure, but he doesn't seem as economy-minded toward China as he is toward Europe." His was an aggressive position intended "to show that the administration isn't tough enough in its attitude toward Communism."[22]

Taft was indeed busy revamping his stance on foreign relations. At an appearance in Detroit early in the year, he characterized bipartisan foreign policy as a failure that "resulted from the character of the New Deal administration."[23] He went on to give a (somewhat reserved) endorsement of Chiang: "[H]e is today, regardless of his faults, the only hope to prevent the spread of Communism in China.[24] The Republican tradition of the Open Door and his own belief that the United States should be concerned with Asia first provided stronger motivation: "I believe very strongly that the Far East is ultimately even more important to our future peace and safety than is Europe. We should at least be as much concerned about the advance of Communism to the shores of the Pacific . . . as we are to its possible advance to the shores of the Atlantic."[25]

At that point, China was just a means to a diversified platform, not a moral or emotional issue for Taft. One indicator was his lack of faith in the Chinese people themselves. He classified the country as "ready to accept dictatorship" and "likely to acquiesce." He trusted the United States' capability to prevent catastrophe, not China's resistance to Communism. Far from entrenched in ideology, his criticism of Asia policy was mercenary, designed to keep up with Dewey and more established internationalists.

Of course 1948 was not to be for either conservatives or the GOP as a whole. Taft lost the nomination to Dewey, who in turn lost to Truman in stunning fashion.[26] Shortly after November, GOP moderates took the opportunity to air their grievances about conservative control of the party. Sen. Irving M. Ives (R-NY) stated that, even if Taft was not a reactionary, he had become a symbol of reaction, to the detriment of the entire party.[27]

Despite the turmoil, conservative internationalism had taken important first steps during Taft's campaign. Just one year later, events in China would afford the GOP right ample opportunity to label liberal containment as a weak foundation for American diplomacy. Furthermore, the presumption of internal subversion of US China policy aligned with conservatives' arguments that a large bureaucratic federal state facilitated the weakening of democratic interests both at home and abroad. The conclusion of the Chinese Revolution represented a point of no return in more ways than one.

Year of the Ox

1949 opened with the capture of Beijing on January 23 and unfolded with Communist troops gaining control of other major cities. By June, Mao was established enough to declare his willingness to open diplomatic relations with any country that showed respect for the new Communist state. In early August, the US State Department preempted Chiang's imminent defeat and released a 1,054-page white paper specifying all the ways in which the Truman administration could not be held responsible for the fall of the Guomindang government.

The escalation of events in East Asia was a potential goldmine for Republicans. As John Davies described it, the "violent transformation of China" was incredibly distressing to an American people that had come to equate the Red Chinese with the Red Russians.[28] Any posture of bipartisanship regarding China disintegrated in the face of such upheaval. The exclusion of Vandenberg from Asian affairs allowed all Republicans to claim that a GOP executive would never have failed as badly in China. Even he, the face of bipartisanship in foreign affairs, began to wonder if continued GOP cooperation would mean "more Chinas and more Hisses and more Russian bombs hanging over us."[29] "It would be absurd to expect the opposition to share the responsibility for the Administration's dismal record in China," wrote former Henry P. Fletcher, undersecretary of state, in the conservative journal *Human Events*.[30] Joseph Martin called the white paper "a confession of inexcusable failure" and stated Republicans had no choice but to pursue the China issue alone.[31]

Still, the realistic future of American China policy remained unresolved because accurate information was hard to come by. GOP leaders who sought a practicable response, like Vandenberg and Rep. H. Alexander Smith (R-NJ), were limited by a lack of firsthand knowledge. A member of the Foreign Policy and Armed Services Committee, Smith embarked on a fact-finding tour of East Asia in autumn 1949 and in November released a report that illustrated the GOP's rather awkward position. There was the expected washing of hands: "[W]e have never been consulted about policy in the Far East . . . those of us who have felt alarm over this unfortunate situation have been given the feeling that we were unwelcome meddlers in matters of policy that had already been settled."[32] He also included a startling, though somewhat restrained, critique of Chiang: "The weakness of the Nationalists has not primarily been corruption . . . but as a leadership that has not really understood Western democracy."[33] With references to the continent's gigantic landmass and manpower, Smith painted a frightening portrait of an Asian menace that posed a far greater danger than any European threat: "[W]hile we are preoccupied with Europe the real threat of World War III may be approaching us from the Asiatic side."[34] In his synopsis for Republican colleagues, Smith suggested they adopt a position of wait and see while demanding the president refuse to recognize the CCP government. In a suggestion that foreshadowed events soon to come, he also called for a "united command in the Far Pacific" to be led by Gen. Douglas MacArthur.[35]

Judging from Smith's report, the GOP had difficulty determining a way forward. Its author was one of the party's most knowledgeable members on Asia, but as he admitted a few years later, "In 1949, I was very much concerned about the Far Eastern situation and [Vandenberg] was also. We felt that our Far Eastern policy was completely futile and yet we were not entirely clear at the time what direction we should move."[36] If the relatively informed Smith was stymied, then someone like Taft was at sea. Caught in the middle between caution and growing hysteria, any policy ideas he had on the subject of China were rapidly eroding. He confessed to Smith, "There is no subject which puzzles me so much. I know we should not be in the mess that we are in, but it is difficult to see how we can get out of it. I suppose now that Nationalist China is pretty well done for."[37] Taft achieved a degree of clarity by avoiding the subject of Chiang and instead focusing more generally on Taiwan. He even briefly flirted with the idea of official recognition of Communist China if PRC forces did not attempt to occupy the island. Still, despite identifying Taiwanese independence as a goal, the senator remained hazy about its future, whether it should resume its status as a Japanese territory or remain in the hands of Chiang's Nationalists. "I suppose only time can prove what the nature of the Communist government is, and there seems little to do now except wait."[38]

That uncertainty and hesitance to rally behind Chiang demonstrated the degree to which the Guomindang had yet to win over what should have been a receptive audience. For even those Republicans eager to exploit the situation in East Asia, the China Question remained a policy conundrum—if not a rhetorical one—until the mainland was officially added to the list of territories under Communist control and Chiang fled to Taiwan in December 1949. Media outlets noted that, from the ordinary citizen's perspective, catastrophe in China appeared to be an overnight development rather than the culmination of a long-standing civil war.[39] It had been a grueling six months, marked by the detonation of the first Soviet atomic bomb and Alger Hiss's trial and eventual conviction for perjury in January 1950. The establishment of the People's Republic of China (PRC) only deepened existing impressions that America was losing the Cold War.[40]

A map featured in *U.S. News & World Report* shortly after Chiang's flight illustrated that notion. "Nationalist Formosa," population 7.5 million, was tiny in comparison to Communist China with its nearly half a billion inhabitants and vast geographic territory. Readers were immediately struck by the imbalance between "What Is Left" and "What Is Lost." More so than the other two events, China engendered fear of an all-pervasive menace. An Open Door myth that cast the United States as China's protector transformed into suspicions of internal subversion once that portal had been slammed shut. The fall of this one particular ally magnified threats to both American democracy and national security.

Such impressions easily compounded perceptions of the free world rapidly disintegrating, which in turn led to a belated appreciation of Free China as a bulwark against the spread of communism and an assumption that the American Pacific Rim was in danger. China's long-standing place within the national imagination guaranteed that the issue would not readily dissipate. The implications of "Who lost China?" haunted the Truman administration, despite the State Department's best efforts to dissipate impressions of negligence. Secretary of State Acheson's irritation with the query remained evident ten years after the fact: "We never 'had' China. . . . Chiang Kai-shek lost

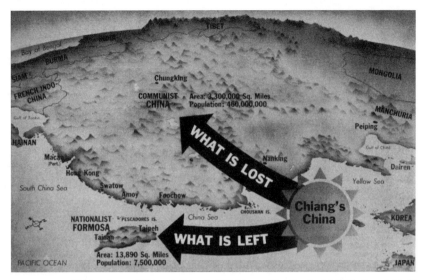

FIGURE 1.1. Illustrated map of Chiang's China, in "U.S. Draws a New Line in Asia," *U.S. News & World Report*, 13 January 1950, 24.

what authority he had—and it was not every much—over the vast areas and population of China." The suggestion that the Truman administration was at fault was patently "untrue."[41] The US government had done all it could to help Chiang, including providing military advisors and approximately three billion dollars in grants, credits, and surplus property from the end of war with Japan until early 1949.[42]

The fall-out over China's communization had yet to be fully determined, but the political benefits of questioning the White House's decision making were already enormous. It did not take long for Republicans, both conservative and moderate, to capitalize on the situation in earnest. According to an intraparty memo, Republican leaders had recognized the value of China as Democrats' Achilles heel during the earliest days of World War II. The text noted the disparity between Roosevelt's Atlantic policy and the "lukewarmness" of his strategy in the Pacific: "This policy [the Open Door] is distinctly a Republican contribution and one of which we can be very proud. In speaking out strongly on the matter, we are true not only to national interests, but to our very finest Party traditions."[43] A decade later, the right opportunity presented itself, and as the accusations and denials flew, Republicans transformed China into an unequivocally partisan issue.

For conservatives in particular, 1949 cemented the formula of their nascent foreign relations strategy. China was to be the steppingstone to a broader platform. Taft's own rapid transformation exemplified the currents shaping American conservatism. The post-1949 Taft stood in stark, remarkable contrast to his public profile before the conclusion of the Chinese civil war. His first major speech on Asia showed how quickly his foreign policy had changed. While he vacillated on exactly what type of official commitment should be made, Taft did approve of using US naval ships already in the area as deterrents against communist occupation, and his emphasis on continued and extensive commitment relegated Taiwan to client state status.[44]

During this transition period the senator revealed some surprising dimensions to his understanding of the relationship between the USSR and the new Beijing government. Unlike many of his colleagues, Taft saw the Chinese Communists as independent from the Kremlin. He also predicted American intervention in East Asia did not run the risk of martial conflict with the Soviet Union: "There is not the slightest evidence that Russia will go to war with us because we interfere with a (PRC) crossing to Formosa."[45] Taft went even further shortly thereafter, stating that US aid to a Guomindang invasion of mainland China would not provoke Soviet action, nor would aid to Greece, Turkey, and Iran.[46]

While such assertions may have been overconfident, they were meant to show that Taft and other conservatives were formulating their own theories of Cold War relations. Conservatism and isolationism were no longer to be considered as one and the same. The *Dayton Journal-Herald* informed Ohio readers that they "should scotch once and for all, charges that he is an isolationist."[47] "Apparently those who make the charge (of isolationism) feel that anyone who varies from the pattern established by our state department is to be cast into outer darkness and labeled as an isolationist," said Taft.[48] Translation: Conservatives were not isolationist; they were blameless, unlike proponents of liberal containment. What the right offered was an alternative to the bipartisan foreign policy that had imperiled American interests abroad by losing China.

Factionalism between GOP elites appeared to abate somewhat as moderates and conservatives both surpassed their efforts in 1948 and made China a keystone issue early in 1950, an election year. Press analysis varied. The *Washington Evening Star* described all Republicans' turn to China as "an adventure in politics" and cited partisanship as the sole motivation.[49] The *New York Times* was more perceptive. It recognized that conservatives' desire for control had not dissipated despite the semblance of unity on China: On one side were conservatives who proposed increased US military presence in the Taiwan region, though whether that was actual troop occupation or a concentration of naval or air power was still subject to debate. On the other stood moderates who wanted to take advantage of political opportunity but hesitated to advocate drastic measures.[50] This was not just a battle between two political parties; it was also a fight for the Republican institution.

Conservatives still harbored just as many, if not more, complaints against the moderates of their own party as they did Democrats. Older leaders partnered with younger conservatives like Smith and Sen. William Knowland, and together they entered the foreign policy debate to save their vision for Republicanism. Once Asia was framed an ideological issue, with defense of Free China as the vehicle for a return to bedrock American principles, the transition proved less fraught and unnatural than before.

Even if support for Free China was immediately associated with Chiang, not all who spoke out on the issue personally supported his leadership. Marked by a distinct utilitarianism, the right's adoption of China attempted to skirt the fine line between endorsement of a more aggressive foreign policy and wholehearted investment in Chiang. In a classified memorandum, MacArthur summed up the delicate position in which conservatives found themselves. The general declared the island's fate "largely rests with the United States," yet in the next paragraph admitted he was "unable to recommend the exact political, economic, and military measures which should be taken."[51] Arming Chiang and setting him on his way was not an option, even for a prominent supporter of the Guomindang like MacArthur. The barest risk of a third world war was not worth it. Rather than as a panacea for China, the most productive way to use Chiang was as an instrument to criticize liberal consensus in the United States.

Yalta: Questions of Executive Power

Accordingly, conservative officials highlighted what they considered to be a tradition of special democratic friendship between the United States and China, presenting a narrative of how Democrats betrayed that relationship via unchecked executive power. By connecting China and Cold War strategy to familiar political issues like federal growth, the Republican right was able to make Cold War policy more legible to its members and their core constituents.

Conservatives had protested the expansion of executive authority within both domestic and international affairs since the 1930s. Taft's own urging of strict American neutrality before Pearl Harbor highlighted conservatives' long-standing fear of the link between wartime and increased executive power.[52] With military conflict consuming Europe, he warned against a president who could seize hold of the economy and use military intervention as a conduit to unlimited growth of New Deal programs if the United States entered World War II. "There are some who say that politics should stop at the water's edge and that the nations must present a united front," he stated. "I do not at all agree. . . . There is no principle of subjection to the Executive in foreign policy. Only Hitler or Stalin would assert it."[53] Taft saw the combination of unchecked power and demagoguery as a potential path to dictatorship. A vigilant Congress was the sole entity that could maintain fiscal responsibility and protect citizens from an overly active government; the legislative branch therefore had a duty to serve as a counterweight to White House unilateralism. Republican opponents to war might be branded "isolationists," but Taft used a different term: "They are the peace party," he asserted.[54]

With the transition from antifascism to anticommunism, the Yalta agreement of 1945 was an ideal way to link the national and the global using a familiar narrative of liberalism's failures. Conservatives had long held doubts about the confidential compacts.[55] "I am not happy about the country's foreign policy. Through the agreements made at Tehran and Yalta by President Roosevelt, and at Potsdam by President Truman, we practically abandoned all of the ideals for which the war was fought," Taft asserted in 1947.[56] After 1949, backlash against decisions made at the conference itself raised larger questions about who controlled US foreign policy and how such a concentration of power could potentially damage national interests both at home and abroad. The blame rested, conservatives argued, with an executive branch that was allowed to wield too much power over a large federal apparatus as well as the nation's participation in multilateral organizations.[57]

It was the provision that granted Soviet troops access to Manchuria during the final weeks of World War II and the subsequent fate of China that raised the outcry against Yalta to full volume. Faced with the reality of a China under communism and the demise of what they believed was a special US-China relationship that dated back half a century, American supporters of the Guomindang—some of whom had the money to make sure that their opinions were heard—mobilized to lay blame for the "loss."[58] Denunciation of East Asian policy grew more frenetic with each passing week. In 1950 alone, Knowland delivered 115 hard-charging speeches on the Far East, a feat that earned him the nickname "the senator from Formosa."[59] Even former isolationists like Taft began to openly advocate intervention to combat communism in the Pacific.

Agreements like Yalta had also exacted costs closer to home. In practical terms, Taft charged that American taxpayers would have to pay for federal agencies expanded to administer foreign aid. The moral price was even higher: "I am not happy about the country's foreign policy. Through the agreements made at Tehran and Yalta by President Roosevelt, and at Potsdam by President Truman, we practically abandoned all of the ideals for which the war was fought."[60] Taft's allegation was clear that, through secret wartime negotiations, an American president had abandoned the nation's public promises to uphold freedom around the world.

Decrying the erosion of traditional morals and values was easy; translating critique into policy was another task altogether. Former president Herbert Hoover was among the first to offer a reconsideration of Taiwan's status vis-à-vis Yalta and other wartime agreements. Immediately after Chiang's flight from the mainland, he wrote to remind Knowland that the Cairo Declaration of 1943, which stipulated Japanese imperial territories would be returned to the Republic of China in the event of Allied victory, and the 1945 Potsdam proclamation, which specified the terms for Japanese surrender, were "executive agreements." That status meant they were never ratified as treaties by the Senate and were therefore legally questionable. Hoover suggested, "You might think over an argument that could be made; namely, that Formosa and the Pescadores are still in MacArthur's jurisdiction."[61]

If Cairo and Potsdam were null and void, and if Taiwan and other offshore islands were still technically Japanese, not Chinese, possessions, then they would fall under the general's authority as head of the Supreme Command of Allied Powers (SCAP) in Japan. Exactly what that meant for the security of Taiwan was left undefined—perhaps the occupation government in Japan would be expected to intervene if Mao moved across the strait. Whatever the possibilities, MacArthur's status as a popular conservative figure offered reassurance that Taiwan would be defended. Hoover's plan demonstrated a remarkable willingness to intercede to protect the island from communist aggression, even if it meant nullifying its status as an independent, sovereign government.

Although the details of his suggestion were rather drastic, Hoover raised the larger issue about growth of executive power at the hands of an expanded US foreign policy, particularly when it came to postwar settlement in East Asia. Other Republican conservatives had also been thinking along similar lines. For example, in response to the State Department's 1949 white paper on China, Sen. Bridges described Yalta as "a trade of territory which did not belong to either the United States or Great Britain."[62] In other words, Roosevelt and Winston Churchill had flouted the principles of self-determination outlined in the 1941 Atlantic Charter in the name of striking a quick bargain with Stalin; an American president had broken a public promise during secret negotiations. Increasingly, conservative leaders treated their suspicions as fact, and they presented them as such when evaluating both China policy and the entire relationship between US foreign relations and executive power.

As Hoover's early example suggested, the shift from reactionary rhetoric to policy proposals would soon follow.

Republican conservatives were certainly the loudest, but they were not the only members of the GOP who believed the United States owed non-Communist China a debt because of wartime negotiations. In 1950 John Foster Dulles argued American interest in Taiwan was "deep and legitimate." The nation owed a "special responsibility because of close connection between disposition of Formosa and conclusion of Japanese Peace Treaty." Dulles did not wish to cast doubt on the validity of Potsdam and Cairo, though he argued the existing Chinese mainland government was not in power when those agreements were negotiated and Taiwan should not be subjected to Communist rule as a Chinese territory. Acheson agreed. He even indicated an interest in providing aid for the Chinese on Taiwan to overthrow the CCP on one condition: They were under new leadership that was not Chiang Kai-shek's.[63]

Indeed, Chiang proved the dividing line. On one side stood Democrats and moderate Republicans whose incredulity about the Guomindang yielded a vague, piecemeal China policy. On the other, conservative Republican officials, relatively inexperienced (and often ill informed), came to view Chiang's anticommunism as the only credential that mattered. Any reservations they previously held dissipated in the face of communism's rapid expansion in Asia.

War Abroad, War at Home

Given prevalent doubts about the Guomindang's government's abilities, reactionary responses to developments in China might have been short-lived if the Cold War in Asia had run a quieter course after 1949. Michael Schaller describes how the rebuilding of Japan and securing a "great crescent" of capitalism and military defense along the Pacific Rim were the cornerstones of containment in Asia.[64] Such a strategy never made China the centerpiece of US Asia policy after World War II. However, political tension over its fate reached a new crescendo after North Korean troops crossed the 38th parallel on June 25, 1950. Eager to counter claims that he was soft on communism in Asia, Truman acted almost immediately, committing significant amounts of American resources in support of United Nations (UN) Security Council Resolutions 82 and 83.

The intervention was expected to quickly succeed, and for the moment, Truman enjoyed an unusual level of bipartisan support.[65] However, Republican conservatives refused to commit to the show of harmony. Just three days after the conflict began, they went on the offensive. "[T]his entirely unfortunate crisis has been produced first, by the outrageous, aggressive attitude of Soviet Russia, and second, by the bungling and inconsistent foreign policy of the administration," Taft stated in a Senate address. "The Chinese policy of the administration gave basic encouragement to the North Korean aggression."[66] The message he intended was obvious: Democratic foreign policy had been ineffective on all fronts, resulting in another hot war in the Pacific.

Truman's choice of MacArthur to lead UN forces in Korea certainly helped to quell such accusations. The general's record of service as a military commander and tenure as head of SCAP during the occupation of Japan made him one of the most celebrated military figures of the era. Moreover, he was enormously popular with conservative Republicans who often floated his name as a candidate for office.[67] Truman accomplished the dual task of outflanking right-wing critics who said he was soft on Asian communism while negating the possibility of the general becoming a nearby asset for the GOP during midterm elections.[68] The general's appointment could also temper notice of the fact that the Truman administration (with MacArthur's concurrence) took pains to forbid Chiang from contributing manpower in Korea for fear of the PRC joining the war. Ostensibly, the Seventh Fleet was deployed to protect Taiwan from aggression, but it was also there to ensure that Nationalist forces "cease all air and sea operations against the mainland."[69]

Bipartisanship proved short-lived as military stalemate replaced the prospect of quick, sure victory. Indeed, there was fundamental disagreement between the Truman administration and its conservative critics as to what actually constituted victory: containment of communism to the 38th parallel versus its eradication on the Korean peninsula and beyond. UN forces' October campaign into North Korea and toward the Yalu River brought those competing views to full light. As Truman ordered MacArthur to pull back for fear of Chinese mobilization, Asia Firsters decried the wasted opportunity to drive allied forces northward into China. The more virulent among them asserted the president was keeping MacArthur and, by extension, Chiang on a leash. The use of Nationalist troops came to be considered a potential cost-saving measure and, ultimately, a way to spare American lives.[70]

That theory held even after the momentum had reversed. When PRC troops entered the conflict on November 26 and UN forces suffered two withdrawals south of the 38th parallel, conservatives framed those developments as preventable. They argued Truman had circumvented Congress by going to the UN, and once war was underway, he had refused to take necessary steps toward total victory by decisively engaging the PRC when MacArthur had momentum on his side. If only Truman had chosen to act aggressively rather than remain committed to mere containment.[71] Angered by the stalemate, conservatives raised the familiar argument about executive overreach. Lest anybody forget, Truman had "usurped his powers as Commander in Chief" and had "no legal authority" to bypass Congress by going to the UN. There were also economic repercussions to monitor, including "arbitrary government control," inflation, and a drastic increase in the national debt.[72]

Conservatives redoubled their support of MacArthur, who still sought expanded engagement with Communist forces via a blockade of the China coast, air and naval attacks of the Chinese mainland, and the acceptance of Chiang's earlier offer of Guomindang troops.[73] "[W]e can release Chiang Kai-shek from the restraints we have imposed upon him, and it may be that he can create enough diversion to occupy the Chinese Communists. . . . We need commit no American soldiers and should not."[74] The United States ostensibly had only to liberate Chiang and donate a relatively small amount of aid to secure its own interests.

Given that PRC engagement in Korea began almost simultaneously, the November 1950 elections bore the imprimatur of the Cold War in Asia. As products of the first national campaigns since the fall of China in 1949 and onset of the Korean conflict, they highlighted the degree to which the right's agenda and prospects for political relevance had been overhauled.[75] Taft's reelection campaign in Ohio was a telling example of how conservatives buttressed their foreign policy credentials. His campaign workers strove to connect with a growing ethnic electorate that included Poles, Italians, Rumanians, Hungarians, Greeks, Jews, and Czechs—groups that usually voted Democrat—by playing up international affairs. When relevant, Taft supporters reminded those voters that the senator had opposed the agreements at Tehran, Yalta, and Potsdam, urging naturalized citizens to vote for an official who had not betrayed their homelands.[76] The ballot tallies confirmed the success of his new platform as Taft won by a massive margin of over 430,000 votes, the second-largest Senate election plurality in Ohio history.[77]

That mandate all but guaranteed Taft's third run for the White House during the next national election cycle, and he began to build his candidacy almost immediately with a lengthy Senate address on January 5, 1951. This was the speech that launched the so-called Great Debate over foreign policy and how it should be executed.[78] "The principle purpose of the foreign policy of the United States is to maintain the liberty of our people. . . . [W]e must avoid war like poison," Taft stated.[79] He protested the extensive use of American land forces overseas. Directly echoing a plan for "victory on the cheap" advocated earlier by Lt. Gen. Claire Lee Chennault (the famous fighter pilot who helped train the Chinese air force), the senator recommended development of naval and air power as a cost-effective substitute for on-the-ground presence overseas.[80] Not only did he consider extensive American military deployment extraneous to the achievement of peace, it was a long-term expense that would trigger "inflation and decrease in the value of the dollar."[81]

Even as conservatism experienced significant validation at the ballot box, the Korean conflict remained unresolved and the rift between Truman and MacArthur deepened. In April 1951, the general wrote to House Speaker Joseph Martin in a fit of frustration. "[I]f we lose this war to Communism in Asia," he averred, "the fall of Europe is inevitable; win it, and Europe most probably would avoid war and yet preserve freedom."[82] MacArthur interpreted the president's adherence to containment as defeatist. After Martin, who had been demanding a second front and use of Guomindang troops in Korea, read the letter aloud in the Senate, Truman announced the general's recall on grounds of insubordination on April 11.

Asia Firsters took the dismissal as a symptom of long-standing US failure on mainland Asia. During the Senate's inquiry, William Knowland tied MacArthur's removal from duty to post-Yalta China and inappropriate executive privilege: "When actions are taken that lead to hundreds of millions of Chinese going into the Soviet orbit with the destruction of their lives and their liberty, is this private business? Is it comparable to the relationship of a doctor and his patient, attorney and his client, priest and the parishioner? I think not."[83] The loss of China and the ensuing Korean conflict were traceable to a secretive White House. That vital decisions could be made without regulation indicated that the president wielded too much power over the direction of US diplomacy and the new national security state. MacArthur's appearance during a joint session of Congress made the ongoing debate over balance of power all the more heated. From the House podium, at the behest of conservative Republicans, the general launched his public retaliation against Truman: "War's very object is victory, not prolonged indecision. In war, there is no substitute for victory," aimed directly at executive leadership that claimed the status quo of containment as its foreign policy goal.[84] Richard Rovere and Arthur Schlesinger Jr. noted the enormous impact of the MacArthur controversy. Millions of listeners heard the radio broadcast while newspapers ran reprints of the address the next morning—Broadway even released recordings of the song "Old Soldiers Never Die." The situation in East Asia "galvanized deep and spreading national bafflement and discontent."[85]

In the wake of such public response lay further opportunity for Republicans to ratchet up their attack on the Truman administration. An April episode of the radio program "Meet Your Congress" demonstrated how the MacArthur controversy had intensified partisan divides on Asia policy. The panel that week consisted of two Democrats (Herbert Lehman [NY] and Hu-

bert Humphrey [MN]) and two conservative Republican senators (Taft and
Homer Capeheart). Never entirely civil, the discussion devolved into a verbal
brawl. Taft channeled MacArthur, asking, "What is the purpose of war except
to win a war?" Capeheart accused Lehman and Humphrey of harboring
procommunist sympathies.[86] Their remarks reflected how conservatives had
latched on to Korea as tangible evidence of Truman's refusal to win against
global communism.[87]

Just weeks later, MacArthur himself gave extended testimony before joint
meetings of the Senate Armed Services and Foreign Relations Committees.
During one appearance, he asserted the United States should act on its own
in China if the UN would not give its approval. Anything less was "appeasement" that could lead to another world war: "[I]f they can't see exactly the
road that they are following in Asia, why then we had better protect ourselves and go it alone." Unilateral action buttressed by cutting edge military
technology was preferable to war applied in a "piecemeal way."[88] If there was
a distinction between appeasement of communism and appeasement of the
UN, MacArthur left it undefined. What was clear was how his hopes for the
reprioritization and realization of US foreign policy complemented that of
Asia Firsters.

Nevertheless, the scope of what to do for Chiang remained a crucial point
of difference between MacArthur and conservative leaders. While both recommended aid to Taiwan for quick victory in Korea, the latter never seriously considered using the Korean War as a gateway for restoration of the
Guomindang on mainland China.[89] For example, on "Meet Your Congress,"
Taft stated, "In recent months, it has, of course, been very doubtful whether
aid to Nationalist Government could be effective, and no one desires to waste
American efforts."[90] His more tempered view demonstrated a healthy degree
of pragmatism about Chiang and an emphasis on the feasible. After recent
engagement with PRC troops in Korea, investment in the Guomindang was a
dubious prospect not worth the risk of World War III.

The more useable elements of MacArthur's proposals bolstered a sustainable conservative foreign-policy ethos by emphasizing the preservation of
national unilateralism, as well as the use of available military and technological means to claim decisive victory in any war, hot or cold. As Rovere
and Schlesinger recognized, response to the United States' latest war in East
Asia and the MacArthur controversy was "a direct reaction to the Chinese
catastrophe itself."[91] The tandem of China and Korea, combined with internal
fears of communist subversion, meant conservative internationalism reaped
significant dividends from perceptions of a domino effect in the Pacific. With
the renewal of military conflict in East Asia, Asia Firsters could continue at-

tempts to question executive power and the endgame of liberal containment. The prolonged timeline of armistice negotiations (June 1951 to July 1953) meant they could persistently claim the liberal brand of anticommunism was unwilling or unable to end armed conflict quickly and favorably.

Moreover, the war overseas engendered extensive political warfare at home. By the time a peace settlement was signed, Korea had provided an effective backdrop for the notoriety of Sen. Joseph McCarthy, as well as a host of issues reemphasized by the phenomenon that bore his name.

McCarthy

McCarthy's rapid rise seemingly went hand in hand with Asia First internationalism. Because the two phenomena overlapped so much, assuming that their influences on conservatism were one and the same was easy. Both originated out of criticism of US Asia policy. Both articulated an antistatism that denounced liberalism and a large federal state as the culprits behind recent setbacks in the Cold War. Above all, both capitalized on a heightened climate of fear that the United States was somehow losing the fight against communism from the inside out. The Hiss and Rosenberg trials, the crusade led by Sen. Patrick McCarran (D-NV) to restrict immigration and monitor suspicious individuals and groups, and the stalemate in Korea helped to buttress that perception.[92]

In short order, "Tail-gunner Joe" seized on established themes of internal leaks and treason in East Asian affairs and expanded their applicability to a wide variety of federal agencies, including the armed forces. "In examining the record, it will be necessary to discuss the actions of certain individuals because history does not just happen. It is made by men—men with names and faces, and the only way that the course of history can be changed is by getting rid of the specific individuals who we find are bad for America," McCarthy avowed.[93] Such rhetoric struck a deep chord. One enthusiastic supporter from Oakland, California, wrote, "All real Americans who love America above any foreign group of ideologiests [sic] are with you. They are sick and tired and have a belly ful [sic] of our foreign ideology boys."[94] Truman told Acheson that he believed McCarthy to be "a pathological liar"—then immediately acknowledged he could hardly repeat such an opinion in public. Even the president could do little in the face of an ingrained system of institutional deference and the long-standing history of anticommunism that helped sustain McCarthy's individual quest for the limelight.[95]

Despite the fact that Republican conservatism stood to profit from this new wave of anticommunism, fault lines did exist between McCarthy and more established leaders. As one of Taft's advisors noted, "I cannot feel that any sense of loyalty to any of us or to any one at all has any part in the picture."[96] Taft himself was divided about McCarthyism. His public statements on communist subversion suggested unalloyed support for the new climate in Washington, and biographer William S. White described Taft's attitude on McCarthy as "fundamentally pro."[97] Yet in private moments the senator expressed apprehension about the way in which his colleague operated, fretting that a witch hunt could sully the party's reputation.[98] Herbert Hoover reinforced that instinct, describing McCarthy as a pressing concern. "He has had a great life by the dismissal of (John) Service," Hoover wrote. The measures the unpredictable McCarthy would take with his newfound fame and power were deeply concerning.[99]

In sum, McCarthy was a volatile asset. His status as an elite GOP official and his efforts in the name of anticommunism complemented long-term plans for conservative internationalism. At the same time, he could not entirely be trusted to do the right thing for the party. The senator's personal popularity forced senior officials to make a choice. Resolution of the issue came when the White House attempted to intervene in Senate operations, namely, the Tydings Committee investigations into McCarthy's allegations. Any executive mitigation was subject to interpretation as a violation of constitutional balance of power. It also triggered Republican partisanship. Taft lashed out at Truman in a Senate address, labeling the president's appeal for reform a "bitter and prejudiced attack on Republicans in the Senate." He presented a united GOP front in the face of Democratic aggression and took the opportunity to again assert Republican innocence in the foreign policy that lost China: "There never was any consultation regarding the policy in China or the Far East. . . . 'Bi-partisan foreign policy' is being used by Mr. Truman as a slogan to condemn any Republican who disagrees with Mr. Truman's unilateral foreign policy secretly initiated and put into effect without any real consultation with Congress." Returning to the issue of presidential fault, Taft called for "an investigation unhampered by executive obstinacy and name calling."[100] It was one of his strongest outbursts since battles with Roosevelt and the New Deal in the late 1930s.

McCarthy's longest lasting contribution to conservatism was perhaps the way in which his crusade highlighted the fundamental issue of congressional authority. Support for him symbolized minority opposition to the administration while challenging his intent could be construed as complicity in a "rubber stamp" Congress. In his leadership position, Taft attempted to bridge caution and partisan support by claiming McCarthy had done much to arouse a public previously ignorant of the communist threat. Although it was "unfortunate" the Wisconsin senator failed to thoroughly check his facts, Taft on balance believed McCarthy had provided the country "a real service."[101] With the next round of national elections fast approaching, the junior senator stood to make a significant contribution to Republican victories if he continued to heighten impressions of the GOP as the party that was proactively tough on internal subversion.

A Foreign Policy for Americans

It fell to Taft to demonstrate that the heart of conservatism had incorporated internationalism in a well-rounded, sustainable way. Blunt rejection of a strict interpretation of the Monroe Doctrine was a major step. "I do not agree with those who think we can completely abandon the rest of the world and rely solely upon the defense of the continent," he stated in the Senate at the beginning of 1951.[102] The logical follow-up was to articulate the conservative answer to liberal internationalism. Released in November 1951, *A Foreign Policy for Americans* marked Taft's official coming out as a "conservative Cold Warrior."[103]

The introduction quickly set an aggressive tone that challenged both containment and Truman himself: "I have written this book to emphasize the fact that the freedom of the people of the United States is in serious danger from the foreign policy of the present Administration. I have frequently written of the danger to liberty from the constant increase in the activity, spending, and the power of the Federal Government, but today the threat from foreign policy is even greater."[104] *A Foreign Policy* was an overtly partisan piece of writing; after all, it was the springboard from which Taft planned to launch his third campaign for the White House. His leadership status within the party also meant the book was widely significant from a political perspective. The slim volume articulated a diplomatic ethos that represented a turning point for the GOP right's agenda, one that signaled that all of conservatism—even the staunchest old guard—had undergone a fundamental shift.

As could be expected, Taft tackled issues and institutions that had long been thorns in the right's side. In many ways his book read like a compendium of familiar conservative complaints about the growth of executive power, the UN, and how US policy helped the "Russian Menace" to expand.

Yet the book was no mere knee-jerk rejection of Democratic policy. Using a combination of political philosophy, history, and geographic case studies, Taft called for selective intervention, tactical anticommunism via arms and economic aid, and defensive military deployment, as well as underground infiltration of communist states. Ironically, his assessment plainly bore the influence of George Kennan, but it was that very similarity that showed how the very backbone of the GOP right had embraced a multifaceted approach to global anticommunism. Unlike previous eras, diplomatic isolationism and armed intervention were no longer the only options for those who identified with conservatism. An approach that provided an alternative to liberal containment—however modest in variation—was a subtle but sure mark of change.

The text also dealt with philosophical matters that transcended the immediacy of the next election cycle. Of chief concern was how the nation could balance an unprecedented role in the global community with its responsibility to its own citizens. According to Taft, US foreign policy should take the well-being of the American people as its primary goal. If the United States protected them from external threats (i.e., communists, entangling diplomatic alliances) as well as internal ones (e.g., subversion, a dictatorial presidency), the entire world would be better off. "We cannot afford to destroy at home the very liberty which we must sell to the rest of the world as the basis for progress and happiness."[105] Taft and other conservatives had used the same line of reasoning during World War II, when foreign intervention threatened to make permanent the programs of the New Deal and grant the president sweeping powers.[106] The Cold War demanded the same, if not a higher, degree of vigilance against forces that imperiled American exceptionalism from within and without.

The book's last chapters were its most effective. They compared two case studies of US postwar intervention, one in Western Europe and one in East Asia, and together illustrated regional contours within conservative internationalism. The contrast between Taft's proposals for the two areas was indeed striking. For Europe, the senator relied on familiar complaints regarding economic and military aid, collective security commitments, and peacetime troop contributions.[107] His overarching concern was that Western European states use their own material and human resources to protect themselves from Soviet aggression. The United States should sell arms, not give them away. It should donate manpower only under specific circumstances. Its policies should not "speak of Western Europe as if it were a single country," but rather differentiate between nations worth going to war for (England and Germany) and those that were not (France and Italy).[108] At bottom, the nation's security commitments in Europe, via the North Atlantic Treaty Organization (NATO) and a weak UN, were overtaxing in all senses of the word. In a foreshadowing of the Nixon Doctrine, Taft inferred that the United States could not be expected to address crises everywhere and thereby expend its own resources; allies needed to contribute much more fully. When it did choose to act, the United States should be able to do so without compromising its unilateralism.[109]

Taft could not but help raise the examples of China and Korea even as he ostensibly addressed Atlantic affairs. If Europe received the "lion's share" of assistance, it came at the expense of allies in East Asia who did not get the arms and equipment they needed to combat the communist threat before and after 1949.[110] In previous conversations, the senator had denied prioritizing the Pacific over the Atlantic: "What I object to is that while we didn't mind risking a war in Europe, we weren't willing to risk any war in Asia. . . . I want the same treatment in the East as in the West; in the West as in the East."[111] *A Foreign Policy* repeated that this was a matter of basic fairness. Why would US policy refuse to grant Asian partners the same attention and support they did European ones, some of whom were less deserving? Providing the same "treatment" for Chinese Nationalist and South Korean allies meant arming and training them so they could combat communist aggression themselves, with a sensible amount of American support that did not include deploying American soldiers.[112]

Taft frequently cited what happened in China during the late 1940s as the best example to date of communist methods and diplomatic errors made by liberals. Roosevelt had conceded too much in the face of Stalin's aggressive demands and secretly "bargained away" Manchuria at Yalta. Truman was accused of having completely "abandoned" the Guomindang after 1947.[113] The disparity between US action in Europe (decisive and effective) and policy on Asia (weak and compromising) was US foreign policy's Achilles heel, Taft argued. "I only insist that we apply to Asia the same basic policy which we apply to Europe. . . . [M]y quarrel is with those who wish to go all-out in Europe, even beyond our capacity, and who at the same time refuse to apply our general program and strategy to the Far East."[114]

With such statements about arming the Guomindang, any initial misgivings about Chiang and his government had been set aside. The Nationalists, along with the British, were the standard by which foreign allies should be judged, heralded as the type of stalwart anticommunist allies that should be cultivated and helped. Qualifying nations like Nationalist China were willing to fight for themselves and had experience with democracy; in other words, they possessed attributes similar to those of the United States. Consciously or not, Taft translated "Asia First" into a Cold War, internationalized version of "America First."

During the early 1950s, the mere suggestion of arming Chiang and supporting his invasion of mainland China was bound to provoke controversy. Britain and France vehemently opposed such a plan, and while the nature of the Sino-Soviet alliance remained unclear, there was the danger of major consequences if such a campaign failed. In an uncharacteristic show of bravado, Taft scoffed at the suggestion. He downplayed theories that intervention beyond containment in Asia could lead to another worldwide conflict. An invasion of mainland China, led by Chiang and sponsored by the United States, would be "no possible threat" to Russia's sense of security. Such a maneuver could hardly compare to the menace of NATO forces encircling the Soviet Union and its satellites, about which Moscow had yet to do anything. Even if there was a chance the Soviets would react, it was a risk worth taking.[115]

The theory relied on two presumptions. The first was that Stalin would not hazard a third world war for Mao; second, Chinese communism could not withstand an Allied assault without the Kremlin's patronage. Like many American officials at the time, Taft held the misimpression that Chinese Communism marched in lockstep with, and was dependent on, the Soviet state. He therefore framed Mao's victory as a Russian triumph and Chiang's loss the result of American errors. Neither development was Chinese, per se.

Although a fundamental misunderstanding of the CCP's depth, as well as Beijing's relationship with the Soviet Union, skewed many conservatives' perception of what could be accomplished in East Asia, the influence of an Asia First platform extended beyond proposals for the region itself. In fact, it shaped conservative internationalism's entire defense platform. From calls for reformation of executive power to criticism of the American involvement in the UN, events of the Korean War in particular served as direct inspiration.

For example, the demand for a stronger air force that could deploy necessary atomic weaponry and expand quickly in times of war was central to *A Foreign Policy*'s defense proposals. Not only would the United States hold a technological and geopolitical edge over the Soviet Union, it could do so while relying less on traditional manpower.[116] As demonstrated by their fierce opposition to the "time tax" of Universal Military Training, conservatives had long protested the expansion of a standing army.[117] After the Truman administration rebuffed MacArthur's desire to engage Chinese Communist forces above the Yalu River for fear of awakening China's military masses, the GOP right argued liberal containment lacked the will to win. Taft agreed US forces could not hope to match Soviet and Chinese numbers on the ground, but that was not the point: "The same old-fashioned obsession for ground combat is dominating our policy today" when it was within the United States' power to dominate the Cold War via air and tactical weaponry.[118]

The text emphasized themes of thrift and efficiency as crucial to protection of national interests around the world. After all, intervention was expensive. In war, US officials needed to be unafraid to use the force necessary to bring

missions like Korea to decisive, successful conclusion. Conservative internationalism was presented as a way not only to minimize the loss of American
lives and money in the event of conflict but also to prevent communist aggression so that it was unnecessary for vital resources to be expended in the
first place.

As its most visible leader, Taft was in a position to show just how much
the GOP right had changed on foreign policy. His words represented a firm
dedication to expansion of the armed forces and the defense state, something
that was not integral to the conservative platform just a decade earlier. At the
same time, retention of traditional values, such as a balanced budget and an
unapologetic vision of American exceptionalism, tempered all the change.[119]
The building up of the nation's air force meant a cutting back of its spending;
it was a policy designed to keep an eye on a balanced budget and appealed to
voters concerned about that bottom line. Finally, Taft's foreign policy was a
public commitment to technology, which allowed an ex-isolationist to now
dub Democratic foreign policy as "old-fashioned." Conservatism now styled
itself an innovator in a new political and diplomatic age.

By early 1952, 52,500 copies of *A Foreign Policy* were in circulation.[120]
Shortly after its publication, MacArthur reached out to congratulate Taft on
a "masterly" effort: "I have read the book and believe that its issuance will
greatly strengthen your position with the American people. It is unequivocal
and clears away many of the cobwebs of uncertainty which are spun so carefully by propagandists and the invisible government," he wrote. "Your aggressive and energetic campaign is splendid in every way. You are immeasurably
improving your position, and everywhere I go I find this to be the case."[121]
MacArthur's encouragement was essential, for he was a potential contender
for the White House himself. Such words indicated that the general was un-
likely to run himself and, in turn, could be open to formally endorsing Taft.
Engaging the former's outsized personality had its downsides, however. As
cartoonist Newton Pratt deftly pointed out, MacArthur beating the drum
threatened to claim the spotlight and disrupt the campaign at hand, a pattern
all too familiar to Truman.

Media response to the book varied between high commendation and
harsh criticism with little in between. *The Atlantic*, for example, featured reviews of the book in two consecutive issues. Arthur Schlesinger Jr. dubbed its
ideas "The New Isolationism"—a "fundamental attack" on the nation's God-
given responsibility to promote democracy around the world. Much more
dangerous than its predecessor, this new doctrine sought an active place
within the crafting of foreign policy, yet it refused to relinquish the spirit of
the Monroe Doctrine. Schlesinger was perhaps even more perplexed by the

FIGURE 1.2. Newton Pratt, "The Voice of Experience," *Sacramento Bee*, 5 March 1952, Harry S. Truman Library Photographs, Accession No. 60-345.

lapse in judgment by the "ordinarily logical" Taft: "There is something deeper here—some essential perplexity of a powerful mind confounded by events which he cannot quite fit into a consistent scheme of interpretation," he wrote. "Senator Taft, indeed, is a man in transition, an Old Isolationist trying hard to come to terms with the modern world." In the end, Schlesinger was not about to let empathy obstruct progress. "Once we have exorcised this latest version of isolationism, we may at last begin to live in the twentieth century," he concluded.[122]

Political science professor W. Reed West had a very different assessment. He praised the book as a reflection of its author's "well-defined foreign policy—a positive program within a global philosophy." It was true that Taft was susceptible to criticism because of his past reputation and a personal tendency toward absolute frankness, but he deserved credit. His foreign policy outlay took into account the nation's financial resources and the burden born by taxpayers. While Schlesinger moaned about New Isolationists "tainted with unilateralism, McCarthyism, and capitalism," West saw a foreign policy ethos based on common sense. From his perspective, this new conservative position "appear[ed] not to be isolationism but internationalism translated into practical statesmanship."[123]

Early in 1952, Taft spoke before a group of Denver Republicans on the subject of international affairs. In a few brief sentences he summed up the transformation conservatism had experienced over the past few years: "How can any Republican avoid the foreign policy issue? It affects every feature of domestic policy."[124] The entire GOP, not just moderate Republicans who participated in bipartisan diplomacy, had to engage with foreign policy because it had a direct impact on matters at home. From taxes to executive power to internal subversion, the Cold War made its presence known in everyday American life. Therefore, conservatives, many of them former neutralists or isolationists, needed to understand that foreign policy was domestic policy, and vice versa.

China and East Asia were the catalysts for that decompartmentalization. Even if Taft seemed at times to struggle with uneven analysis, his book showcased the partnership between the GOP right and the Guomindang. The bond made perfect sense. Frustration with the Korean War, the Cold War dynamics of the GOP, and the public's lingering receptiveness to the Open Door ideal that Chiang represented meant emphasis on East Asia could yield considerable electoral gains. Chiang himself benefitted from the efforts of a political faction that needed him to present its internationalism as much as he needed them to keep his hopes afloat.

A major part of the American narrative of global benevolence, the open door to a "free China" was a salient way for rightwing Republicans to craft a more popular, widely relatable approach to foreign policy. As the title of Taft's book suggested, he and fellow conservatives aimed for a broader audience than the relatively esoteric one familiar with George Kennan's "Article X." The turn to an Asia First strategy empowered each reader: "We are embarked on a voyage at this moment in which a continued failure of understanding and judgment may wreck the greatest adventure in freedom the human race has ever known."[125] All Americans, not just elite State Department bureaucrats, were responsible to stay the course of "freedom" and give the rest of the world hope. That undiluted articulation of exceptionalism created a sense of national community, as well as destiny, to be fulfilled by all citizens.

The strategy adopted by elite conservative officials dovetailed perfectly with developments within the private sector. As early as the 1930s, activists in the United States had considered the Guomindang government to be a democratic counterpart in East Asia. After the Communist revolution, grassroots efforts to force the direction of US China policy in favor of increasing aid to Chiang's efforts on Taiwan and beyond tested the traditional boundaries of formal diplomacy. Waged outside of government with the hopes of influencing public policy, the campaign also engendered one of the enduring myths of Cold War politics, that of the so-called China Lobby.

No Such Thing: The China Lobby

On July 26, 1951, Sen. Wayne Morse (Ind.-OR) stood in chambers to introduce S. Res. 170, which he and Sen. Brien McMahon (D-CT) had drafted together. The measure proposed to grant the Foreign Relations Committee the
power to investigate individual or group representatives of foreign states that
had attempted to manipulate US policy since September 2, 1945, the day the
Japanese government surrendered and World War II officially ended. Of special interest were the methods and financing those agents used to accomplish
their objectives.

Morse named only two regimes outright: the Chinese Nationalists and the
Chinese Communists, both of which claimed rights to govern all of China.
Given the content and context of his address, Morse was clearly taking aim at
the former: "The China Lobby has for several years been conducting a violent
campaign against American policies in China."[1] Interest and concern over
the operations of Chiang Kai-shek's government had been steadily increasing
since Joseph McCarthy made the State Department's Far Eastern desk the target of his initial allegations. Disquiet was evident at the highest levels of government as Harry Truman himself indicated he was ready to investigate the
China Lobby from "hell to breakfast."[2] S. Res. 170 intended to illuminate the
machinations of an apparatus that appeared to exert undue power in Washington, possibly through the use of bribery or other unlawful means.

Morse was bound to fail if he sought to investigate an actual organization
with a set group of affiliates. The "China Lobby" was an inconsistent conglomeration of American individuals and interest groups that advocated an
overhaul of US foreign policy in favor of Chiang's Guomindang government.
It was neither formalized as a political entity nor registered as such. Contem-

poraneous observers and historians alike have noted that the phrase was a convenient catchall description for people in the United States who supported the Chinese Nationalists.[3]

Chiang supporters in the United States were indeed a motley group. Individuals who participated in lobby activities—the names listed on the letterhead of pro-Guomindang organizations, people who donated funds (or just their reputations), and those who volunteered their time—came from a wide variety of backgrounds. Despite a lack of cohesion, the group appeared to wield considerable political reach. Prominent names like Congressman Joseph Martin Jr. (Speaker of the House and former head of the Republican National Committee) participated firsthand, whereas others like US Senators Styles Bridges, Patrick McCarran, William Knowland, and Richard Nixon appeared to take lobby directives on Asia policy. It was scarcely any wonder that concerned parties such as Morse wanted to investigate an organization that seemed at once to be nowhere, yet everywhere.

Even if it had only an unofficial existence, the China Lobby made a lasting impact on national politics. It was an activist form of Asia First orientalism that paralleled the revolt over bipartisan foreign policy waged by conservative Republican officials. Practitioners generated alternatives to "liberal" institutions that they believed tainted by communism, including the State Department, academia, and the majority of mainstream media. Spurred by events in East Asia, these activists worked mostly outside the state to influence the shape and tenor of US intervention in China. They also established news outlets and partnered with publishing houses to combat what they saw as insufficient levels of anticommunism at home.

The success of their labor is best measured by the fact that traces of a powerful lobby existed at all, rather than actual changes in policy or public opinion. Asia First orientalism, in the guise of extrastate activity to aid Nationalist China, connected groups of citizens who otherwise appeared to have little in common. It simultaneously gave shape to fears regarding the Cold War and offered a potential protagonist in the form of Chiang. From the late 1940s through the mid-1950s, the American network in support of Guomindang restoration demonstrated how disparate factions and organizations banded together around a common complaint. An examination of its membership, ideology, and methods reveals how the China Lobby could ultimately provide a template for future conservative mobilization at the grassroots level, as well as a narrative of US-China relations that endured as an inspirational cornerstone of rightwing mythology.

Because the China Lobby was an informal grouping, trying to identify its

American membership without the benefit of official rolls or literature has historically been a difficult task. Ross Y. Koen's investigative study, *The China Lobby in American Politics* (1960), broke new ground by identifying a galaxy of figures and organizations that worked to promote the Free China cause.[4] He outlined the lobby as "a kaleidoscopic array of affiliates who were increasingly allied to the Chiang regime in their sympathies." In 1975, E. J. Kahn described them as "legislators, publishers, writers, businessmen, religious leaders, crackpots, and plain folk."[5] A wide variety of individuals, including ex-Communists turned anticommunist crusaders, found a place under the umbrella of the China Lobby.[6]

Koen was the first scholar to look seriously at the China Lobby. He classified its members into two categories based on their individual motivations: those who were impelled by financial interests (i.e., a paid agent whose income depended on the Nationalist regime retaining control, or a business that would lose revenue if Chiang fell from power) and those who supported the Guomindang because of "politics, ideology, or a particular set of assumptions regarding the requirements of American security."[7] Koen listed their names and those of China-related groups, though he omitted explanation as to why they showed such commitment toward a geographically distant issue.

Thanks in no small part to *The China Lobby*, pro-Chiang activism in the United States came to be considered an example of zealotry run amok. The book depicted the China Lobby as a group whose members possessed varying motivations but were nonetheless synchronized, almost monolithic, in their operations. The negativity of Koen's interpretation was largely understandable, for the author experienced firsthand the zealousness of those who wished US policy to maintain a close alliance with the Guomindang: Supporters of Chiang successfully campaigned to halt his book's distribution when Macmillan first printed it in 1960.[8]

After its second publication the text became a standard reference for scholars of US-China relations, but that did not mean its arguments were accepted wholesale. In a 1975 review, Warren Cohen pointed out that the book was somewhat misleading because it discounted efforts in favor of Nationalist China from figures across the political spectrum and gave the lobby "the characteristics of its most obscene participants." Nevertheless, Koen's characterization continues to resonate. The term "China Lobby" has been used as shorthand to describe practitioners of a virulent form of anticommunism that wielded outsized influence despite a rather single-minded focus on American aid to Chiang Kai-shek.[9] As a result, the group's connections to wider political trends (other than McCarthyism) have gone largely overlooked.

Personal Orientalisms

When considering Asia First activists and how their efforts complemented the emergence of a revitalized conservatism, *The China Lobby in American Politics* offers the salient observation that many Americans' involvement with China was deeply individual and emotional. It was that category of Asia First activists—those who fought for China for reasons other than money—who comprised the majority of the lobby and included its most recognizable members.

Personal connections that bound three prominent members of pro-Chiang circles to East Asia provide insight into the orientalism that drove Asia First activists. Among them, publisher Henry Luce, Congressman Walter Judd, and businessman Alfred Kohlberg offer examples of how a specific vision of China inspired certain US citizens to political and diplomatic action.

Henry Robinson Luce, the publisher of *Time* and *Life* magazines, was the most well known of the three. Both his parents served as YMCA missionary educators in Shandong Province, where Luce was born in 1898, just as the United States joined the scramble for overseas empire. His relationship with Chiang began in the 1920s during a pivotal journey back to China. He found the place of his birth and childhood drastically changed by Guomindang campaigns to run off Japanese forces and combat the growing influence of communism. Robert Herzstein's excellent biographical study of the publishing magnate describes the close link between Luce's orientalism and the Nationalist government. Persuaded by Chiang's brother-in law, T. V. Soong, Luce by the early 1930s came to the conclusion that "Chiang and other Christian Chinese leaders were the instruments at hand. With American help, they would modernize and Christianize their ancient country."[10] It was a sentiment that would endure. Luce habitually ignored allegations of corruption within the Guomindang because they countered his own ideals about Chiang's Christian leadership and what it could do to reaffirm the US-China bond. One editor at *Fortune* held that his boss was "stuck utterly and completely to Chiang Kai-shek until the day of his death."[11]

With a vast media empire at his disposal, Luce had the power to influence American public opinion like no other individual. Throughout the 1930s he tirelessly promoted Chiang and his wife as international heroes, even naming them "Man and Wife of the Year" in 1937.[12] After World War II, Luce's capacity to project his brand of internationalism reached new heights: In 1947, *Life*'s subscription rate reached 4.7 million, while *Time*—which was published on every continent except Antarctica—had a readership of well over 1.5 million.[13]

With the Cold War unfolding and Free China no closer to stability, let alone meaningful collaboration with the United States, Luce intensified his efforts and allowed his advocacy to color reportage of subjects varying from overseas philanthropy ("China's Children Shift for Themselves," *Life*, January 14, 1946) to Tom Dewey's presidential campaign and pro-China plank ("Republicans: Victory in the Air," *Time*, October 18, 1948). Through mass communication, he attempted to raise a groundswell of public opinion in favor of alliance between the United States and Nationalist China.[14]

Walter H. Judd stood as a sort of federal counterpart to Luce's extrastate activism. The congressman's China credentials were impressive. For ten years of the interwar period, Judd served as a medical missionary and witnessed the Japanese invasion in 1937. In 1939 he testified before both the Senate and House Foreign Relations Committees about the Sino-Japanese War, urging officials to curtail Japan's access to American-made supplies.[15] By the time he was elected to represent Minnesota in the House in 1942, Judd was a well-known authority on China, thanks to the 1,400 lectures he delivered across the country for the American Committee for Non-Participation in Japanese Aggression.[16] During the waning days of World War II, he delivered one of the first articulations of Asia First and cautioned Americans to look to East Asia: "[W]hen the war ends in Europe . . . America's attention will inevitably shift more and more to the far Pacific and we must know and understand the situations there better than we have in the past. . . . We got into this war through Asia; and if America gets into another war, almost certainly it will be through Asia."[17]

Judd continued to fight for the interests of the Chinese Nationalist regime after 1945. On the House floor he compared the conflict in China to the American Civil War, an equation that saw the Chinese Communist Party (CCP) as the "slavery faction" that had seceded and Chiang as the Lincoln-like leader who was fighting to reunite his country.[18] In October 1947, Secretary of State George Marshall dispatched Gen. Albert Wedemeyer on a fact-finding mission to China to placate Republican critics headed by Judd.[19] Predictably, the Wedemeyer Report recommended increased aid to the Guomindang. After just a handful of years in government, Judd emerged as a leading voice on US-China affairs, a prominent critic of the Democrats' East Asia policy and a principal of the "China Bloc" in Congress. Foreign Service officer John Davies described him as "the most dogged campaigner for the Nationalists and against the Truman administration."[20] Decades later Judd still had harsh words for Truman: "He tried to appease Communism. He sent Marshall to China to tell the Chinese we wouldn't help them unless they took the Communists into their government. His policy was right in Europe, it succeeded. His policy was wrong in Asia, it failed."[21]

His actions also extended beyond the bounds of his office. Four years after the establishment of the PRC, he was a force behind the Committee of One Million Against the Admission of Communist China to the United Nations.[22] The group's name is self-explanatory, but Judd's work to further its mission— including directing organizers, fundraising, and crafting petition language— demands examination. Even as he was serving his home state in Congress, Judd advanced the agenda of a private special interest group that aggressively (and quite successfully) represented the concerns of a foreign government that he described as the "cream of the crop," the very best that China had to offer.[23] In his role as Asia First activist he tested the boundaries that separated personal interest and public duty—and then pushed through them. According to historian Michael Schaller, Judd, in contrast to some of his fellow politicians who exploited China for electoral gain, truly believed in Chiang's abilities.[24] Like Luce, his missionary background fundamentally shaped his perspective on US intervention in the Pacific, and though he later denied letting emotions cloud his judgment, his actions suggested that he genuinely hoped American paternalism channeled via Chiang would save China.[25]

Luce and Judd waged their work on behalf of Nationalist China largely in the public sphere. Yet the press, government officials, and scholars of Asian affairs all identified a little-known man named Alfred Kohlberg as the shadowy mastermind behind the China Lobby. The *New York Post* described him as an "[a]gitator, prophet, Cassandra." He was the subject of endless supposition, and his activities—both rumored and real—made him the common denominator between the almost absurdly diverse factions of pro-Chiang activists.[26]

Kohlberg had been speaking and writing about the importance of Asia well before Republican politicians turned East Asia into a domestic political issue in the late 1940s. A devout anticommunist, Kohlberg actively sought to refute, defame, or silence all those whom he perceived as threats to his China-related causes and beliefs. He was initially dismissed as a crank, but Kohlberg accomplished a considerable amount while working alone behind the scenes. During the mid-1940s, he helped to instigate the slow demise of the Institute of Pacific Relations (IPR), an organization founded in 1925 to promote mutual understanding among Pacific Rim nations.[27] Kohlberg was convinced that IPR's staff was "almost 100% Red" and that its publications espoused a communist line.[28] He waged a research campaign that culminated in a federal investigation that irreparably damaged the group's reputation.[29] He also had a hand in the destruction of many promising careers, including those of Owen Lattimore and John Service. Unwaveringly committed to his vision of China—an ideal that was, not coincidentally, shared by many others—Kohlberg was a serious adversary who did not hesitate to use a range of aggressive tactics, from writing letters to supplying Joseph McCarthy with information.[30]

Kohlberg was born in San Francisco in 1887 to German immigrants of Jewish descent. His love affair with China began at the 1915 Pan-Pacific Exposition, where he saw an exhibit of Chinese fabrics that inspired him to become a textile importer. He traveled to Asia soon after and was immediately enchanted by China. His writings at the time described a preference for China over the more Westernized Japan: "[I]ts swift-running rickshaw coolies as opposed to the plod, plod of the Japanese coolies; China with its swarming population; China with its good-natured laughing street coolies as opposed to the more serious crowds in Japan; China immediately took itself to my heart."[31] That sentimental first impression would only grow more vivid as years passed, and it eventually would form the basis of his Asia First activism.

Meanwhile, Kohlberg made his headquarters in New York. Business thrived throughout the 1920s and even during the lean years of the Depression, its success largely due to the "Kohlkerchiefs" for which the firm became famous. Kohlberg's considerable wealth was bound to the manufacture of his textiles. According to biographer Joseph Keeley, he employed "an army" of Chinese women who embroidered handkerchiefs throughout southeastern China.[32] That arrangement ended after the Japanese attack on Pearl Harbor stifled American trade with Asia. Kohlberg reestablished his business once the war ended but was stymied again by the outcome of the Chinese Communist revolution. He finally liquidated his inventory in 1957. By then he had already devoted himself to resurrecting "the China that was."[33]

On the surface, Kohlberg's interest in China was easily interpreted as a financial matter. He reportedly earned about $1.5 million a year before World War II.[34] But his silence on the subject of reopening American trade to China complicated that explanation; unlike many other businessmen who had operated there before 1949, he never spoke out on the matter.[35] Given his utter devotion to Chiang, as well as his extensive efforts on behalf of Asia First, for Kohlberg monetary gain appeared to pale in comparison to the political eradication of those who threatened his romanticized notions of Chinese life.

Reopening the Door

The goal of Asia First activism was to realize a China that was accessible to the United States, a nation that benefitted from the influence of democratic empire. Together, Luce, Judd, and Kohlberg represented a particular strain of American orientalism that took the idea of Asia First quite literally. They and other activists who worked to restore Chiang shared a central belief: America's fate was inextricably tied to that of China. Correspondingly, Mao's victory symbolized a great blow to democracy everywhere. Clearly referencing national security, Judd declared that US citizens needed to "wake up to the real nature of the Communist movement in China and to the fact that its real target is ourselves. . . . [I]t is plain that to all that the Communists have all of Asia and ourselves, not just China, as their aim."[36] If China under Chiang was once a bulwark against communism, its demise meant danger for its neighbors across the Pacific. By helping China, Americans helped themselves.

Beyond the idea of geopolitical containment, Judd's statement carried a note of sentimentality that emphasized a moral element to reestablishment of the Guomindang state on mainland China. If the Chinese were indeed potential counterparts who had long looked to the United States for leadership and protection, then national morality was also in jeopardy if US policy did not change. In a manner that paralleled the federal government's concurrent programs to further what Christina Klein has dubbed a "sentimental education," China Lobby activists declared that Washington had a paternal duty to China that transcended the normal state-to-state relationship.[37] Their emotional rhetoric differed from that of former isolationists like Robert Taft and Arthur Vandenberg. The latter had approached the issue with a certain degree of sangfroid, viewing China primarily as a strategy to counter political adversity at home. China Lobbyists, on the other hand, played to their audiences' goodwill or baser fears, often both. Through a personalization of the United States' connection to China, they became willing to go to great (some would say undue) lengths to see their version of world order restored.

As the variety of orientalist expression suggests, the doctrine of "Asia First" adapted to shifting diplomatic, political, and even personal contexts. It is best understood as a set of beliefs that had a few core tenets and many malleable ones. Strident anti-communism and fear of Mao were constants even as many fine points of disagreement existed—the actual effectiveness of Chiang among those. Nevertheless, the mere existence of the People's Republic of China (PRC) provided a unity of purpose.

The historical origins of those impulses can be traced to a misunderstanding of Secretary of State John Hay's "Open Door" notes of 1899 and 1900. In a 1970 interview Judd averred, "In the Far East—our west—our policy was 'Maintaining the Open Door in China'" to keep China "free and independent."[38] The memos' original, mercenary goal of granting US commercial interests equal opportunity to exploit Chinese resources was overlooked, as was the fact that Hay's messages did little to slow the territorialization of a weak country by European states and the Japanese government.[39]

A revision of diplomatic history led to the arrogant assumption that

America's relationship with China before 1949 had been a proprietary one, that China, as an overseas territory of US democratic empire, was a sort of protectorate. Such a line of reasoning made it possible to believe that the United States could "lose" China in the first place.[40] *How the Far East Was Lost* (1963) by Anthony Kubeck was a representative example of this line of interpretation. It directly blamed Democratic presidents for a series of poor decisions, ranging from cooperation with the Soviet Union on the UN to allowing communist interests in Washington to prevent adequate aid from being transmitted Chiang, that led to the "loss." This version of Asia First argued for a return to a state of foreign affairs that never really existed. As one critical review of Kubeck's book concluded, "The United States never 'lost' the Far East because it never could have 'won' it."[41] While the notion that China somehow belonged to the United States lacked logic, it still managed to hold sway over the imaginations of many, perhaps because it was so historically ingrained. Numerous scholars have analyzed how the longing for a benevolently paternalistic US-China relationship had deep-seated roots dating back decades.[42] An attitude that colored a wide range of Chinese-American interaction, it was driven by a sense of nostalgia rather than political partisanship, though it was difficult to discern the difference at times.

Conversely, the impulse toward interventionism was unambiguous. Unlike the old-guard conservative elites of the GOP, Asia First activists never saw themselves as isolationist. They consistently pushed for the US government to participate in international affairs if only to protect American interests, be they economic or cultural, or related to national security. "The American Century," an essay published by Luce in the February before Pearl Harbor, urged readers to recognize that geopolitics and moral commitments made isolationism untenable. "We are *in* the war," he insisted.[43] Rather than resisting involvement, citizens could "bring forth a vision of America as a world power which [was] authentically American." Armed with the characteristics of the Western frontier—"imagination," "vigor," and "enthusiasm"—they could remake the twentieth century, and the world, in their own image.[44] Similarly, Judd showed impatience with those who had their heads in the sand, including senior members of his own party who believed that domestic conservatism required isolation from international developments. "I was totally non-isolationist. . . . I knew that it was an impossible policy for the United States," he recalled, adding that his firm belief in collective security and other forms of permanent alliance dovetailed more often with the Democrats than the GOP.[45]

The rhetoric of Asia First reconstructed Hay's memos as acts of benevolent intervention. For example, Judd proposed a pairing of the Open Door and the Monroe Doctrine of 1823 and suggested they both be revived as corner-stones of the nation's foreign policy.[46] Failure to recognize how an Open Door could contradict the Monroe Doctrine and its declaration of hemispheric iso-lationism demonstrated a strong sense of proprietorship toward China. While many strict isolationists cited the doctrine as historical proof that the United States' interests should stay close to home, pro-Chiang activists considered China to be a territory that fell under the mandates of Monroe's edict. Yet the vision of a divided world still remained. For example, Kohlberg declared "Old World" Europe to be decadent and corrupt, a lost cause; on the other hand, China and Asia were partners in America's Pacific destiny and should therefore be spared from communist tyranny.[47]

Free China activism also built on a long tradition of nongovernmental interventionism in Asia, namely, American missionary campaigns. It was a tactic ideal for the early struggle against international communism, since politicians and other leaders divided the world into absolute halves: light and dark, good and evil, democratic and dictatorial. The idea that communism represented atheism and therefore jeopardized China's five hundred million souls combined Cold War fears with notions of Christian paternalism. Many China Lobbyists were actively involved in their religious communities and used the language of salvation to underscore their anticommunism. Half a billion behind the Bamboo Curtain needed to be saved, and the United States would only be able to fulfill its obligation to them through the deliverance of aid to the Chinese Nationalists.

What made the Chinese a worthy cause was their seeming possession of the correct traits for conversion. The *Christian Century* provided a typical description of the Chinese as "patient, industrious, tolerant, peace-loving, and democratic" people who looked to the United States for their faith in free-dom.[48] Any overture of conciliation toward the Communist regime in Peking would "shake the confidence in us of the peoples in Asia still on the fence," reasoned Judd. The pendulum could just as easily swing the other way. Claire Chennault offered his own analysis: "Many Chinese are now accepting the Communists only because they feel the United States has abandoned China to its fate. At the first real sign of American interest in China these marginal millions would abandon the Communists."[49]

In either scenario, the United States was responsible for extending the hope for democratic salvation, as though the vast majority of Chinese people were passive entities incapable of sovereignty. Statements made by public figures like Judd and Chennault revealed fundamental doubts about China's ability to sustain its own best interests. They dismissed the possibility that Chinese communism was indigenous or ideologically distinct from Soviet communism; Marxism was supposed to be an anomaly in democratically inclined China. At the same time, they refused to believe that the Chiang regime could win a civil war against Mao's Communists without astronomical sums of military and financial aid, which the Roosevelt and Truman administrations refused to grant. As a result, China's fall reflected badly on powerful Americans who should have known better than the weak, if brave, Chinese, and it was left to the United States to rectify the matter.[50]

That set of ideals led Asia First activists to extraordinary measures on behalf of a foreign regime. They spoke out against their own government, spent untold sums of money and other resources, and risked reputations. A few, like Kohlberg, became notorious. Their sentimental orientalism was not purely organic, however. Guomindang representatives were careful to stoke any initial impulses favorable to them, waging an extensive public relations campaign in the mass media and on the ground. American China Lobbyists were themselves being lobbied.

The Chiangs at Work

One hallmark of Asia First activism was a belief that Chiang Kai-shek should be allowed to resume leadership of all China. That sentiment varied from romanticization of Chiang and his wife Soong Mei-ling as embodiments of democratic leadership, morality, and military bravery to the more guarded argument that Chiang deserved support simply because he was the obvious alternative to Mao and was to play a part in the mainland's liberation. The most ardent Asia Firsters considered "Chiang" and "China" to be interchangeable entities. They dismissed negative reports of the Guomindang regime as Soviet propaganda and expressed the belief that the Generalissimo, like China itself, was capable of great things if given adequate support.

Since the 1930s, the Nationalist government had systematically curried favor with the American public via mass media. Even as knowledgeable US officials, skeptical journalists, and GIs stationed in China saw the Guomindang as a weak ally, Chiang's personal popularity in the United States held steady thanks to rigorous campaigning.[51] Jonathan Fenby's recent biography describes Chiang as a man obsessed with his international public image who once used violent means to thwart the publication of his second wife's potentially damaging memoir.[52] The Guomindang public relations machine, combined with favorable coverage from Luce's large-circulation publications, meant China remained on the public's radar.

The theme of the United States' betrayal of Chiang recurred on both sides of the Pacific.[53] Nationalist leaders were careful to stress that redemption could still be achieved if Washington would only act. For example, in 1950 Chiang asserted, "The future of Asia depends basically on the firmness of American Far Eastern foreign policy rather than any temporary or local fortunes of war. I firmly believe that, through timely American leadership of a fighting union of Asiatic countries, this huge pool of man power may yet be saved from Communist domination and thereby the world may yet be spared a third world war."[54] As GOP conservatives castigated Truman for not prioritizing Asia over Europe, Chiang compounded the pressure with demands for an international alliance in the Pacific that resembled the North Atlantic Treaty Organization (NATO) and assured mutual defense for member countries. Chiang's tone of deference did little to mask an extreme frustration with the lack of tangible support from the US government. The very public venue of his statements, *U.S. News & World Report*, suggested that he never intended it to. His words were addressed to the reading masses rather than the White House or State Department.

Faced with lack of enthusiasm from official quarters, the Guomindang often took its pleas directly to the American people. In their ongoing campaign to educate overseas readers about China, Chiang and Soong Mei-ling frequently granted interviews and played host to friendly journalists. The goal was to cultivate consciousness among the voting public to pressure federal officials to funnel more foreign aid to the Nationalist government. If that failed, hopefully new leaders more sympathetic to the Guomindang would come to power.

Even before the resumption of the Chinese civil war, the regime had amassed a considerable amount of experience in mass persuasion. Mme Chiang regularly visited American cities during her tenure as First Lady. In 1943 she addressed both the House and the Senate and then subsequently embarked on a national tour that stretched from New York to Los Angeles. John Service recalled that her tour created a "furor of propaganda favorable to the Kuomintang. . . . She was appealing over the head of the president by going directly to Congress."[55] During the early 1950s, she made New York her secondary headquarters and the frequency of her public appearances intensified. Her topic of choice was almost always China's need for American aid, and her effectiveness as a sympathetic figure was undeniable. In China itself, the Guomindang had experienced a long decline in popularity that dated from misguided decisions Chiang made throughout the 1930s.[56] Thanks to his industrious spouse, Chiang's popularity in the United States far outpaced the goodwill felt by the people he wanted to govern.

Soong Mei-ling was a woman modern by common standards for Western women and revolutionary by American ones for Chinese women, the per-

fect Westernized foil to her husband. Her fluent English even bore traces of
a Southern accent, a reminder of time spent in Macon, Georgia, when she
was a young girl. As a student at Wellesley College, she excelled academi-
cally and was remembered as a popular figure on campus.[57] During the long
war with Japan, she acted as the humanitarian face of Chiang's government,
fronting sewing drives, visiting hospitals, and opening orphanages. In private,
she often served as his translator and intermediary at strategic meetings with
Allied officials.[58] Soong's charm was legendary when it served her needs, and
more than a few American politicians were smitten. "You may ask how to win
the hearts of the people? My idea of learning would be simply to sit at the feet
of Mme. Chiang," Thomas Dewey remarked after Soong's wartime visit.[59] Her
magnetic personality and a background that combined East and West allowed
Soong to appear as the attractive embodiment of a China open to America's
influence.[60]

    If her persona underscored an imagined close relationship between the
two nations, so, too, did her words. According to Soong, one of their shared
connections was an impulse toward Christianity, which led to a common
set of basic democratic principles. Unfortunately for the Chinese, an atheistic government prevented them from exercising their civil rights. "It has
been part of the Communist technique to rob us of our faith," she averred to
Readers Digest in August 1955. "We Christians of the present generation have
lacked the spiritual fire to insist on a better world. We can have a better world
only if we care enough." Her message was a deft balance of respect and indict-
ment. "We" and "us" designated a US-China community of Christian nations.
The United States and China were bound by a common faith, yet the former
had done nothing to redeem its brethren from atheistic totalitarianism. She
concluded by describing her husband in Christlike terms: He was a Methodist
and willing to die for "the Cause" but could not keep fighting until more of
"us" were ready to do the same.[61]

    The mien put forth by Soong Mei-ling was designed to make Nationalist
China more legible to US citizens by aligning her husband's government with
the Christian, democratic values that Americans stereotypically cherished.
What most of the latter did not recognize was how such a presentation directly countered Guomindang policies implemented as recently as the 1930s
and 1940s. Historians of modern China have long debated the Nationalists'
militaristic tendencies, with some going so far as to describe the regime as
fascist.[62] Whether or not Chiang himself could be labeled as such remains
open for interpretation. In the Cold War United States, however, the political
aftermath of the Chinese civil war made anticommunism an overriding quali-
fication for public sympathy. Moreover, a dearth of knowledge about wartime

China, let alone the specifics of Guomindang directives, allowed an emissary like Soong to portray Chiang as she saw fit.

Mme Chiang was deft at endearing herself to readers and listeners even as she attempted to arouse their self-reproach. She was a familiar face during and after the war, and her pleas for American aid found receptive audiences from coast to coast.[63] Nonetheless, the US government did not grant the amount of foreign aid the Nationalists would have liked. The 1948 China Aid Act provided for $463 million overall, but promised only to supervise $125 million in military procurement rather than provide arms firsthand—amounts in sharp contrast to the $13 billion allocated by the Marshall Plan to rebuild Western Europe.[64] Soong's high profile did manage to extract concessions like the repeal of the 1882 Chinese Exclusion Act (the law that had attempted to ban Chinese immigration to the United States), a gesture of goodwill made a few months after her visit in 1943.[65] As late as 1958, when it was clear that the Guomindang was not going to be (and perhaps never had been) a viable option for China, the New York Times still described her as "fragile, charming, eloquent."[66]

She may have conveyed an aura of fragility, but Soong possessed power in her own right and was integral to the Guomindang's plans for securing foreign funding. Faced with the reconstruction of European allies, conflict on the Korean peninsula, and a dearth of practical knowledge about the Sino-Soviet relationship, Washington was in no position to underwrite a foolhardy venture in China. After it became apparent that the desired aid was not forthcoming, Nationalist fundraising within the American private sector became even more vital.

During the early 1950s, Mme Chiang's overseas work extended beyond convocation speeches and radio addresses as she increasingly waged business behind closed doors. In the privacy of the Riverdale, Bronx, home of her brother-in-law, financier H. H. Kung, she presided over salons for people invested in helping the Nationalist government. Those in attendance ranged from leaders of the Chinese American community to former military personnel and diplomats. They also included individuals who held emotional ties to China, if not ethnic or professional ones. Sessions resulted with attendees pledging substantial donations to show their support.[67]

Guomindang leaders made certain their American sympathizers felt valued, and they went to great lengths to personalize their gratitude. The relationship between V. K. Wellington Koo, the Republic of China's ambassador to the United States, and Alfred Kohlberg provides a case in point. In late 1949, just as the civil war was reaching its conclusion, Koo made the New Yorker a member of the Order of the Auspicious Star, an honorary decoration reserved for foreign supporters (Henry Luce also received one in 1947).[68] The gesture triggered an emotional response from Kohlberg: "In this time of trial I especially appreciate the thoughtfulness displayed by your government and shall greatly treasure this decoration as a token of your appreciation."[69] In following years Koo sent holiday gifts—a poinsettia in 1950 and a gift basket in 1952—to maintain the friendship.[70]

The Soong family also extended its hand. Mme Chiang's older brother, T. V. Soong, invited Kohlberg to dinner while Soong Mei-ling herself singled him out for special attention. When she sent him a telegram of condolence after the death of his wife, Kohlberg's response described the late Jane as he would himself: "Jane was a great admirer of you and your husband, and was deeply involved, in every way, in the cause for which you and he so nobly stand."[71] Their relationship spanned over a decade. It evolved to the point where the textile importer could invite the First Lady of Free China to take in a performance of *Flower Drum Song* on Broadway.[72]

That leaders of the Guomindang invested so much to cultivate overseas support was significant on a number of levels. Above all, it demonstrated the limited options at the disposal of a severely weakened Nationalist regime. Doubts about Chiang's ability proved bipartisan, and regime change from Truman to the Republican Dwight Eisenhower did little to improve chances of a Guomindang restoration. While Washington was careful to keep friendship alive with mutual defense treaties and positive remarks, support of a mainland takeover was never in the offing. Without a large degree of help forthcoming from the federal government, the Guomindang increasingly turned to private citizens and politicians willing to defy their party's mainstream.

Indeed, the Guomindang found a greater success with grassroots activists in the United States than in efforts to sway official US policy. Its ability to motivate citizens overseas to the cause of Free China, as well as the alacrity with which China Lobbyists worked to change foreign policy and public opinion, demonstrated the plausibility of international relations practiced on an extrastate basis. The American Cold War experience emphasized communism as both a domestic and foreign threat. When, how, and where to fight the enemy was consequently at once a much more individualized and immediate matter than perhaps was formal warfare. By personally reaching out to China supporters, the Nationalists provided an outlet for citizens frustrated with the situation in Asia.

Alfred Kohlberg's writings and actions collectively reveal a deep-seated need for approval from recognized authorities. The attention lavished on him by such illustrious personages would be enough to turn anyone's head, but he was particularly vulnerable. Personal contact with Mme Chiang and other

Nationalist officials catapulted his organic interest in China into the realm of obsession. At her behest, Kohlberg redoubled his commitment to "re-educate America about China" and counter the confusion instigated by a "barrage of Communist propaganda."[73]

On the surface, Kohlberg was the least likely of candidates to emerge as the force behind an American China lobby. He was not so well known as other Free China advocates and his credentials as an expert on East Asia were relatively weak. Whatever authority Kohlberg claimed as an "expert" was derived from travel to China for both business and charity, including a 1941 trip as a representative of the American Bureau for Medical Aid to China.[74] He did not speak the Chinese language and much of his first-hand experience of the country was restricted to tours led by Nationalist guides and tea with Soong Mei-ling.

Although Kohlberg's understanding of China was narrow, few other civilians could claim they were as informed. Even before the Sino-Japanese War and World War II broke out, most US citizens did not have first-hand knowledge of China and relied on competing external sources (e.g., the press, missionaries, and diplomats) to explain East Asian events. As *Cosmopolitan* observed in 1945: "We have a tremendous stake in China, whose very life we save and whose continued welfare traditionally engages us. Yet we know little about China and less about the Chinese."[75]

Armed with Mme Chiang's personal blessing, Kohlberg sought to fill that information vacuum with the help of like-minded activists. What Luce did with his magazines and Judd in Congress, he accomplished behind the scenes. His efforts on the ground constituted a major share of Asia First activism, and their largely private nature has obscured Kohlberg's long-term significance. An examination of the American China Lobby's formation points to a popular dimension of Cold War foreign relations, one that demonstrates how grassroots action shaped the intersection of international affairs and domestic politics in surprising and significant ways.

An Asia First Network

Working mostly out of the public eye, Kohlberg coordinated disparate groups into a convincingly united front. The singularity of their shared purpose — support for Chiang — belied the rather scattershot methods used to create an impression of organizational unity. A preliminary strategy was to contact just about any public or powerful figure that expressed an interest in Asia and solicit their support for Chiang. Kohlberg approached people ranging from anticommunist cronies like Albert Wedemeyer and William. J. Loeb (publisher of the *Manchester* [NH] *Union-Leader*) to much more distant acquaintances, such as Pearl S. Buck and comedienne Lucille Ball.

Buck's endorsement in particular was a potentially powerful resource. Her best-selling novel *The Good Earth* (1931) had given millions of Americans their first impressions of Asia, and her approval would have provided significant cultural cache.[76] Kohlberg approached the author numerous times to no avail. Not one to take rejection well, he labeled her "naïve politically."[77] "I think your humanitarianism is being used by less scrupulous persons," he condescended. "Frankly I think you are confused and I fear you are the victim of propaganda."[78] Buck fired back that she was wary of extremism on either end of the political spectrum. She likened Kohlberg's pushiness to tactics used by communists—both "would drive all human beings into one camp or the other" and both were "dangerous in their desire to control the world."[79]

Failure to enlist the author hardly slowed down Kohlberg's campaign. There was logic behind his wide-ranging choice of correspondents, since the diversity of people that he tried to enlist reflected the multifronted battle he hoped to wage. The fundamental goal was to reestablish Chiang's government in China, but there was more than one way to make Americans understand East Asia as vital to their own survival. China had been lost due to a combination of diplomatic, religious, intellectual, and media factors; accordingly, the reeducation program he promised Mme Chiang needed to cover all those areas. With his business affairs suspended, Kohlberg's attention span for anything related to the cause was limitless and his motivation boundless. No one was better suited to the challenge of harnessing and coordinating the energy of those left unsatisfied by US China policy.

A structural groundwork was already in place. In early 1946, Kohlberg founded the American China Policy Association (ACPA) in response to the continued existence of the IPR, the organization he had accused of communism three years earlier.[80] Both groups sought to strengthen international relations along the Pacific Rim, but the similarities ended there. The ACPA's geographic focus was much narrower (the United States and China only) and it promoted a strict anticommunist stance that eradicated any claim to objectivity. Its goal was not revenge but rather the power to exert, as Mme Chiang suggested, a "corrective influence."[81] During the late 1940s and into the 1950s, the ACPA functioned as a major source of nongovernmental information on China. It served as a think tank/press office/fundraising center, an umbrella organization for Nationalist Chinese interests in the United States. If there was a single group that constituted the backbone of the China Lobby, the ACPA was it.

The original plan was for the ACPA to exist alongside the State Department and make some sort of imprint over the latter's formal policy. In 1946 Dean Acheson had assured Kohlberg the PRC would never receive aid from American quarters until it cooperated with the Nationalists.[82] As long as the State Department continued to recognize the Guomindang above all other parties in China, it could be considered a partner in anticommunism. Collaboration became impossible after the August 1949 release of the department's China White Paper, which squarely blamed Chiang for Mao's imminent victory. The ACPA hurriedly mailed a statement to all members of Congress, seven hundred newspapers, and other media outlets, while Kohlberg wrote personal reassurances to Chiang and Soong Mei-ling. After reading the report, Kohlberg concluded the State Department was primarily at fault for Nationalist defeat and that Acheson and his officers had been unwilling to combat a growing threat. From his perspective, Foreign Service bureaucrats like John Service, John Carter Vincent, and John Paton Davies had caused incalculable damage by mistaking Chinese Communists as "agrarian reformers" and recommending that the Guomindang broker peace with them. That tendency toward appeasement presumably made the department incapable of containing communism, let alone spreading democracy throughout the world.[83]

From late 1949 onward, ACPA press releases and publications questioned all aspects of official American action in East Asia. In his own writings, Kohlberg applied the adjectives he had earlier used against the IPR to describe State Department officials. Animosity toward the agency did not abate even after John Foster Dulles replaced Acheson. The ACPA claimed to be the sole source for acceptable American policy on China, an alternative to the State Department itself. The standard, and only, line it promoted was that the United States should properly equip Chiang so that he could become an asset in the global fight against communism.

Because the organization so closely followed Kohlberg's own interpretations and beliefs, it might be easily dismissed as a vanity project. But its founder in fact wanted the group to wield real influence over US China policy, as he believed the IPR had, so he enlisted the help of more illustrious and powerful figures. At his request, J. B. Powell (editor of *China Weekly Review*), Clare Luce, and Loeb successively occupied the ACPA presidency and acted as the group's public face. Other famous "China Associates" could lend their good names on a lesser scale. Kohlberg himself would stay out of the spotlight as a vice president and chairman of Board of Directors, although power still rested firmly in his hands since only he could designate the organization's president.[84] The point was to attract attention and project legitimacy through the power of association. The "Manchurian Manifesto" of 1946, which bore the names of dozens of public figures and had decried the Yalta settlement, was one of its earliest public relations efforts.

Another inroad to influence was through the two major political parties. Despite its idiosyncratic nature, the China Lobby was willing to partner with *either* Democrats or Republicans, as long as they were willing to advocate an Asia First stance.[85] The GOP was the obvious fit. The internal debate over Cold War foreign policy forced dissatisfied members to look outside party confines for other options. As previously isolationist conservatives began to agitate for a foreign policy platform that was distinct from bipartisan containment, Kohlberg simultaneously reinforced his contacts among Republican politicians throughout the late 1940s.

Of all the well-known names that participated in the ACPA, Walter Judd proved the most useful. He and Kohlberg held nearly identical views on the past and future of US-China relations. Both were concerned about internal communism only as far as it impacted foreign policy decisions. Judd complained to his friend in 1948 that the House Un-American Activities Committee spent too much time investigating Hollywood celebrities rather than seeking out the real threats, "the pro-Reds who have been influencing our policy toward Asia for so long."[86] Kohlberg himself espoused the same theory. For over a decade he and Judd forged a close working relationship through frequent correspondence and trading of information. The congressman sat on the ACPA's Board of Directors and lent his name to its letterhead, while Kohlberg made donations to Judd's reelection campaigns.[87] Judd's solid reputation and increasing House seniority were major assets, and Kohlberg valued him as a key player in the Free China cause.

Judd was just one of the links that connected Kohlberg to the GOP; others were forged as the result of opportune timing. Resumption of civil war in China coincided with the presidential election of 1948, a race that Republicans believed they might actually win. Dogged by his predecessor's shadow and crises in Europe, the Middle East, and Asia, Truman's candidacy appeared weak. Major news outlets predicted that a strong Republican contender could easily take the race. As the second-time GOP nominee, Thomas Dewey appeared poised to achieve the goal that had eluded him in 1944. One of his strategies was to exploit perceptions of the Democratic administration's weaknesses in diplomatic affairs. Since China was the major exception to bipartisan foreign policy, Dewey began by demanding the US government give more guns and more money to Chiang Kai-shek.[88]

A major party nominee had finally made China a priority. Kohlberg was ecstatic and willing to show his appreciation through generous contributions. A $5,000 check accompanied his note to Dewey's campaign manager:

"THOMAS E. DEWEY IS THE MAN TO GET THE GOVERNMENT OUT OF THE RED AND THE RED OUT OF THE GOVERNMENT."[89] He also freely offered advice on anticommunism and East Asia, even going so far as to outline "The Dewey Plan" for foreign policy: "It does not enlarge the commitments of the Truman Doctrine and Marshall Plan. It merely requires every ally prove itself by choosing our side now and burning its bridges through destruction of its fifth column and restriction of trade. It creates an allied world cleansed of fifth columns and pledges to principles that permit no further sell-outs."[90] In note after note and memo after memo, Kohlberg attempted to position himself as Dewey's teacher and biggest fan, cautioning the nominee against misguided liberals while lauding him as the solution to "the Communist-slave-state-tyranny."[91]

The candidate himself did not reciprocate that level of enthusiasm. Dewey was much more moderate than his admirer was perhaps willing to acknowledge, and his interest in China extended no further than a shallow critique of Democratic policy. There is little evidence of his taking Kohlberg's aggressive directives seriously. Yet that mattered little in the long run. The Dewey candidacy had served its purpose for Kohlberg. He was thrilled that Republicans had chosen to stake their claim in the Pacific and that China became a theme of the campaign, and he vested more and more in the GOP as a vehicle for Free China as a result.[92]

Such goodwill did not extend to all Republican elites. At the moment he built Dewey up, Kohlberg was tearing down GOP officials he thought guilty of appeasing communism. Arthur Vandenberg, whose cooperation was so vital to bipartisan foreign policy, was singled out for special attention. In an ill-timed maneuver, conservative hardliners complained Vandenberg had turned Congress into a rubber stamp body that approved any foreign policy Truman wanted.[93] Kohlberg joined in the fray by writing a series of incendiary letters that accused the senator of rendering the GOP indistinguishable from the Democrats and marching it toward extinction.[94] Vandenberg's attackers failed to appreciate that his deliberate silence on China during postwar negotiations had preserved Republicans' ability to blame Democrats for the situation in Asia.

Dewey lost in November, and the photograph of a jubilant Truman hoisting the *Chicago Tribune*'s erroneous front-page headline became part of election lore. Kohlberg's mourning period was brief. Undaunted, he continued to court other politicians, mostly from the Republican ranks, and he kept an eye out for more public officials willing to speak out about China. As the 1950s unfolded, the majority of those belonged to the newly internationalized conservative wing of the GOP. Joseph Martin, Robert Taft, and Richard Nixon subsequently earned his esteem.[95]

Kohlberg was also busy at the grassroots level consolidating various China-related groups into what looked liked a well-funded and monolithic network. The public nature of his relationship to the Chinese Nationalists coupled with his prominent activism heightened the impression that the Guomindang had amassed a vast collective of American influence. What he managed to achieve was a masterpiece of illusion, and it propelled Asia First forward on the grassroots level.

In return for their endorsement of the ACPA, Kohlberg sat on the boards of multiple advocacy groups and charities established by other activists. If he did not act as an officer, he made donations. United China Relief, Association for the Chinese Blind, and the Committee for One Million were just a few of the groups pulled into orbit. Because his name was associated with so many organizations, even a keen observer could come to the conclusion that all China-related groups were interchangeable and the former textile importer was some sort of omnipresent mastermind. "Alfred Kohlberg" became synonymous with "China Lobby." Kohlberg himself reinforced that notion. He increasingly stepped from behind the scenes and into the public spotlight. Besides acting as a liaison between discrete groups, he agreed to public speaking engagements to educate audiences about Chiang and China. He took to the podium as "a distinguished American patriot; an authority on Oriental problems, the friend and supporter of Generalissimo Chiang Kai-shek."[96]

There was only so much one individual could undertake. Kohlberg was acutely aware of the history of American missionaries in East Asia and realized that the religious sector would have to play a vital part in any China lobby. Like Luce and Judd, a significant number of Asia First activists were the children of missionaries to China or had served as missionaries themselves. Kohlberg's own impressions of Chinese Communism had been informed by bulletins and letters forwarded by missionary home offices. Dating from 1945 to 1949, these documents told of CCP atrocities committed against Chinese and American civilians alike. They described the destruction of property, military torture, and murder. Intended to raise both sympathy and money, the dispatches depicted atheistic communism as not only resistant to Western civilization but also threatening to all that was just and righteous. Missionaries often testified that Communist China was directly tied to Soviet Russia.[97] Then there were those Americans simply active in their local church communities who were more likely to view Chiang favorably as the Christian alternative to Mao; it was crucial to tap into that potential wellspring of support.

Following the lead of Mme Chiang, Kohlberg sought to enlist the nation's Christians to fight against Chinese Communism. Through him the ACPA solicited the support of spiritual organizations like the American Christian

Alliance, American Council of Christian Laymen, and various theological seminaries.[98] Kohlberg often adopted spiritual rhetoric when asking for their support. Whether they were Protestant or Catholic, he made frequent references to "good," "evil," and God. If communism were overthrown, he reasoned, Christian leaders could once again enjoy a significant presence in China and continue their good work saving heathen souls.[99]

The strongest tie between the Free China cause and religious groups was a shared hatred of how their respective beliefs were in decline, allegedly because of communism. Unable to realize that his visibility had increased due to the outcome of the Chinese civil war, Kohlberg was concerned that his patriotic views were being pushed from the mainstream of public opinion. William H. Anderson of the American Christian Alliance made the same complaint, fretting, "Communism has already invaded both Politics and Religion" and a coalition was needed to "achieve unity in self-defense against this sinister, subversive force."[100] Solidarity was to be achieved by standing shoulder to shoulder with other anticommunist organizations, including the ACPA.

It is important to note that, although Kohlberg actively courted religious groups, the China Lobby did not adopt an overtly theocratic stance. Religious conversion was the not the end goal. Rather, China was to be redeemed, first and foremost, by anticommunism and renewed American intervention on the mainland. The appeal to religious organizations stemmed from Kohlberg's belief that they were more receptive to an Asia First message, not because he wanted to further the missionary endeavor specifically.

Just as significantly, some Christian leaders were neither convinced by Kohlberg's argument nor interested in collaboration, despite how eagerly he sought their help. More than a few vehemently disagreed with the blindly pro-Chiang, Nationalist interpretation of events. "What is not so well known, or at least so well remembered, is that China has been in revolution for half a century," stated Frank T. Cartwright of the Methodist Church's Board of Missions. "In appraising universal unrest, we should remember that the Kuomintang rode into power on military successes that were largely based on promises of social reform. Some of these promises were kept, but not enough of them . . ." International Missionary Council Secretary J. W. Decker concurred: "No doubt our Government has been guilty of mistake . . . but the determining factor has been a sharp cleavage in the Chinese nation." Not wishing to risk alienating such key groups, Kohlberg responded quite meekly: "Our only disagreement is that you feel that there is nothing that could properly be done and I feel that there is. . . . [W]e do not seem far apart and I wonder whether most Americans, except those few of the extreme left, are not in agreement with us thus far."[101]

There were other fissures beneath the surface. Not all people who wanted China free of communism worked with the ACPA. As mentioned above, Pearl Buck resisted Kohlberg very early on. Henry Luce was another case in point. Because his wife was closely involved with the ACPA and he, too, was deeply connected to China, Luce seemed like he would be a natural ally. Nonetheless, the *Time-Life* publisher was put off by Kohlberg's constant finger pointing and rejected many overtures of friendship, leaving the latter bewildered.[102] In his zeal, Kohlberg could alienate even his closest allies. He once suggested that Judd shortchanged Rep. Martin Dies (D-TX), who "was really right about the Communists, when you and I weren't taking them too seriously, not even in China, back in the '30s." Judd strenuously rebuffed the accusation: "[Y]ou take me to task because I do not give all my effort to the same sort of anti-Communist activity that you diligently advocate and pursue." Their relationship cooled dramatically after that exchange, despite Kohlberg's feeble explanation that he was only joking.[103] Other times it was Kohlberg who did the rejecting. He deplored John T. Flynn, the author of *While You Slept: America's Tragedy in Asia and Who Made It.* Flynn's America First organization and his associate Charles Lindbergh were both praised by the German-American Bund, a fact that Kohlberg, who was Jewish, could not abide.[104]

If there was one ally the China Lobby could count on to take unequivocal action, it was Joseph McCarthy, Kohlberg's most apt pupil. "As you may know," he wrote to Herbert Hoover in 1950, "I have been of some slight assistance to Senator Joseph McCarthy with background material and have managed to keep informed of the developments and the character of the testimony that will be forthcoming." Kohlberg described his contributions as mere supplements to the senator's organic impulse to investigate the State Department.[105] He was being modest: The disproportionate number of Foreign Service officers who worked the Far East desk and IPR affiliates among McCarthyism's early victims demonstrated the pivotal nature of the information Kohlberg supplied.[106] Later he seemed to take took fuller ownership of the inquiries, bristling when the media alleged that McCarthy had fabricated evidence. The senator's statements, he averred, were "packed with facts."[107]

Because Kohlberg supplied the ambitious, attention-hungry senator with information, China Lobby interests were able to manipulate the course of early McCarthyism. The consequences for US foreign policy and the field of East Asian studies were immediate as the careers of scholars and diplomats were hindered or destroyed outright. In the long term, American understanding of Pacific relations regressed because few were willing to take risks by opposing the view that communism was monolithic and that the CCP took direction from the Soviet Union.[108] The senator and his aides' ea-

gerness to prove that Americans had made a mess of East Asia, in conjunc-
tion with the public's apparent willingness to believe the charges, made the
early phases of the postwar Red Scare almost like a national self-flagellation
over the loss of China. Ultimately, as Ernest May has astutely highlighted, it
was a Democratic administration that justifiably purged the China hands.
But pressure from Congress, as well as internal discomfort over those Foreign
Service officers' ability to act on behalf of the national interest, forced Dean
Acheson to act.[109]

McCarthyism's campaign against disloyalty and internal subversion renewed the domestic front in the war against communism. It has been pointed
out that the McCarthy-Kohlberg connection introduced treason as a new dimension to Cold War anxiety.[110] What has gone unnoted, however, is how
McCarthyism raised the profile of Free China and lengthened its shelf life
as a relevant issue. The charges of State Department officials pushing China
to communism actually prolonged Chiang's time in the limelight, even after
a new foreign policy in his favor became impossible. McCarthyism not only
sustained Asia First activism, it attracted new anticommunist recruits and
increased notoriety for Kohlberg. And the latter was grateful. Even as Mc-
Carthy veered off course and faced censure, Kohlberg defended him as "an
honest patriot who makes mistakes" and extended his largesse to those close
to the senator, such as Roy Cohn.[111]

Backlash

The search for communists in government raised the profile of Asia First
as well, and by 1952, breathless reports of Guomindang operatives skulking
around Capitol corridors abounded.[112] The most extensive came from the left-
ist biweekly *The Reporter*, which named names both Chinese and American.
Over the course of two issues in April 1952, editor Max Ascoli and his staff ran
lengthy articles detailing the financial and political activities of high-ranking
Nationalist officials and their supporters in the United States.[113] The series
painted a sweeping panorama of US-China relations since 1940 complete
with unflattering portraits of alleged lobbyists. Its authors saw the hand of
the China Lobby everywhere. Their focus was money—how it moved and
whom it went to.

Judd and Kohlberg were prominently featured as prime agents behind
the American branch. The magazine let Judd down relatively easily, describing him as "a selfless altogether dedicated man who had seen China suffer and
had suffered with it."[114] By contrast, special ire was reserved for Kohlberg. He
was described as a "clever, complex" individual who had transformed into a

Alfred Kohlberg

FIGURE 2.1. Illustration of Alfred Kohlberg before Republic of China flag, in Charles Wertenbaker, "The Pattern of Enrichment," *The Reporter*, 15 April 1952, 9.

"zealot"; for all intents and purposes, he performed as a professional lobbyist on behalf of Chiang and was motivated by his business interests as well as anticommunist mania.[115] The visual representations of the written description were even more critical: In one, Kohlberg's short, squat figure stands in front of a Republic of China flag, cigar in hand. Ugly lines like deep ravines etch his face, which features flared nostrils and is framed by prominent ears. His mouth is partially open, as if to level yet another accusation.

The Reporter's examination of the China Lobby was an extremely thorough and nuanced piece of investigative journalism. The series' lead writer was Charles Wertenbaker, the former Foreign Editor and European correspondent for *Time*. Its analysis differentiated between a "good" lobby (support for China during World War II) and the "bad" one dominated by Kohlberg.

As best they could, the articles traced a flow of money from Guomindang coffers to public relations firms, political campaigns, and other operations that had promoted Chiang's government in America. Their text stands as the most comprehensive primary reportage on the subject and has been referenced extensively by any serious inquiry on the lobby.

While Wertenbaker and Ascoli did a fine job in portraying the lobby's myriad American members, their depiction of the Chinese demonstrated how liberals, too, used stereotypical imagery to explain the US-China relationship. But rather than viewing China as needy and ripe for American paternalism, the articles' rhetoric was reminiscent of anti-immigration language from the Gilded Age. As a result, the Chinese and the Chinese in America were reduced to two-dimensional caricatures. For example, members of the extended Soong family were described in dynastic terms as an internally divided clan that remained "exotic" and inscrutable to outsiders.[116] Editorial cartoons were sprinkled throughout the series like punctuation marks. One group depicts a slant-eyed Chinese agent dressed in a suit similar to Uncle Sam's. The illustrations show him traversing from New York to San Francisco to Washington holding a bulging briefcase presumably filled with money. A few pages later, a dragon is shown having just devoured a victim—a bowler hat, briefcase, and dollar bills lay scattered in the foreground. Another cartoon shows an enormous dragon curled into the "S" of a dollar sign; the sinister creature looms over the Capitol, poised to strike at the heart of American democracy. The fundamental message was clear and would have pleased even nineteenth-century labor leader Denis Kearney: The Chinese acted out of greed, and they used nefarious means, including infiltration of federal systems and duping of private citizens, to achieve their goals. The Chinese had to go.

The title "China Lobby" itself connoted invasion by numerous agents or a sort of Cold War Yellow Peril. Its use represented a smear, for "lobby" had become something of a dirty word in postwar government.[117] After the passage of the Legislative Reorganization Act of 1946, all formal interest groups were required to register with the federal government and disclose their finances and membership rolls.[118] With the ongoing McCarthy and McCarran investigations, anxiety enveloped Washington, and it was not difficult to convince liberals or moderates that sinister forces were at work. They loudly denounced what they saw as an unregulated foreign lobby that threatened national security and domestic political processes.

Conservative politicians showed they also wanted nothing to do with any lobby representing Nationalist China. In fact, they averred there was no such thing. Sen. Harry Cain (R-WA) best expressed those sentiments in a lengthy speech made the month after *The Reporter*'s investigation was published. He ridiculed the notion that any formal organization existed. Cain argued that if there was a China Lobby at work in America, it represented communist interests because all recent US foreign policy had been skewed in their favor. Moreover, there had been no investigations into foreign lobbies resulting from the Morse-McMahon resolution because the Democratic administration had not "a Chinaman's chance" of surviving unscathed. He then proceeded to insert the entire *Reporter* series into the *Congressional Record* as proof of the Communist Chinese Lobby at work.[119]

Yet, Kohlberg was unperturbed by the wealth of negative exposure. The reams of paper devoted to exposing the China Lobby only increased general awareness of Free China. According to his calculus, any publicity was good publicity. He relished his role in the process and wrote essays with titles such as "My China Lobby" and "I Am the China Lobby."[120] The purpose was to poke fun at liberals struggling to pin down his network of Asia First activism. The only point he challenged involved money. "Never have I had any business or financial transaction with the Government of the Republic of China, or any of its subsidiaries or with any individual Chinese even connected with the Government," Kohlberg avowed. He would make variations of that statement again and again. Any discernible financial connection between him and the Guomindang made an illegal, unregistered China lobby tangible. Moreover, an inability to prove that Kohlberg received any Nationalist money forced critics to complicate their assumptions regarding his motives.[121]

Even if he did helm a formal organization under the radar, it was far from effective. Judd's Committee for/of One Million was the only pro-Nationalist agency that succeeded in its mission. The lobby's power was based on the *presumption* of relationships and unity. Outsiders easily assumed that all the pro-Chiang groups and figures acted in coordination. Through name-dropping and his own ubiquity, Kohlberg had done an excellent job of presenting a solid front.[122] As William F. Buckley Jr. chortled, "*The Reporter* cannot wholly be blamed if, on seeing a thousand bullets whiz by, they assume they are shot by a thousand men."[123]

Grassroots Alternatives

The single-mindedness of Asia First activism could have resulted in a static pattern of behavior if the Korean War had not dramatically changed the tone of public discussion regarding East Asia. As Rosemary Foot has discussed, 60 percent of Americans surveyed in 1951 wanted the United States to give Nationalist forces "all the help they needed" to retake the mainland.[124] The looming question of PRC involvement in the conflict, coupled with Mac-

Arthur's dismissal, gave momentum to the theory that China's fall had initiated a domino effect soon to destroy a huge swath of the Pacific Rim.

For his part, Kohlberg felt vindicated by current events and became more confident in his persona as foreign affairs prophet. He was further buoyed by how some Republican leaders echoed ACPA press releases: "Can anyone expect the State Department to accept the blame for the fact that American boys are now being killed by Chinese Reds?," asked House Leader Martin in 1951.[125] Korea was a turning point that inspired Kohlberg to adopt new methods if not a new message. The resulting partnerships between those eager to provide alternatives to moderate consensus granted the China Lobby a certain solidity as well as ubiquity, cementing Asia First's place within nascent grassroots conservatism. That network would endure even after the possibility of Free China began to fade.

In the past, Kohlberg had focused on well-known names to give his cause legitimacy and heft. Once his name earned a reputation in its own right, he became less dependent on the help of others and more willing to criticize adversaries in an extremely personal fashion. He flooded the desks of politicians, White House administrators, and newspaper editors with letters. Kohlberg was a prodigious correspondent and rarely let a day go by without sending a missive to some major official or shaper of public opinion.[126]

Those communiqués became a trademark. In 1960, Buckley noted, "I myself count it a day lost when I do not see a letter Mr. Kohlberg has written to the President, or to Khrushchev, or to Allan Dulles, or J. Edgar Hoover, or Mrs. Roosevelt, or de Gaulle, or Churchill, or you, or me, copy to the *New York Times,* the *New York Herald Tribune,* the CIA, etc."[127] From a less accommodating perspective, one observer wrote that the correspondence was part of a "ceaseless endeavor" to brainwash Washington when it came to China.[128] Some of the missives received by Kohlberg's enemies could only be described as poisonous, and they could provoke deep anger. "I am unwilling to any longer run the chance of having my acceptance of your letters interpreted as indicating any measure of support either of your political views in regard to China or of your efforts to smear those who do not accept your interpretation of events in that unhappy country," wrote one recipient.[129]

Endeavors to convince or attack individuals one by one would never result in the rapid change in China policy that Kohlberg wanted. Mass communication was the most effective way to reach a large audience. But, excepting such figures as columnist George Sokolsky and *Chicago Tribune* publisher Robert McCormick, he distrusted the mainstream media. Foreign bureau dispatches and coverage of the Owen Lattimore investigation had convinced him that most reporters were communist sympathizers unwilling to tell the truth about China.[130] Edgar Snow, Theodore White, Drew Pearson, and Edward R. Murrow were particularly egregious examples. Academia, where those who crafted policy were trained, also posed a problem, especially since it allowed men like John King Fairbank and Lattimore to thrive: "Are they [the academic community] really so stupid, or is Communism and pro-Communism much more wide-spread than even I suspect?"[131]

The lack of sustained public outcry about China and Korea signaled that America needed outlets that told of communist infiltration into federal government and the repercussions for foreign policy. Kohlberg established the journal *Plain Talk* to counter accounts like Theodore White and Annalee Jacoby's *Thunder Out of China*—tellingly, both publications were released in 1946. The runs of *Plain Talk* and its successor, *The Freeman*, were relatively brief and their circulation numbers never quite high enough to be considered widely influential.[132] Churning out editions on a regular basis proved difficult for a one-note operation. Even so, the journals' titles clearly reflected Kohlberg's intention to establish sources for an audience interested in politics but supposedly ignored by the liberal media and the Washington elite: honest, hard-working Americans who refused to take the words of communist appeasers for granted.[133]

Books were by far the best vehicles for expressing the theories of Asia First anticommunism. Unlike journal articles, their format allowed for lengthy ruminations of conspiracy theories. A single volume could amend decades of history. While he was not directly involved in the cultivation of authors, Kohlberg still wanted to support them and their publishers by recommending pro-Chiang texts to his growing mailing list. The Regnery Company of Chicago was a natural partner.

In business only since 1947, Regnery was already influential among American conservatives. The company specialized in books that the traditional publishing establishment would not touch. In a letter to the editor of *Publisher's Weekly*, Henry Regnery protested the industry's bias:

> I have published more "revisionist" books than any other publisher—books, that is, which have opposed, or questioned the foreign policy of the administration. On the basis of my experience, I am convinced that a book which takes a position contrary to that of the administration, especially in matters of foreign policy, does not get a fair chance. Such books have difficulty finding a publisher, and once published are more often than not given unfair or inadequate treatment by the influential reviews.[134]

He and Kohlberg shared a desire to provide alternatives to "liberal" institutions, to even destroy them. With the China Lobby cultivating a wider audience for Regnery's publications, and vice versa, their collaboration was poised to be a fruitful one.

Regnery had long trusted Kohlberg as an authority on East Asia. In September 1949 he requested the latter serve as a consultant for Freda Utely's upcoming project.[135] The manuscript in question, *The China Story* (1951), was the publisher's first foray into Asian affairs. As could be expected, it was an unequivocal validation of Chiang. "It is a book which should have great influence if we can get it into the hands of the right people," Regnery wrote.[136] Interest in Asia First titles was a growing trend among right-wing publishers. Devin-Adair put out John T. Flynn's *While You Slept* (1951) and Frazier Hunt's *The Untold Story of Douglas MacArthur* (1954). Caxton Press also released texts to Kohlberg's liking.[137] The readers his magazines had failed to reach were responding positively to the story of China's fall in book format.

As the bibliography of anticommunism grew, so too did the right's formation of conservative intellectualism. The early 1950s saw the production of Buckley's *God and Man at Yale* (Regnery: 1951) and *The Conservative Mind* by Russell Kirk (Regnery: 1953), two texts that proved foundational to the postwar conservative movement. Kohlberg was delighted. He fancied himself an independent scholar of foreign policy and always made much of the months he spent in 1944 at the New York Public Library preparing his charges against the IPR. Ever since that campaign, he had harbored special animus toward the academy. From attacking publications that gave Clinton Rossiter poor reviews to condemning Arthur M. Schlesinger Jr., Kohlberg eagerly helped conservative intellectuals in any way he could.[138]

Kohlberg wanted to outflank liberal academia in institutional ways as well by donating his personal papers and other documents to a conservative archive. Herbert Hoover had established a collection at his alma mater, Stanford University, and the former president had been amassing documents from various government bureaus and important personages since the 1920s. By the 1950s, the holdings at the Hoover Institute and Library were distinctly Republican, if not transparently conservative. Stanford became the repository for the papers of many Chiang supporters, including Claire Chennault and Albert Wedemeyer. Kohlberg actively monitored the acquisitions of the Hoover Library, and he would make loud commentary on the occasions when it acquired material produced by leftists.[139] In 1952, after learning that Lattimore was conducting research there, Kohlberg complained to Sen. McCarran: "This seems like academic freedom with a vengeance, which I doubt Mr. Hoover will appreciate."[140] Despite the library's occasional lapses in library selections or authorizations, Kohlberg remained a firm ally, partly to ingratiate Hoover and mostly to encourage oppositional thinking within the Ivory Tower.

On that subject and many others he found a kindred spirit in Bill Buckley, who became a special pet. In the summer of 1954, the self-styled enfant terrible of the right was trying to get his own conservative journal off the ground. He turned to Kohlberg and submitted a draft prospectus for a publication to be called *National Weekly*: "This magazine will forthrightly oppose the prevailing trend of public opinion; its purpose, indeed, is to *change* the nation's intellectual and political climate. . . . The magazine will begin publication as a minority voice—not only in the sense that America's 'respectable' press has ordained that such voices as ours are of the past and not worth serious attention."[141] Kohlberg responded enthusiastically with pledges of moral and financial support.[142] After Buckley established his magazine and changed its name to *National Review*, he and his editorial staff maintained a regular, cordial correspondence with Kohlberg, who in turn liked to provide them with information as he had for so many other conservatives in the public sphere.[143] The alliance between the two was so close that Buckley delivered an affectionate testimonial at a celebratory dinner at the Waldorf-Astoria in July 1960. During the speech Kohlberg beamed like "a benign oriental idol." Just a few months later he was dead, and Buckley's remarks would become the preface to Joseph Keeley's hagiographic biography *The China Lobby Man*.[144]

While his was certainly not the only case of Asia First activism, Kohlberg's support of Chiang Kai-shek stands as a prominent example of how nostalgic, sentimental orientalism could drive private citizens to great lengths. From the ACPA to the publishing world to academia, Kohlberg fostered alternatives to mainstream institutions with the purpose of revitalizing an idealized version of the US-China relationship. Perhaps Kohlberg's underlying achievement was not that he created a China "lobby": Rather, he demonstrated how believable the idea of a China lobby really was and revealed some of consensus liberalism's insecurities. In the process, a few of the individuals he enveloped into his grassroots network—Buckley and Robert Welch, in particular—sought his advice and borrowed the lobby's methods. They would then go on to play major roles in the postwar conservative movement.

Joining Forces

If not for the battle within the Republican Party, the China Lobby might have remained on the fringes of party politics after Dewey's loss in 1948. At first glance, conservative internationalists and Asia First activists had little in common beyond a desire to prove the Democrats wrong. Even after Robert Taft became aware of Asia and its implications for his own career, he kept the Chiang fanatic at bay by repeatedly refusing Kohlberg's requests to meet.[145] At the same time, consistent partisanship was not exactly the latter's forte. Kohlberg was a lifelong Republican, yet his loyalty belonged to Free China only. He attempted to commandeer any vehicle that might advance the cause, including the Democratic national platforms of 1944, 1948, and 1952. The ACPA likewise refused to reveal any symptoms of overt partisanship.[146] Despite the claims of historians and contemporary pundits alike, Kohlberg did not completely rely on Republican elites for his political future, and vice versa.

What allowed Asia First to bring the GOP right and grassroots activists together was the innate conservatism the doctrine advocated: It demanded the return to a US-China relationship that had supposedly once existed. Rightwing elites argued for the unilateralism that marked US action in the Pacific at the turn of the century, and activists stressed ideas of traditional friendship and moral obligation. Whether a democratic China was a deeply cherished ideal or a vehicle for political gain, the doctrine filled a niche for Americans concerned with the alarming trajectory of the early Cold War.

The partnership between grassroots activists and the specifically *conservative* wing of the Republican Party is best described as utilitarian and designed for mutual benefit. It was forged after 1949, when foreign policy became a distinctly partisan issue. They shared a desire to define the GOP—what it had been and what it could be. Conservative elites wanted to win back control of their party while Kohlberg wanted to use it to save China, but both sought a break from consensus. Though the gateway to China may have been closed, public nostalgia for the Open Door still allowed willing Republicans to reap certain political benefits.

Kohlberg was also a conservative at heart, if only in the sense that he was unfailingly loyal to the (revisionist) past. His ideology stemmed from a dedication to a special US-China relationship and a belief that socialists in the government and the media had conspired to destroy a sacred tradition. Since it was his fundamental conviction that America should intervene in China, he was by no means isolationist in the literal sense. Unlike Taft, Kohlberg never thought the nation should avoid foreign entanglements, just postwar commitments in Europe that extended beyond national security.[147]

To strengthen his relationship with conservative officials, Kohlberg expanded on the correlations he saw between domestic issues and the fall of China. In 1947 he had guffawed at the "nutty liberals" who said they loved the New Deal and hated Communists "without realizing that the one cannot live without the other."[148] Snide jokes turned into accusations of treachery and socialism. "[I]t is time for our Republican Party to hit the sawdust trail, publicly express its repentance, and take leadership of the millions of Americans who view with anger and disgust the murder of our sons in Korea at the behest of, and under the limitation imposed by India, Britain, and our Stalinist State Department," Kohlberg wrote to Joseph Martin.[149] In an appeal to Taft's well-known hatred of expanded government at the cost of higher federal spending, he told the senator that the GOP had been "tied to the New Deal's apron strings by our so-called bi-partisan foreign policy."[150] With Hoover, the grandfather of American conservatism, he felt comfortable enough to tender advice on the GOP's function in the American delegation to the UN.[151]

When asked about the senate investigation of the China Lobby, Taft gamely defended the man whose magazine once compared him to the reviled Neville Chamberlain: "[Kohlberg's] very anti-communist and as far as I know he's putting his own money on it. . . . I think he would give reasons—and very, very sincere and earnest reasons—as to why he has acted in that way." Four months later, he deigned to ask Kohlberg for guidance on how to create publicity for East Asian affairs.[152] Members of the Republican right needed the China Lobby nearly as much as its leader wanted to work with them. Calamity in the Pacific offered the means to an electoral comeback, and conservative elites were therefore willing to put up with Kohlberg's volatility and reputation for extremism. The man was a resource they could not afford to ignore.

"If a citizen is dissatisfied, he is free to organize his own society to advance his own cause," wrote V. O. Key in his classic 1952 study *Politics, Parties, and Pressure Groups.*[153] Alfred Kohlberg possessed dissatisfaction in abundance, and he acted to remedy what he considered to be an outrageous situation up until his death in 1960. Asia First activism outside the government offered a broad, ambitious agenda for organization and mobilization. In the process of implementing those structures, it provided an organizational template for activism that the growing grassroots right would follow well into the 1960s.

The unique nature of the China Lobby defied conventional definitions of political machinery. The lobby model not only addressed the press, intellectual life, and federal policy but also allowed an exaggeration of popular support for any one issue. With savvy enough management, even extremism could feign a grassroots groundswell and thus wield influence over the direction of national politics. The solution was to create an umbrella cause that appealed, however obliquely, to groups and individuals that were like-minded but disparate. With the Cold War being waged on both foreign and domestic fronts, radical anticommunism promised to be that umbrella.

However, when it came to formal politics, Kohlberg's strategy resembled conversion more than it did Key's suggestion of outright replacement: The failure of multiple "Draft MacArthur" attempts emphasized the need for practicality. Time was of the essence for China and a third party movement was not going to succeed in the near future. Kohlberg was exceedingly practical when he needed to be. He recognized that the Republican right's desire for its own foreign policy presented a promising conduit to advance Free China. Nevertheless, in another demonstration of pragmatism, he had no qualms about cultivating support among GOP moderates after the possibility of a conservative victory via Taft slipped away in 1952.

Given due consideration, such fickleness was unsurprising. Kohlberg was a one-track activist whose conscience remained untroubled by extra- or intra-party distinctions. Ingratiating those in power was the only thing that really mattered. On a larger scale, the China Lobby's wavering partisanship was the precursor to other issue-based conservative groups whose commitment to the GOP could be tenuous at best. In order to harness their dynamism, elites on the right would have to overcome their attachment to traditionalism. The conservative establishment ultimately needed to cultivate party leadership that condoned, if not embraced, fundamental change in its ideology and tactics.

3

Firefights: China's Meanings after the Korean War

The 1952 national elections were an excellent opportunity to test the efficacy of an Asia First strategy and conservative internationalism in general. Indeed, national and global affairs were dovetailing to lift Republicans' hopes for 1952. The Korea stalemate, the spotlight of McCarthyism, and questions about Stalin's health and future Soviet leadership provided ammunition that complemented domestic opposition to Truman's Fair Deal legislation. The question was which type of Republicanism—conservative or moderate—would dominate to capture the presidential nomination and hopefully the White House.

After failing with Thomas Dewey in 1948, the entire party was determined to win in 1952. When surveying the potential field of GOP candidates, conservatives had reason to believe they stood a good chance of capturing the nomination. Robert Taft was an obvious choice: a national figure with presidential lineage, a seasoned campaigner (1952 would be his third run for the White House), and a reputation as both a stalwart conservative and Republican leader. Moreover, his turn to internationalism came at the necessary moment. With *A Foreign Policy for Americans*, Taft demonstrated that the GOP right as a whole had its own ideas on how to handle the challenges of a Cold War world. If nothing else, the campaign marked the culmination of conservatism's transition from isolationism to internationalism.

Taft would find a nomination anything but easily achievable because, despite a common party goal, rifts between factions widened rather than closed. Moderate Republicans wanted to nominate Gen. Dwight Eisenhower. Eisenhower was a proven global leader, but there were grassroots activists who found his anticommunist credentials considerably lacking. Some, including Alfred Kohlberg, wanted Douglas MacArthur: "If can be of service," he telegrammed the general, "am yours to command."[1] Due to Eisenhower's popularity, the GOP convention came and went with neither of the conservative favorites securing the nomination. Taft was finished, and because his name appeared in only a few state primaries, MacArthur was never a serious candidate. Without missing a beat, Kohlberg began currying favor with the winning ticket. "My dear Dick," he telegrammed Richard Nixon, "As you may know, Taft was my choice but now that decision is made I whole-heartedly back ticket which is made easy for me by your nomination." He even offered counsel on how to win over the "sore" Taft wing of the party.[2]

The lingering bitterness between conservatives and moderates threatened to discolor the GOP's triumph at the polls. "It looks as if the result of Eisenhower's election will be to put into power a New Deal Republican Administration. . . . It would be more difficult against a Republican New Deal Administration than a Democratic New Deal Administration," Taft sourly observed. He also had serious reservations about Eisenhower's political savoir faire. "My principle reason for being uncertain," he continued, "is that I don't believe General Eisenhower really understands the differences which exist between the two branches of the Republican Party."[3] The new president tried his best to mend fences, thanking Taft for his "true cooperation."[4]

The White House's efforts to bring the GOP Senate conservatives into line faced difficult challenges, mainly because the right had undergone so much change over the last few years. Under Taft's leadership in the Senate, the conclusion of the Chinese civil war and its immediate aftermath provided conservative officials a toehold into the debate over foreign policy through the early 1950s. At the same moment, the China Lobby organized a grassroots response intended to complement efforts within the GOP. An Asia First approach had strengthened the bridge between elites and activists—and conservatism overall—despite the disappointment of 1952.

Asia First hardly faded away after that November. Neither short-lived nor restrictive, its influence continued as a series of conflicts in East Asia, including the ongoing Korean War and crises in the Taiwan Strait, fueled debates over fundamental issues such as executive power and the efficacy of collective security. They provided American conservatism the opportunity to use Congress as a base for a legislative approach to anticommunist internationalism long after the ideal of a democratic Chinese mainland no longer seemed a viable possibility.

The strategy's longevity also owed much to broader postwar developments that signaled a distinct regional shift of electoral power and with that shift, increased consciousness of the challenges posed by communism in East Asia. Even if conservatives did not see their candidate reach the White House, the GOP right scored major victories in key congressional races. Invigorated leadership from a younger generation of conservative politicians, many of whom came from the western United States, ensured that concern for the Pacific became a lasting feature of postwar conservative politics.

Western Promises

Boasting the nickname "the Golden State," California exemplified the American West's increased prominence during and after World War II. A unique economic, demographic, and cultural vigor allowed it to emerge as a new national epicenter as movements within its borders radiated outward and shaped a variety of fields, from popular culture to the dialogue of diplomacy. By 1969, political analyst Kevin Phillips described the state as a sociopolitical microcosm: "Not only does California reflect contemporary trends, but the state probably anticipates the future better than any other."[5]

Much of that influence stemmed from the fact that California was elemental to security in the Pacific after Pearl Harbor, a status that owed much to its transformation during wartime. Historian Marilynn Johnson has called the influx of federal defense dollars "the second Gold Rush," a wave of unprecedented government spending that subsidized the exponential growth of the state's industrial capacity and fueled the call for workers. Sleepy small towns transformed into bustling cities, and concentric rings of suburbs sprang up virtually overnight. Many of those locations remained population centers long after the war as defense funding spurred by a Cold War arms race created jobs and required services from the private sector. Thanks to a steady stream of new arrivals attracted by the region's continued promise, California overtook New York as the most populous state in the union by 1962—a marked sign of how happenings on the American Pacific Rim were transforming the electoral as well as physical landscape.[6]

An economic well-being increasingly based on Cold War defense, coupled with a strategic geopolitical position, produced a regional anticommunism that naturally prioritized Asia over Europe. The Chinese civil war moved many Californians to express their concerns in no uncertain terms. One anonymous voter insisted that the public be fully informed on the situation in China: "The American people don't know why we have failed. They do not even know to what extent our policy in China is responsible for the present debacle there. And the American people have the right to know!" Donald Armstrong of Sonoma wrote: "A billion people of Asia allied with international communism would present a picture of far reaching consequences to the remaining nations outside of the 'Iron Curtain.'" "The Pacific has been neglected," asserted San Francisco resident Ed A. Borden, "And we have lost billions in trade, to say nothing of some of the friendship we had in China . . . officialdom in Washington must be made to realize how important the Pacific is relative to the European situation."[7]

Anxiety about Asia transcended social and professional divisions. A bulletin released by the World Affairs Council revealed that nearly six hundred Northern Californians attended the organization's December 1949 conference on China. The majority were educators from places like Berkeley and Stanford. However, the second and third most numerous groups in attendance were business professionals and "housewives," respectively. Labor leaders, journalists, government workers, and social workers comprised the remainder.

One of the elected officials invited to speak at the conference was Sen. William F. Knowland. His talk was called "Our Far Eastern Policy," a rather benign title that belied the senator's established reputation as a strident Asia First politician and a rising star in the GOP.[8] "I happen to come from a state where the waters of the Pacific wash upon our shores, and we saw World War II break out there," he had declared earlier in the year during an appearance on the radio program *American Forum of the Air.* "And we certainly do not believe they are giving proper attention to that part of the world."[9] Such a stance was natural for somebody who called the Pacific Coast home. When asked to trace the origins of her father's interest in Taiwan, Estelle Knowland Johnson pointed to the vulnerability of California cities to Japanese attack: "[W]hether it was 'San Francisco is going to be bombed next,' or whatever, our western focus was strong."[10]

Once the Cold War began, Knowland supported extensive aid to combat communism in Europe, but he also argued that Washington fell short when it came to the Asian front. An allied China friendly to the United States was an issue close to his heart and to his constituency. His background as a Californian granted him authority to speak as one with firsthand knowledge of American life on the Pacific Rim. In particular, he could confidently relate what Free China meant to the West Coast and the danger that Red China posed to national security.

Knowland was uniquely positioned among a new generation of postwar conservatives who were eager to capitalize on voters' dissatisfaction with developments in East Asia. The precocious scion of an influential publishing family from Oakland, he entered office in 1945 as a gubernatorial appointee to the US Senate. Because of experience in office gained during the crucial years between World War II and the Korean War, he emerged during the late 1940s as a key face for Asia First.[11]

Less than a decade after arriving in Washington, Knowland became Senate majority leader, handpicked by Taft himself. That he did so after garnering the dubious moniker of "the senator from Formosa" reflected the sustained development of right-wing internationalism during the period following the Korean War. His tenure as leader of Senate Republicans (1952–58) spanned key moments ranging from the censure of Joseph McCarthy to the Bricker Amendment to the Taiwan Strait Crises. By the end of the decade, the emerging face of the right had clear, distinguishing features: virulent anticommunism, a focus on the Pacific for both diplomatic and political strength, and calls to expand the defense state.

An evolving stance on Taiwan and China was part of that development. In the wake of war in Korea, there was a marked de-emphasis of Chiang Kai-shek as panacea to the China problem. Under Knowland's stewardship, Asia First shifted from a largely reactionary position to one that attempted real policymaking, evidenced by the proactive nature of conservative officials' positions on foreign affairs. Coupled with the West's new status as electoral powerhouse, that new emphasis effectively ensured that anti-communist orientalism would become a long-standing fixture of national political life.[11]

"The Senator from Formosa"

Knowland's rapid rise was due in large part to his reputation as an expert on East Asia, which itself was founded on his early, vociferous efforts to raise public awareness of events in China. As one of the strongest Republican voices urging more aggressive support for Taiwan, Knowland quickly gained a reputation as a strident critic of the White House and the State Department.[12]

A flair for the dramatic, as well as sheer volume, made for excellent copy throughout his Washington career. "Communist China," read one typical statement, "is a symbol of slavery, regimentation, and irreligion. She is no different in these respects from Nazi Germany, Fascist Italy, or the Soviet Union. Mass murders, brainwashing, and a denial of man's higher being are conditions that have revolted the consciences of free people everywhere."[13] Thanks to his rhetorical excesses, Knowland deserved much of the credit for turning China into a hot-button issue in Congress. Knowland's influence was not limited to the capitol as he supported Free China in large-circulation publications and on the public-speaking circuit

A range of media outlets, from the University of California, Berkeley, student newspaper to national magazines, derided those efforts. Dick Hafner, editor of the *Daily Californian*, described the GOP's position on Taiwan as an "asinine" political strategy: "How many more times is the party going to cut its throat before November, 1950?"[14] Journalist Walter Lippmann was even

SENATOR KNOWLAND POINTS TO FORMOSA
The State Department sees it differently

FIGURE 3.1. Senator William Knowland, *U.S. News and World Report*, 13 January 1950, 23.

more pointed: "I have always thought that foreign affairs should be conducted for specific objects, and that the less grandiose generalities we proclaimed, the better," he admonished Knowland. "My first experience in international affairs was working for Woodrow Wilson, and I have learned from that the danger of a rhetorical diplomacy." He ended by suggesting they have a "good long discussion on the whole problem of Asia."[15] By the mid-1950s, the *New York Times* portrayed the senator as using China to create his own sect of Republicanism—"Knowlandism"—in opposition to the White House.[16]

Such critique owed a great deal to the presumption that the senator was sympathetic to the China Lobby. The press described Knowland as a "Chiang-backer"; both *The Reporter* and *Congressional Quarterly* identified him as the lobby's most important Senate contact, an integral part of the "Soong-Kung-Kohlberg-Knowland" axis. Although Kohlberg denied the allegations as "unsupported smears and no investigation," as a discerning observer of political trends, he was well aware of Knowland's potential and assumed the latter could be incorporated into his network.[17]

Both the media and Kohlberg overlooked the fact that Knowland's stance on China was far more complex and flexible than mere knee-jerk support of Guomindang desires to retake the mainland. Biographers Gayle B. Montgomery and James W. Johnson have argued that Knowland's commitment to the issue of China can be traced back to the West Coast's strategic importance and the senator's own "vociferous," principled stubbornness.[18] However, they too equated support for Taiwan as allegiance to the Nationalist regime and the China Lobby without consideration for how such a position might evolve.[19] Most recently, Nancy Tucker's study on the Eisenhower administration and China simply labels Knowland as one of several "China Lobby activists."[20]

While his support for the dream of a China aligned with the West was unwavering, the senator held independent ideas and convictions that, in practice, never entirely dovetailed with the demagoguery that many supporters of Free China so prominently displayed. He remained essentially independent of private associations and organizations and spoke out without waiting for any sort of go-ahead from elder statesmen, imagined or real.

Two key issues illustrated that early self-determination and offered clues as to how the senator would later lead conservatives in his capacity as a party leader. The first was his stance on Douglas MacArthur's removal from Korea in 1951; the second, his mitigated views of Chiang Kai-shek himself.

After MacArthur's recall, reactionaries expressed sentiments such as, "I hope we'll get responsibility out of the hands of the pink 'teacup' boys into the hands of an American like Douglas MacArthur."[21] A few even clamored for presidential impeachment. In contrast, Knowland exercised more forethought by heeding his longtime advisors, with whom he exchanged significant correspondence on the matter. O. D. Keep, publisher of *Fortnight,* counseled that MacArthur was "one of the most overrated military figures this country ever had, and this fact is bound to emerge and become generally known to the public, making him more of a liability than an asset to the GOP."[22] He urged Knowland to decenter MacArthur in favor of emphasizing that Truman had overstepped his executive powers by involving US armed forces in Korea without Congressional consent: "If . . . the Congress of the United States is to be foreclosed in finding out what took place we will have gone a long way toward the modification of our constitutional system."[23] MacArthur was a shaky foundation on which to rest GOP hopes; it was a safer wager to let the Democrats self-destruct. Knowland's father Joseph shared that view: "Do not advocate impeachment. However too bad Americans chose an unbalanced child to do a man's job as President. MacArthur will never die but Truman just did."[24] By letting the dismissed general remain a martyr, Republicans could add to their pantheon of popular heroes. In the ensuing months Knowland remained tacitly supportive of MacArthur's valorization, but he refused to let any individual figure overshadow the entire Asia First cause.

That strategic levelness carried over into his perspective regarding the leader of Nationalist China. As so many others had, he could have advocated unquestioning support of Chiang. Not only was Knowland a fervent anticommunist, he had also witnessed firsthand the Guomindang struggle to stay in power. During a fact-finding tour of East Asia, Knowland and his wife Helen were Chiang and Soong Mei-ling's fellow passengers aboard the last plane to leave Chongqing before Communist forces took the city in December 1949.[25] The Guomindang later attempted to enlist his support, praising his comprehension of "the importance of Asia both to America and to world peace and security as a whole."[26]

Despite such dramatic moments and rhetoric, Knowland was circumspect on the topic of Chiang. He and Sen. H. Alexander Smith exchanged misgivings, asserting that Chiang's usefulness lay only in his nominal status as a democratic leader. Smith even expressed his belief that the incumbent leadership "has not really understood Western democracy" and located hope for reform in the next generation of Guomindang officials.[27] Others urged Knowland to use his position to urge Chiang to leave office. "You would be rendering a constructive and statesman [sic] service if you could use your influence to get Chiang Kai-shek to give up his dictatorship and to rule that island under a constitution," Choy Jun-ke of the Chinese World newspaper wrote in 1950.[28]

Barring that, there were other potential options. For instance, encouragement of opposition parties like Young China and the Social Democratic Party could force the Guomindang to reform.[29] Another route was to cultivate a Chinese ally not even on Taiwan. Knowland saved documents regarding a "Third Force," a group of overseas Chinese, anti-Chiang as well as anti-Mao, who might prove an alternative. If the US government provided training, supplies, and transport, Third Force members proposed to invade mainland China with the goal of overthrowing Mao.[30] Based on the assumption that a popular uprising would occur, the idea foreshadowed the Eisenhower and Kennedy administrations' involvement in the Bay of Pigs invasion on Cuba a decade later. That someone in Knowland's capacity would entertain such a notion, even in passing, indicated support for a Free China not inextricably tied to Chiang's Nationalists, despite the Guomindang representing the most plausible ally.

Despite growing consciousness of Guomindang shortcomings, conservative officials refused to let the issue die. Certainly the political benefits were considerable as foreign policy on Asia provided the Republican right with continuing critique of moderate consensus. But China was also too important of an ideal and symbol to relinquish even as the Generalissimo began to fade. The unwillingness to accept Chiang as the sole face of Chinese anticommunism showed how Asia First conservatism could persevere. There were other opportunities that could be exploited. Even if retaking the mainland was impossible, other battles could be waged in the name of Taiwan. There was a great deal of promise in the use of Free China as an avenue to advance the right's agenda at home as diplomatic concerns were increasingly melded with national ones.

Redefining "Conservative"

Before the Republican right could fully transition into this new phase, there had to be resolution among conservative elites as to the new direction. Framed by a war in Korea that appeared to bear out dire predictions of communist expansion, the 1952 election suggested that all Republicans might be able to unite under the banner of change in foreign and national security policy, thus achieving the modicum of unity that had eluded their party. It helped that up-and-comers in the GOP spearheaded the effort to revamp the right's call for stronger resistance against threats from within and without.

Knowland was among the first to articulate this new agenda to Republican delegates and voters. In a speech at the national convention, he insisted that "non-military expenditures be limited drastically and that even in the field of military expenditures that the American people get a dollar's worth of value for every dollar spent and that the funds be spent on building muscle and not fat in the defense organization." By being careful not to call for a decrease in military spending even while urging fiscal responsibility, Knowland established the tone for future conservatives who would consider defense reductions out of the question. In an appeal to conservatives still wary of federal growth, he buttressed his novel approach with classic right-wing principles. During the same speech he railed against high taxes and the erosion of states' rights, concluding the GOP should adopt his attitude and "give to the people of this nation a clear-cut choice in the elections."[31]

Another address Knowland delivered before a large crowd in California demonstrated how conservative internationalism started to connect perceived errors in federal government to global affairs: "Americans are facing one of the most critical election campaigns in 1952 that our people have been called upon to face. . . . [T]he issues we face are not any narrow, partisan issues. We want to rally the Constitutional Democrats and Republicans who believe we should preserve our free way of life under the Constitution of the United States of America." Voters were polarized into two camps. They were either on the side of liberty as delineated by constitutional originalism or they were no better than communists.

According to Knowland, the disease that threatened the nation's future was statism. Precise symptoms, let alone mechanics, remained vague, but its consequences were absolute. Above all, statism infringed on "the right of the individual to be free from an all-powerful state."[32] It impaired the workings of a well-run government—from majority rule to the secretary of state's ability to communicate with Foreign Service officers—and insulted the memory of soldiers who died overseas to make the world safe for democracy. A bloated federal bureaucracy could also harm the country's international reputation. By setting an example of poor government, the United States betrayed foreign nations who looked to it as an exceptional beacon of freedom. The fine line between American citizens and foreign peoples under totalitarian rule was a constant theme. Domestic appeasement was apparently a slippery downward slope toward joining the victims of communist expansion.

Without a constant definition, the specter of statism was allowed unlimited growth, a trait it held in common with the specter of communism. Whatever its form, the condition was a "menace" that threatened to steer the nation off the course laid by the Founding Fathers. If allowed to continue, it would lead to "a collapse of our economic and political system," and America would "take the entire free world down with us." Every fiscal and political decision, Knowland warned, had global consequences, and for twenty years liberals had led the United States down the path of dictatorship, financial ruin, and global instability. From Yalta to Korea, Democrats and their allies had immorally endangered global security, especially when it came to China.[33]

This line of reasoning was a familiar one by the time Knowland spoke, yet he made it fresh by connecting the communist revolution in China to domestic wrongs wrought by the Democrats. By casting bygone foreign policy as an explicitly partisan issue, he inserted an alternative version of the US-China relationship that was admittedly wishful thinking but an infinitely useful construction nonetheless.[34]

Success at the polls depended on an ability to present voters with a genuine alternative, one that was fundamentally based on a vision of state that could confront the global communist threat. Rather than stressing intervention or generous financial aid, US foreign relations were to be reshaped along lines of defense and, if need be, unilateral military action. This position encompassed conservative mores of fiscal thrift and militant anticommunism, applying them to an entirely new field.

Thanks to efforts by both the old guard (Taft's advocacy of increased air power) and the new (Knowland's defense-centered federalism), the conservative platform was diversified to include the party's official association with the building of a defense state. According to McIntyre Faries, a member of the GOP National Committee, the California senator's ability to make global issues relevant on local and state levels fed his personal appeal: "Knowland went up and down the state thundering about the Korean War," Faries recalled. "Knowland's issue was a natural and he won very handily. Other Republicans did, too, but Knowland was the big winner and he did because he carried the burden in the race."[35]

A strong demonstration of muscle would be vital to postvictory negotiations back in Washington. His constituents proved receptive to a platform of boosting the state economy through protracted defense spending. By emphasizing the Pacific, the senator won reelection in November 1952 with an unprecedented majority. That victory allowed him to take over the chair of the Republican Policy Committee, the second-highest position in the GOP Senate.

Just a few months later, Knowland reached a pinnacle. After learning of his cancer diagnosis in the summer of 1953, Robert Taft asked his junior colleague to serve as acting majority leader. Knowland's earlier support of Earl Warren for the GOP presidential nomination paled in comparison with his party loyalty. "Nobody can push him around," Taft explained.[36] The appointment was a major show of approval from the conservative establishment, and with it, the right's internationalist future was secured. Even more dramatically, Taft made a deathbed demand for unilateral action in Asia: "I believe we might as well abandon any idea of working with the United Nations in the East and reserve to ourselves a completely free hand."[37]

Despite the vote of confidence from his predecessor and a promising new agenda, leading Republicans in the 83rd Senate was no easy task. For one, there were still intraparty divisions to deal with: moderate versus conservative, internationalism versus lingering isolationism, and old guard right versus new guard right. It would be up to GOP leaders in Congress to bridge those divides, and an untested figure could actually compound conflict. Moreover, Democrats still held half the floor votes. Knowland was majority leader only because Nixon, as vice president, presided over the Senate and cast a deciding vote.[38]

Another obstacle was Lyndon Johnson, the Democratic minority leader. A formidable opponent, Johnson was infinitely skilled at the hand-to-hand combat that fulfillment of legislative agendas required. He was "Master of the Senate," as Robert Caro has aptly described.[39] Although their working relationship was far from antagonistic, Johnson constantly got the better of Knowland when it came to winning over colleagues and lining up votes. Johnson did do Knowland one favor, however. The Texan's divisiveness helped to solidify unity among conservative legislators and therefore eased a changing of the guard. Consequently, Knowland, once decried by purists as an Earl Warren liberal, was eventually acknowledged as the embodiment of conservatism by the late 1950s.

Of course, Taft's personal passing of the torch did much to assuage initial uncertainties about his successor's politics. Lingering doubts about the depth and tenor of his conservatism meant Knowland needed the endorsement, and he did his best to invoke Taft's spirit at key moments.[40] The strategy seemed to pay off. *One Man's Opinion*, among the growing number of rightwing publications, proclaimed: "In the Taft election in Ohio in 1950 and the Knowland election in California in 1952 there is tremendous lesson for politicians of this country, especially those who would like—but do not dare—to take a firm conservative stand on domestic issues, and a firm pro-American anti-Communist stand in foreign affairs—if they were not so blind."[41] Using an extension of Taft's nickname, the piece even christened Knowland "Mr. Republican II." He was American conservatism's heir apparent.

The changes championed by the next generation of politicians clearly spurred a literal broadening of conservatism's parameters. "We can no more return to isolationism than an adult can return to childhood, regardless of how pleasant the recollection may be," Knowland told fellow Republicans.[42] He referred to the United States and its newly awakened sense of global responsibility, as well as former isolationists turned reluctant internationalists. The reality of a conservative leader urging his allies to shake off the mentality of the Monroe Doctrine indicated the postwar right was evolving and growing a sense of lasting purpose well before Barry Goldwater's famous dictum of "Let's grow up, conservatives!" at the 1960 GOP convention.[43]

What became clear after the Korean War was how domestic policy, specifically argument for a stricter adherence to constitutional balance of power, became the primary focus of Asia First conservatism as the 1950s continued. Proxy battles against consensus and communism included the Bricker Amendment debate in 1953, the 1954–55 Taiwan Strait crisis, ongoing furor over seating the PRC in the United Nations (UN), and the controversy surrounding publication of previously classified Yalta proceedings. By continuing its emphasis on Pacific issues, the right wing of the GOP could capitalize on the West's growth and present its agenda as adaptable to the new realities of the United States' place in the Cold War world.

No Rubber Stamp: The Bricker Amendment

Even though the GOP won an Eisenhower administration and stronger numbers in Congress by decrying past policy on East Asia, harmony remained difficult to achieve after the election. Conservatives still publicly criticized the United States' approach to Asia, at times even protesting the administration's handling of communist Asia as a compromise of national security and morality. Little deference was spared. If a show of bipartisanship in foreign affairs had been difficult to manage during the Truman years, then party unity on Asia proved just as problematic even as the Korean War came to an end.

The debate over the Bricker Amendment highlighted long-standing conservative frustrations with the executive branch's increasing dominance over Congress. Introduced by Sen. John Bricker (R-OH) in January 1953, the resolution's first clause stated, "A provision of a treaty which denies or abridges any right enumerated in this Constitution shall not be of any force or effect."[44] It immediately targeted executive agreements as dangerous to individual and states' rights.[45] By requiring Congress to strictly regulate presidential agreements with foreign parties, it proposed a distinct transfer of power away from the White House to the legislature.

Against the backdrop of the Yalta agreements and the Korean War, the amendment translated long expressed sentiments into concrete policy proposals. Duane Tananbaum's examination of the Bricker proposal shows how, in a post-1949 world, pacts and treaties of which conservatives disapproved were deemed aspects of totalitarianism. The Cold War had given dictatorship, in the form of an all-powerful executive, ample opportunity to emerge.[46] "In our time the power of government has grown at a rampant rate. Whenever the power of government is enhanced, to the same degree human liberty is suppressed," Bricker proclaimed. "The fundamental rights of the American people are either inalienable, or they may be alienated by treaty."[47] In other words, any president, Republican or Democrat, could singlehandedly implicate the nation in international debacle. Moreover, policy that was ostensibly "foreign" had a direct impact on civil liberties at home.

In remarks on the floor and in a subsequent press release, Bricker specifically cited Yalta as a controversial executive agreement that should be contested.[48] By falling back on the narrative of Roosevelt's unchecked concessions and how they led to Chinese Communist aggression, which in turn provoked conflict in Korea, he and other amendment supporters appeared to fulfill stereotypes of stale, inflexible conservatism that did not square with the realities of American global power. The impression proved a lasting one. In 1956, Eric Goldman dubbed the Bricker Amendment "the isolationist's dream"; nearly four decades later, fellow historian Cathal J. Nolan still deemed it "the last hurrah" of isolationism.[49]

The Bricker episode warrants interpretation in a different light. The bill and the support it garnered are better understood as evidence that conservatives had significantly altered their views of the nation's diplomatic responsibilities. Their brand of Asia First internationalism demonstrated an ability to exploit the crossover between domestic and foreign concerns. By again

raising the specter of Yalta, the amendment framed constitutional constructivism as the safeguard against mistakes made by errant presidents (even if
the executive had the best of intentions when striking international bargains).

The bill ostensibly sought to protect constitutional principle during a conflict that had already wrought an incredible amount of change in government.
Executive agreements and other acts of imprudent diplomacy supposedly exposed the nation, but they were above all interpreted as omens of something
awry at home. In other words, constructivism dictated that executives should
not be accorded such unilateral power in the first place. The potential of presidents to repeat follies like Yalta indicated that the very fabric of democracy
was imperiled from the inside out. The Senate had a duty to stem the growth
of dictatorship.

From a partisan standpoint, the timing was a disaster. Republicans on the
right raised the issue of executive power shortly after the GOP regained control of the presidency and a senate majority. Such a display of disunity and
insubordination so early in the new Eisenhower administration put a severe
damper on the party's comeback, which was two decades in the making.[50]
But the GOP Senate, its party leadership dominated by conservatives, had a
ready answer for that critique: "I am certain that this President, Eisenhower,
does not believe that Congress should be a rubber-stamp body," declared
Knowland.[51]

By defying *even* a Republican executive, conservative legislators presented
themselves as dedicated to national ideals, not just partisan ones. Out of the
ninety-one senators present, sixty voted for the final possible version of the
legislation and thirty-one voted against (the final "nay" vote came from an
inebriated Harley Kilgore, a Democrat from Virginia, who stumbled into the
Senate chamber at the last moment).[52] Although their efforts fell short of a
two-thirds majority, the message they managed to send was quite clear. Moreover, the boldness of questioning executive power while a Republican president sat in office—and the rhetorical targeting of Democrats Roosevelt and
Truman only after the fact—demonstrated that the right's dedication to Asia
First extended beyond the scope of pure politics. Conservative principles
were still waging a battle against consensus as usual.

The episode was Knowland's first real test as leader of the Republican Senate. Personally he had nothing negative to say about the president himself and
had even drafted a (rejected) compromise amendment.[53] But in the end the
GOP floor leader threw his support behind Bricker by emphasizing preservation: "I think the thing that has preserved our freedom and will preserve it is
the maintenance of our constitutional balance of powers between our three
great branches of Government—the executive, legislative, and judicial."[54] It

was the Senate majority leader's responsibility to preserve the integrity of the legislative branch by voicing his opinion, perhaps never more so than when the executive happened to be a member of his own party.

Those sentiments were rooted in the symbolism of the Senate as a long-standing stronghold of conservative power. It was where the GOP right thrived, its interests promoted and safeguarded by both a tradition of deference, as well as a chain of leadership that saw its latest link in Knowland. On a personal note, the California senator also continually sought to wield a wider influence on the direction of foreign policy from his place on Capitol Hill. With a vested interest in safeguarding his sphere, Knowland granted himself leave to challenge, on behalf of "freedom," any White House or Supreme Court mandate.

Conservative officials' relationship with the White House sustained a major hit and confrontations related to balance of power and China continued. Two more occurred the following year. In November 1954, Knowland called for Congress to summon testimony from State and Defense officials "to fully inquire into our foreign and defense policy," intimating that "a basic change in the direction of our foreign policy is needed."[55] Shortly thereafter, censure proceedings against Joseph McCarthy took place, and they brought the fissures between the White House/moderate bloc versus Senate conservatives into sharp, public relief. The GOP right unified behind votes not to punish a figure revered as a grassroots hero who had exposed the "China Hands."[56]

Official condemnation of McCarthy hardly began or ended the struggle over balance of power. The overarching issue was still US foreign policy in East Asia, specifically the Eisenhower administration's diminishing protection of Taiwan and what conservatives saw as a weak stance against Chinese and Soviet Communists. The call for policy revision (and defiance of Eisenhower regarding McCarthy) came at an intensely delicate moment, when events unfolding in the Taiwan Strait threatened to demolish attempts by the United States to maintain some semblance of order in the Pacific.

The fervor of the right's protest against consensus foreign policy extended Yalta's influence beyond the crisis of the Korean War. Dealing with the PRC catalyzed and legitimized demands for equilibrium of power in foreign affairs, which remained an ever-present theme. But from that central issue stemmed a host of arguments about how American superpower should be executed. A trio of events in 1955—crisis in the Taiwan Strait and the Formosa Resolution, consequent debate over the UN, and the release of the Yalta papers—demonstrated how conservative internationalism was starting to address diplomatic issues more specifically and in more depth.

Quemoy and Matsu, 1954–55

Armistice in Korea in 1953 hardly dissipated fears that the Cold War could again turn hot in Asia. Certainly, mainstream media heightened public perception of a regional powder keg. *U.S. News & World Report*'s Christmas 1954 cover, for example, blared, "Chances of War in '55: Explosion, If It Comes, Will Probably Be in the Pacific." Inside, the article intimated that China and Soviet Union were marched in monolithic lockstep: "One false step by the Communists toward Formosa can explode into war. Chinese Communists are talking and acting tough—with Moscow's full backing."[57]

The Eisenhower administration's protection of Taiwan aggravated concerns of another military conflict. In 1953, the White House announced that US naval forces would defend the island from attack; the ships would also refrain from interfering in any moves made against the Chinese mainland. In what appeared to be a wholehearted renewal of support for Chiang's government, which continued to represent China in the UN, the president signed a mutual defense treaty with Taiwan on December 2, 1954. The United States was tightly bound to the island, meaning any attack on the latter could be potentially catastrophic.[58]

Yet the vigorous anticommunist rhetoric used by both Eisenhower and Secretary of State Dulles did not reflect the whole of their position. In private, they took care to avoid confrontations from happening in the first place. The White House warned Guomindang envoys that it would refuse to green light any plan that could drag the United States into war.[59] In public, the tough talk was a way to tell Beijing and Moscow that Washington would act if stability were threatened. It also staved off criticism from conservatives who questioned whether Eisenhower was taking a hard enough line against communism.

It was true that the president was no Asia Firster. His career and inclinations led him to put Europe first. Likewise, the National Security Council found the idea of going to war over Taiwan highly objectionable. After all, Dulles had just extricated the United States from the multilateral confines of the Geneva Accords on Vietnam, and with the 1954 founding of the Southeast Asia Treaty Organization (SEATO), US policymakers could sustain flexible response in an increasingly unstable region.[60]

Renewed shelling of Nationalist-held Quemoy and Matsu, two small islands situated between Taiwan and mainland China, in January 1955 placed further strain on the White House's public/private compartmentalization regarding Taiwan. Motivated in part by the formation of SEATO and fears of the United States forging new agreements with Taiwan, Mao ordered a shelling campaign that first began the previous September.[61] The situation quickly escalated as the Nationalists returned fire. In response, Congress overwhelmingly passed the Formosa Resolution on January 29, granting the president unilateral discretion to use all necessary force in the Taiwan Strait, including nuclear intervention.

Rather than immediately exercise that power, the administration made no public move, and Dulles was put in the unusual position of having to quell rumors of war. At a press conference in April, he declared, "We have made it perfectly clear our desire that there shall be no war; our desire that there shall be a cease-fire. So if there is any war, it will be entirely due to the provocation and initiative of those who unfortunately may not be subject to the pacific purpose which they proclaim." Dulles insisted American intervention would be strictly along the lines of the mutual defense treaty. There was "no commitment of any kind, sort, or description" that obligated the United States to protect Quemoy or Matsu.[62]

Dulles's words of calm belied the decision made by Eisenhower. The president was determined to use presidential prerogative if escalation occurred. Although the White House did what it could to prevent such a scenario from happening in the first place—urging the Guomindang to withdraw from the islands or agree to a naval blockade with US military support—the planned course of action was to exercise the full power of the Formosa Resolution.[63] As Gordon Chang has discussed, the president was prepared to resort to nuclear weapons even if he did not communicate as much to either the public or members of Congress.[64]

Because they were not privy to the maneuvering and decision making behind the scenes, Asia Firsters remained unaware of Eisenhower's level of commitment. Impatient for a strong show of support for Taiwan, they had criticized the limitations of the mutual defense treaty when it was first signed. When shelling started again in January, they demanded immediate intervention.[65] Rather than an affirmation of Eisenhower's leadership, their votes in favor of the Formosa Resolution had represented a potential expansion of mutual defense parameters. After giving the president a mandate to guarantee the security of Taiwan and surrounding areas, conservative internationalists expected him to exercise that power. Shortly after the vote, Senator Smith told Chinese Foreign Minister George Yeh that the president "could not have taken a stronger attitude toward Communist China than the resolution which he had just signed." Smith also reassured Yeh that further plans were being discussed in "certain high circles."[66]

They voiced strong opinions in public as well. In response to Dulles's affirmation of nonintervention eleven days earlier, Knowland again pointed out East Asia's importance in relation to Western Europe: "The fact of the matter is that Quemoy and Matsu are as important to free China as Western Berlin is to free Germany." If Soviet forces had stormed West Berlin, he argued, American policy would undoubtedly be more decisive than it was being in the Taiwan Strait. Was it not "time for the Iron Curtain to move backward rather than forward?"[67]

When Senator Wayne Morse moved for reversal of the Formosa Resolution two months after its passage, Knowland rejected the proposition on the grounds that any such action would endanger the islands and begin a chain reaction that could lead to communist control over most of Asia within two years. Chinese Communism was Soviet Communism, and because of a shrinking of the globe, "We are up against Soviet forces just across a river line." Defensible American interests in the Cold War included Quemoy and Matsu, whatever the mutual defense treaty outlined. Eisenhower had to act. "The argument has been made that this is not the place to draw the line. It will never be easy to draw a line," he argued. "A great danger to the peace of the world today is that the Communists may interpret the mere introduction of a resolution which would reverse our policy and which, on its face, would tie the hands of the Commander in Chief."[68]

On the surface, such an endorsement of executive power clashed with the spirit of the recent Bricker Amendment. How could conservatives argue for entrusting a president with such a degree of military power, despite recently attempting to limit the White House's ability to unilaterally strike agreements with foreign nations? The answer rested with legislative process. Bricker's chief complaint was that presidential treaties lacked congressional oversight. On the other hand, the Formosa Resolution was put to a vote, thus adhering to rules that allowed lawmakers to air their opinions. Rather than being antithetical to one another, support for both proposals were examples of how conservatives retained their commitment to a strict interpretation of the Constitution while simultaneously engaging with new Cold War issues. China and Taiwan provided both context and forum for what seemed to be a proactive conservative internationalism, distinct yet also malleable to a mainstream Republican agenda if circumstances demanded.[69]

All or Nothing: Conservatives Take on the UN

Crisis in the Taiwan Strait also yielded further opportunities for conservatives to criticize the UN, an organization with which they had long-standing grievances. Collective peacekeeping through an organization that seated Communist nations and restricted national autonomy had never sat well with the American right. Members of the John Birch Society proudly displayed "Get

U.S. Out of the UN" bumper stickers. Senator Bricker once described the UN Charter as a "a blueprint for slavery."[70] Truman's appeal to the UN rather than Congress for the Korean War cemented that assessment.

In an immediate sense, conservatives fretted over China somehow gaining control of Quemoy and Matsu, perhaps through UN channels. Such a development would constitute a "down payment" toward further communist expansion in the Pacific. Similar to the arguments about Yalta and Manchuria during 1945, the fear was that the People's Republic of China (PRC) would claim more and more territory, and a shoring up of PRC legitimacy might pave the way for its seizure of the Pescadores Islands, or even Taiwan, "through the United Nations or by armed conflict."[71] Admittedly, the odds of such changes actually occurring were extremely slim, especially given the composition of the UN's membership. Yet Dulles, despite a healthy apprehension of the Republican right wing, had raised the idea of seating both Chinas in the UN on multiple occasions.[72] If admittance was even a possibility, the issue was too hot for conservatives to drop.

Their solution was to reform the UN to protect Taiwan. The key was to deemphasize the possibility of a Nationalist return to the mainland (by then almost universally accepted as an impossibility) and instead frame China's exclusion as, first and foremost, a matter of national self-interest. The UN was a potential conduit for growth of Chinese power and corresponding threat to Taiwan; therefore, it impeded what was good for the United States. While somewhat circuitous, this direction went so far as a joint resolution that called for American withdrawal from the UN if Communist China was admitted or its delegation recognized. Hoping to thwart any PRC attempt to "shoot their way into the United Nations organization," Senate Resolution 112 and Senate Concurrent Resolution 29 urged the president to "take such steps as may be necessary to effect the withdrawal of the United States from membership in the United Nations and all organs and agencies thereof."[73]

While clearly hostile, the resolutions were no mere reactions. On a symbolic level they proposed a type of diplomatic isolationism in the age of collective security. Rather than a return to literal, geographic isolationism, this version meant the execution of US foreign policy unfettered by an international body. Conservatives had embraced the view that being an active superpower meant being able to intervene anyplace in the world. However, a perception that an organization dominated by foreign delegates (including representatives of communist states) could jeopardize American sovereignty and potentially usurp the Constitution underscored their criticism of the UN. Extending the discussion that began with reaction to executive power at Yalta, conservative internationalism demanded that neither the president nor an external organization should be able to dictate the United States' overseas commitment without strict oversight.

In the spring of 1955, talk of admitting the PRC reached one of its periodic crescendos, due in part to Zhou Enlai's leadership during the Bandung Conference in Indonesia. China's heightened influence in the Third World via the "Bandung Spirit" sparked renewed debate within US policy circles.[74] The PRC had shown diplomatic initiative separate from the Soviet Union. Even if it was an unexpected rival, Beijing had nonetheless made serious overtures toward newly independent states in Africa, the Middle East, and Southeast Asia, which US officials had long considered to be frontiers of the Cold War.[75] By the time the Bandung Conference ended, *Foreign Affairs* had published an article by Arthur H. Dean, former special envoy to Korea, that argued for formal US recognition of the Communist state—and UN seating—provided Taiwan's interests were still rigorously protected.[76]

Concession of this kind was anathema to Asia First conservatives. Knowland responded by venting complaints focused specifically on how the UN eroded two vital characteristics of American life: national sovereignty and national morality, both of which comprised major elements of national interest. According to his logic, the very inclusion of nations with totalitarian governments was increasingly detrimental to American sovereignty if the United States had to comply with UN measures. Knowland cited the Security Council seat of the Soviet Union ("the most tyrannical government since western civilization entered the modern era") as the organization's fatal flaw: "I am opposed to any form of world government wherein American freedom guaranteed by our Constitution and Bill of Rights is compromised or diluted in the slightest by co-membership with Communist tyranny."[77] Timing was another issue. The organization was potentially constructive, but its rules and bylaws allowed communist nations to hamper timely, streamlined action: "If you exhaust the United Nations before you act, all of these countries could be down the drain."[78]

As the PRC gained a diplomatic status independent from the Soviet Union, and the possibility of its entry into the UN loomed large, Asia Firsters demanded the United States withdraw if Chinese admission became reality. They argued that seating China countered everything for which the UN stood. If the organization was to promote peace worldwide, nations with constitutional governments needed to be the dominant forces within it. Moreover, the UN's potential admission of China, despite PRC aggressions, raised the possibility of an outside organization legitimizing a foreign government that the United States refused to recognize. An international body with such an agenda could hardly promote what was good for American democracy, let alone Taiwan.

Conservatives pushed back, unsurprisingly, by raising familiar arguments about the execution of the Korean War. But conservatives did not rely on old tropes alone. One example specific to the 1955 UN debate on China's admission was the continued imprisonment of fifteen American airmen. POWs from the Korean conflict, they were being held somewhere in China. Knowland used the unresolved situation to highlight what he framed as a fundamental hypocrisy: The UN was considering admission of a nation that respected neither the organization itself nor the ideals it was supposed to uphold. He presented the POW situation as damning evidence. Because Allied participation in Korea was a UN peacekeeping mission, the organization had "an obligation to get the men out of Red China," but "apparently the Communists have not been impressed by the resolution adopted by the United Nations. . . . The men remain there, and they are still in the Communist prisons." Going further, in April 1955 the senator accused UN officials of treating the Korean War armistice as "a scrap of paper," adding, "Either these arrangements mean something, or they mean nothing."[79] He claimed the POW debacle revealed the UN's ineffectualness in the face of a defiant nonmember state that would likely retain that attitude even after it was allowed to join.

Asia Firsters predicted that PRC membership would have disastrous results on hearts and minds around the world. Admission to the UN would bestow prestige on Communist China, transforming a rogue state into a symbol of triumph. Conversely, if the United States failed to vigorously oppose Chinese admission, the Taiwan government could very well lose all hope and collapse. At bottom, weaknesses in prevention might deflate Asian anticommunism to the point where communist revolution would engulf the entire region. If the United States were to let that happen, the Cold War in the Pacific was as good as lost.

In sum, conservative internationalists believed the UN was a conduit through which the PRC could encroach on independent Taiwan. The ostensibly neutral and benign international body undermined America's sovereignty and moral position. Even if the government in Beijing was a reluctantly accepted fact, any avenue through which it could gain recognition and legitimacy had to be closed off. As Knowland avowed, "On the day when Communist China is voted into membership into the United Nations, I shall resign my majority leadership in the Senate, so that without embarrassment to any of my colleagues or to the administration I can devote my full efforts . . . to terminating United States membership in that organization and our financial support to it."[80] This line did not diminish over time. "I still believe that the admission of Communist China would warrant United States withdrawal from the United Nations," he told *American Mercury* several years later.[81] Knowland's florid promise illustrated the tenuous and grudging nature of conservatism's relationship with the UN. It also signaled how initial reservations about centralization of power had evolved to formulate sharp criticism of multilateral peacekeeping. Practitioners of conservative internationalism did not oppose all interventions or multilateral institutions, just those demanding American participation yet not subject to sufficient American control, or those that unduly increased presidential prerogative without oversight. From their perspective, the UN did both.

Yalta, Ten Years Later

The right's ambivalence toward postwar "foreign entanglements" was maybe best represented by its attitude toward Yalta. For nearly a decade, conservatives consistently critiqued the final settlement struck among Roosevelt, Churchill, and Stalin in 1945. And yet it was hard for Asia Firsters to discuss a conference whose records remained classified. Even most federal officials were not privy to the contours of the agreements, and as a result, accusations of mismanagement and double-dealing often lacked substantive detail.

Release of the Yalta proceedings in 1955 dramatically changed knowledge of what happened. As expected, familiar arguments about the betrayal of Chiang Kai-shek, Soviet takeover of Eastern Europe, and expansion in Manchuria again colored discussion of the Cold War. However, this time they were presented with renewed vigor, thanks to the Bricker Amendment and UN controversies. With shelling in the Taiwan Strait still reverberating, the redress of diplomatic missteps regarding China—however dated—took on an urgency that dovetailed with conservatism's ongoing attempts to impose strictures on executive power.

The timing of the papers' publication again illuminated the political faultlines within US diplomacy. In a move that reemphasized how the GOP had parlayed diplomatic discontent into electoral victory, the Eisenhower administration set the release process in motion shortly after entering the White House. In May 1954, the State Department informed the Senate that papers of wartime conferences would be ready for publication by the end of the following month. The June deadline came and went, and State officials who were holdovers from the Truman years were pointedly blamed for the delay.[82] McCarthyism's active targeting of the "China Hands" may have been over, but its effects still lingered.

In anticipation of the release, the right-wing journal *Human Events* offered its own assessment. "Yalta has been a main target of the whitewash brigade of the Roosevelt Administration court historians and apologists," wrote

William Henry Chamberlin. He deemed Yalta the "Pandora's box from which most of international troubles in the postwar era have emerged." In light of recent events in and around China, he warned that the United States was being asked to repeat its wartime mistakes: "Let us not imagine we shall appease Mao Tse-tung and buy peace, in our time or for any long time, if we offer up Free China as a sacrifice in a Formosan Yalta."[83]

Conference proceedings were eventually circulated to Congress on March 19, 1955. They immediately elicited a heated response. Arthur Schlesinger Jr. declared that the publication would "persuade the rest of the world that John Foster Dulles is an idiot, if they need any persuasion." *Foreign Affairs* lamented the obviously partisan motivation behind the release: "The Yalta papers could not have appeared under worse auspices."[84] Conservatives, too, orchestrated a politicized response, as the declassified records seemed to confirm the narrative publicized by the "Manchurian Manifesto" nearly a decade earlier. Sen. Styles Bridges called for the papers to be made available to the general public.[85] For his part, given the backlash, Douglas MacArthur could not distance himself far enough from what had happened at Yalta. In response to the claim that he had influenced decisions made there, the general issued an angry denial: "My views upon the need for Soviet Russia's entry into the war against Japan were never requested and it was only months later that I heard of the territorial and other concessions which had been used as an inducement. . . . Such a statement is utterly unfounded and without the slightest basis in fact."[86]

With elections coming up in 1956, the Yalta papers were an opportunity to show Republican unity in the face of Democratic diplomacy in general and the legacies of Roosevelt in particular. Dulles pointedly stated the president had made the Yalta agreements in secret and never allowed the senate a chance to vote on ratification. The not-so-subtle implication was that the president had overstepped his executive authority and circumvented the Constitution.[87] From a partisan perspective, the proceedings revealed that Democrats had allowed themselves to be bullied by an aggressive, expansionist Stalin and that the president had defied national law to make unnecessary and unwise concessions.

Although the publication of the Yalta proceedings did not drastically alter what Asia Firsters had already said about wartime diplomacy and executive privilege, it did manage to temporarily mend relations between the Eisenhower administration and conservative Republicans. Partisanship trumped differences over the principle of executive agreements—at least temporarily. The secretary of state and his hard-line position against communism in Asia did much to bridge the rift. Dulles diligently cultivated the pro-Nationalist bloc in Congress because he was eager to avoid what had happened to Dean Acheson during McCarthyism's peak.[88] He had proven his anticommunist mettle with his refusal to commit to the Geneva Accords. Moreover, his language on communist China in the UN assured that, at very least, he would not push for official recognition of the Beijing government or allow it any quarter. But, even as Dulles affirmed that the United States could veto a new member, he also stated there was no occasion for American withdrawal from the UN.[89] While his stance met only the halfway mark for Asia First conservatives who would have liked public, armed commitment to Taiwan, the secretary's words suggested he could be a key ally. Publication of what happened at Yalta brought the administration and conservative internationalists marginally closer.

In particular, the friendly working relationship between Dulles and Knowland mitigated any underlying rancor. Indeed, it was Knowland who had personally urged Dulles to release the Yalta papers to expose any cover-up by "Roosevelt-Acheson supporters" lingering in the State Department.[90] Dulles thanked the senator for his "fine leadership" and "attention and assistance" in State Department matters. In 1957, three days before he was to make an appearance in San Francisco, he gave Knowland an advance copy of his speech regarding US policy on China. It detailed opposition to normalizing relations with Beijing, pointed out the ideological ties between the PRC and the Soviet Union (even if the two had "basic rivalries" over Asia), and forcefully rejected the prospect of PRC entry into the UN ("The United Nations is not a reformatory for bad governments"). Knowland described the speech as "outstanding" and of "great help in interest of a peaceful and free world."[91]

Blind Ambition

By the time of that exchange, Knowland had already decided to leave the Senate to run for governor of California in 1958. If he was elected, the plan was then to run for president in 1960. "That man wanted to be President of the United States. He never admitted it publicly, but that's where his whole career was shooting for," daughter Emelyn recalled, "That's where he wanted to be. That's where he thoroughly expected to be at some point in his career."[92] If it were to come to fruition, the election of a Knowland administration would be the culmination of the Republican right's political comeback. It would signify that conservatism was not outside mainstream politics and that the majority of citizens chose to believe in unquestionable American superiority, an expanded defense state, and unilateral military intervention. Knowland had made his reputation by focusing on the Pacific, and his party rewarded him handsomely for his efforts. By the time he announced his plans in early 1957, California's growing numbers made it an obvious launching pad for his ambitions.

The assumption was that the race would be an easy win. Perhaps Knowland suffered from a case of "Potomac myopia" as he failed to consider a host of significant obstacles: a late campaign start; Goodwin J. Knight, a popular incumbent Republican governor who still wanted his job; and the resentment of the California GOP for such an act of political cannibalism.

After a bitter primary battle, Knowland won the nomination, forcing Knight to run for the former's soon-to-be vacant Senate seat. Lingering acrimony within the party compromised chances of winning against Democrat Pat Brown. A mismanaged campaign, public relations blunders, and Knowland's floundering position on right-to-work initiative Proposition 18 only exacerbated the divisiveness of his candidacy.[93] His position as a China expert was also compromised. Torn between campaigning and keeping up with duties in Washington, Knowland was unable to fully participate in discussions of renewed crisis in the Taiwan Strait in late 1958. The final vote count revealed that nearly 59.8 percent of the vote went to Brown while Knowland tallied 40.2 percent.[94] It was a crushing defeat, and its magnitude spelled the conclusion of the senator's career in public office.

Despite that ignominious end, Knowland's leadership in the Senate sparked the continuous development of a conservative internationalism inspired by China. "I began to direct some attention to Asia because I felt not sufficient attention was being given to it," he told one interviewer.[95] His efforts garnered the senator a great deal of criticism, but they also helped to demonstrate that foreign policy was now an integrated part of the right's agenda. Reactionary calls for revision of US China policy were not the entirety of conservatism's approach to the Cold War. Although China remained a major inspiration, and an example Asia Firsters would raise again and again, its usefulness extended beyond Chiang and the Guomindang.

East Asia embodied conservatism's hopes and fears for the future, but for electoral purposes, it was perhaps optimal that Communist China was an irreversible fact. By the mid-1950s, Asia First's goal shifted from restoration of Chiang on the mainland toward curtailment of executive authority and obligations to collective security, broad philosophical issues that raised questions regarding the scope of American commitment overseas and the rapid expansion of presidential power.

As a result, the Republican right was able to hone its overall vision for the nation's responsibilities to the world: The United States acknowledged its heightened stature and corresponding obligations, but that did not mean it was to be bound by compulsory coordination with foreign states. Indeed, as the exemplar of democracy, the nation should have license to act unilaterally when and how it wanted. According to right-wing internationalism, that independent—"free"—mentality was what allowed the United States to succeed where other constitutional nation-states like Britain and France had failed. Conservatives thus constructed a diplomatic approach that managed to skirt traditional definitions of isolationism and internationalism. Their philosophy advocated the preservation of American unilateralism, yet they were eager for intervention in the Pacific, to fight in the name of (or perhaps in memory of) a special US-China relationship.

Labels aside, continuation of the Asia First strategy represented a period of sustained development for conservative internationalism after the Korean War. Although East Asia remained the regional starting point, and the vehicle, for sustained critique of the UN and executive treaties, the methodology changed. Throughout the decade, conservative internationalists toned down the reactionary rhetoric in favor of legitimate steps toward legislative solutions as they fought proxy battles to prove that differences over the shape and purpose of US foreign policy were far from resolved.

Even if they offered no clear resolution, the Bricker Amendment, protests against PRC admission to the UN, and reiteration of critique against Yalta gave the China issue longevity by extending Asia First's reach further into domestic politics, the right's original comfort zone. Ironically, it was precisely the concept of international peacekeeping that allowed China to prolong political warfare at home. Had the United States unilaterally refused to recognize Communist China, there would have been little to discuss. With the questions of UN admission and the organization's impact on the legislative processes at hand, conservatives were able to refresh bygone affairs like the Yalta agreements.

Conservatives had begun to actualize ideological argument through statecraft, and the combination appealed to a specific sector of the electorate that expected forceful activity from its federal representatives. If diversifying Republican conservatism was the key to ensuring its modernization and survival, then the proxy battles over China were vital to attracting support from those who had long harbored doubts about moderation's effectiveness in a Cold War world.

A variety of audiences responded positively to this sustained inspiration from the Pacific, and perhaps none were more crucial than the inhabitants of rapidly growing states like California. The existence of an armed, Moscow-connected enemy in Asia inspired the fear needed to galvanize support for conservatism in the American West. Regional visions of an anticommunist defense state offered economic and ideological benefits, but their effectiveness depended on the impression that the United States' ability to stave off enemy expansion hung in the balance. Ongoing Cold War developments in Asia meant conservative leaders continued to look to the region, and its increasing number of voters, as a potential electoral base that could sway the calculus of national politics.

Meanwhile, Asia Firsters around the country were paying attention. "Congratulations on the stable leadership you are giving to conservative Republicans," Alfred Kohlberg wrote to the senator in 1956.[96] Certainly, Knowland's shepherding of Asia First made a lasting contribution to the future of conservatism, since East Asia policy continued to forge critical links between GOP elites and grassroots activists. Among the latter, even those who did not wholly trust mainstream, institutional politics came to regard the Republican Party in a new light because Knowland demonstrated that the organization could accommodate and even encourage views that paralleled their own. As the decade continued, China and its meanings would bridge the divide between different types of conservatives time and time again.

4

Onward, Christian Soldiers: The John Birch Society

As the 1950s continued, China bridged the divide between elite officials and grassroots activists, even as the latter channeled their energies into mass mobilization efforts rather than the tedium of actual policymaking. A common cause eventually emerged: to rescue the GOP from moderation. That partnership would make a lasting contribution to the right's future.

Unbeknownst to him at the time, William Knowland helped to broker that vital working relationship just as he was beginning to build his own reputation as a spokesman for Asia First conservatism. At the peak of the "Who lost China?" panic in 1950, he introduced, in a Senate address, an individual who eventually became one of the major symbols of the 1960s conservative movement.

The speech unfolded like the plot of a film. On a hot and humid August 25, 1945, John M. Birch, a US Army captain stationed in China, was engaged in a covert intelligence mission. Accompanied by a Lieutenant Tung of the Chinese Nationalist Army, Birch traveled to a small village in a remote northern province where he and his companion encountered a group of Chinese Communist soldiers. After a brief exchange, the Chinese disarmed and detained Birch and Tung for no apparent reason. In the confusion, bayonets were drawn and two shots were fired. One bullet caught Tung in the leg; the other hit Birch. The Chinese soldiers dragged the two men to the village outskirts, dumped their bodies into a roadside ditch, and left. Although Good Samaritans eventually rescued Tung, Birch died of his wounds: "His body was thrown into a ditch . . . even as some of our American soldiers were left for dead quite recently in Korea."[1]

If, as Knowland claimed, Birch was the first casualty of the Cold War in Asia, this incident meant more than the death of one man. The senator used

the soldier to illustrate the conditions American troops faced in Korea and
to criticize what he deemed a pattern of blindness in US Asia policy. Writing
to the secretary of the Air Force, he claimed, "The same type [of] bullets that
killed Captain Birch in 1945 are now killing American troops in Korea. The
same communist military direction existed in 1945 as exists today."[2] Throughout the war in Korea, Knowland pushed for Birch's file (ACO-889028) to be
made public. Military and CIA personnel repeatedly cited security concerns
and denied the request.[3] He nonetheless persisted in disseminating the story,
despite official roadblocks, by passing on copies of the dossier to interested
parties, including one particularly inquisitive seeker named Robert Welch.[4]

The Candy Man

Robert Welch was a sales executive from the Boston area who worked for
his brother's candy company. The James O. Welch Company manufactured
a number of popular treats, including the bestselling "Sugar Daddies" and
"Junior Mints," which boasted tens of millions of dollars in sales.[5] Based on
his success as a businessman, Welch became a regular on the local Republican
lecture circuit. His political ambitions grew, and he eventually ran a failed
nomination campaign for lieutenant governor of Massachusetts in 1950.[6] Despite the disappointment, Welch was motivated to remain politically active
thanks to the Korean War and the recall of Douglas MacArthur, in particular.
He interpreted President Truman's dismissal of the general as an indication
that something was wrong within the American government, and he vowed
not to sit idly by.

Although new to the world of East Asian relations and intrigue, Welch
took to the subject with zeal and began preparing a book manuscript on the
subject of MacArthur's firing. During the year it took him to complete the
project, publisher Henry Regnery passed along an early draft to Alfred Kohlberg, who was perhaps the ultimate test audience for an Asia First author.
Kohlberg responded enthusiastically and told Welch that he would forward a
copy to Chiang Kai-shek himself.[7]

Publisher Henry Regnery quickly released *May God Forgive Us* in 1952.
Written in letter format to the American public, the book tried to raise a
warning about communist infiltration inside the federal state. "It is my utterly
sincere belief that, through whatever puppets activate to exert their combined
insidious pressures, MacArthur was fired by Stalin. He had to be removed,"
Welch argued. "Diplomacy is a wonderful thing if you own all the diplomats
on one side and a sufficient number on the other."[8] As its title suggested, the
text was concerned with issues larger than MacArthur, and it articulated a

broad worldview in which the general's dismissal was just another symptom of America's deterioration. Welch saw Soviet influence in nearly every aspect of American cultural and civic life. "[W]ith every paragraph I shall be hoping, but not believing, that the extent of my fright is not really justified," he wrote.[9] He expressed dismay at the state of labor relations and government spending, and, like many of his fellow conservatives, blamed the liberal establishment of book reviewers, journalists, Hollywood, and Dean Acheson.

Without reservations, Welch linked foreign policy to what he saw as a vast domestic conspiracy that worked around the clock to deliver the United States into enemy hands. He was convinced that both communist global conquest and collectivism at home were parts of a cycle engineered by Stalin and perpetrated by a wide network of agents: "Our enemies are the Communists. Our opponents are their allies, their dupes, and those who support them for whatever cause."[10] Meanwhile he described the "betrayal" of Free China in virtually the same breath as unconstitutional expansion of the federal government. The loss of an allied China was the result of State Department treason as well as welfare programs; each phenomenon was indicative of the other.

Because he linked the result of the Chinese Communist Party (CCP) revolution so closely to alleged missteps within US policy, Welch's attitude on the capabilities of Chiang and the "Free Chinese" correspondingly bordered on the blasé. He agreed the Chinese leader was "badgered, hamstrung, and abandoned," but did not mention the Open Door, expressed no organic humanitarian concern, nor offered any suggestions for future East Asia policy.[11] It appeared that Welch's orientalism had so fully absorbed the idea of China as a reflection of the United States that China itself largely faded from view.

Potential heroism instead came from the ordinary people who read Welch's book. Those who stood against communist subversion were "publicspirited" citizens, much like Welch himself. Just as his text railed against ineptitude within the federal state, it underscored the virtues of extrastate opinions and action. The promotional materials issued by Henry Regnery reflected that focus by painstakingly explaining the genesis of *May God Forgive Us*. The book began as a letter from Welch to three friends, expressing his "indignation at the stupidity and suspicions of treason . . . and his alarm at the continuing course of events." Those friends forwarded copies to their acquaintances, Welch happily obliged requests for more copies, and so on, until his letter effectively became a mass chain letter for a more aggressive US foreign policy. The text had begun as a grassroots phenomenon—there were an estimated seven to ten thousand copies circulating via mimeograph alone.[12] After its official release, Regnery crowed that Welch's text sold twenty-five thousand copies and an additional one hundred thousand ordered in

"Reader's Digest format for newsstand distribution."[13] With mass publication, its addressee was the entire American voting public.

On the institutional side, the best hope for appropriate anticommunism was the conservative wing of the Republican Party. During the 1952 elections, Welch worked feverishly to help Robert Taft win the presidential nomination. He even purchased airtime on a local Boston radio station and began a series of unauthorized broadcasts to drum up support for the Ohio senator. As a Massachusetts delegate, he witnessed Taft's dramatic defeat at the convention and returned home convinced the outcome was proof of communists operating within both political parties.[14] Years later he would still insist that the slogan "I'm for Taft, But He Can't Win" was the brainchild of Soviet agents. "[The slogan] managed to crowd into seven words exactly the right amount of concession, and of apparent realism," Welch fumed in a 1959 editorial.[15] His criticism was aimed squarely at the moderation embodied by Eisenhower's candidacy. Eisenhower was an objectionable leader on more than a few fronts. He was a political dilettante. He was weak on East Asia. He was closely associated with George Marshall, the man who tried to pressure Chiang into cooperation with the Communist Mao. Welch's theories about Eisenhower later took on an irrational slant and were articulated in a manuscript that he shared only with "good friends and outstanding patriots" who could be depended on to safeguard his document.[16] Some years later Welch abandoned secrecy and published the text as *The Politician* (1963). Among other allegations, he accused the "completely opportunistic and unprincipled" president of committing treason against his country by acting as the agent of a worldwide Soviet plot.[17]

Welch's loyalty to the Republican Party was obviously shaken in 1952, and he threatened to make good on his previous threat to defect from the GOP if it refused to actively change the direction of foreign policy. "I am a good Republican," he wrote in *May God Forgive Us*, "But the impact of what is happening in Washington, and of the devious game our State Department is playing in so many parts of the world, transcends even the soundest reasons for my strong partisanship. Rather than cease to fight the dangerous machinations of the Acheson clique at every turn . . . I would abandon the Republican Party in a minute."[18]

Despite those strong words, Welch was not yet prepared to jump ship. All Republicans presumably benefitted from the timely publication of *May God Forgive Us*; in later editions he claimed that it had helped Eisenhower carry Texas. He expected the new president to repay favors he owed conservatives and commanded readers to "make your voice heard and your vote felt."[19] After all, with Taft as Senate majority leader, and others like Joseph McCarthy, Walter Judd, and William Knowland in Congress, anticommunist conservatives were still a force.

Missionary-Soldier

Within the charged postelection atmosphere, Welch stumbled on the story of John Birch. While researching congressional committee hearings on foreign policy in Asia, he came across information on the Army officer's death. His interest piqued, he tracked down the speech Knowland had delivered in 1950 and acquired a copy of Birch's file.

The material consisted mainly of wartime correspondence between Birch and his family. Filled with religious language, the letters composed a portrait of an extremely devout, sometimes self-deprecating young man from Macon, Georgia. Born in India to Baptist missionaries, Birch followed in his parents' footsteps and traveled to China in 1940 as a World's Fundamentalists Baptist Missionary Fellow. He became fluent in Chinese during the course of his work. The United States soon declared war on Japan and Birch joined the Army as an interpreter, eventually becoming an intelligence officer under the command of Lt. Gen. Claire Chennault.[20] In his letters home, Capt. Birch opined that Christians made the best soldiers and described how the Chinese endured relentless persecution by the Japanese.[21] Upon hearing of Soong Mei-ling's 1943 visit to the United States, Birch expressed gladness that she was making a "fine impression."[22] Musings about his place in the world were laced with a combination of hope and apocalyptic prophecy: "I constantly pray that He will forgive my failures and yet use me mightily in China. . . . I believe this war and the ensuing federations will set the world stage, as never before, for the rise of Anti-Christ. What a privilege it will be to stand as witness for the King of Kings on that day, provided Christ does not return and take us out first."[23]

Welch was deeply moved. The same day he received the file, he wrote to Birch's parents, George and Ethel, to introduce himself, inform them of his intentions to write their son's biography, and ask for their cooperation. "I can not [sic] only do justice to a great American patriot and put him in the same category with Nathan Hale, where he belongs," he offered, "but at the same time can point out that patriotism and love of country and honesty and decency and courage still mean something, and are worth the devotion of one's life, even in a world now so badly confused by the long infiltration of Communist doctrine and beastliness."[24] Welch emphasized to the Birches the degree to which his own life resembled that of his potential subject. He and Birch shared Southern backgrounds; they were both raised fundamentalist

Baptists; and each was, in his own way, an anticommunist activist. He believed himself eminently qualified to articulate Birch's ideology. "[T]he faith and sense of brotherhood which motivated John" would guide him in his writing.

After the family granted permission, Welch continued gathering information. He was determined "to make clear the difference between the civilization for which [Birch] gave his life and the pseudo-civilization by which he was murdered."[25] Knowland's original speech had not gone far enough. Whereas the senator used Birch as just one episode of the many he employed to critique US policy in East Asia, Welch planned to make the late soldier the very symbol of democracy betrayed. To him, Birch's death marked the end of innocence and initiated an ongoing age of treason and subversion, which needed to be broadcast as an alarm to the general public. He was going to take his subject's words to heart: "It doesn't make much difference what happens to me, but it is of utmost importance that my country learn now whether these people are friend or foe."[26] When Regnery released *The Life of John Birch* in 1954, Welch succeeded in his and Knowland's mutual desire to make Birch known to a wider audience.

However, the finished product only partially resembled the raw material the senator had forwarded. Access to the classified Army file meant Welch could claim knowledge to which few others were privy. He could therefore selectively use facts, or embellish them, with little fear of reprisal. For example, the book credited Birch with almost supernatural capabilities. It described him as patriotic seer who had the prescience to realize that Mao was not an "agrarian reformer" with good intentions; therefore, CCP forces had to kill him. That portrayal was in direct contrast to the opinion of Col. J. Wilfred Smith, one of Birch's close Army friends, who stated, "At the time John worked under me, his attitude toward the communists was that they were one instrument to get rid of the common enemy. John had no bitterness toward the communists, his attitude was that anybody who helped defeat Japan was to be worked with."[27] Indeed, any antipathy contained in Birch's letters home was reserved for the Japanese, while peasants were the only Chinese group afforded more than a passing mention. But, by casting Birch as a figure that Communists knew by name, feared, and deliberately targeted, Welch wove an international conspiracy theory that implicated both the Chinese who pulled the trigger and American officials who had enabled the alleged plot from the beginning.

The topic of religion was also subject to revisionism. Unlike Knowland, who had identified Birch as a member of the US armed forces, Welch made the captain's religious calling his defining characteristic. The book identified him first and foremost as a missionary whose potential spiritual influence was so great, the Communists needed to destroy him. "Unfortunately, agents of the very anti-Christ, whose rise John foresaw, also recognized what a dangerous antagonist John Birch would be," Welch wrote, "for it was his firm intention, often announced, to remain in China and resume his missionary activities once the war was over."[28] Evangelical proselytizing was a form of conversion that had both spiritual and actively political dimensions, and the stressing of Birch's religious background demonstrated the author's own belief in Christianity's power to triumph over communism in mainland China and other threatened regions of the world.

Such unabashed religiosity was a new angle for Asia First conservatism, which had previously highlighted the duties of the Open Door policy and general humanitarianism. Other authors and politicians alluded to communist atheism as a sign of perversity, but none prescribed spirituality as an anticommunist measure to the extent that Welch did. Even Guomindang supporters who had missionary backgrounds, like Walter Judd and Henry Luce, rarely cited the Bible as a defense against Mao.[29] In fact, the public figure Welch resembled most in his religious rhetoric was Soong Mei-ling, who cited her family's Methodism as proof that the Guomindang qualified for American aid.

Birch's life as a missionary-soldier in China was portrayed as an extended lesson in how to relate to potential converts. Welch extensively quoted Arthur H. Hopkins, a lieutenant who served with Birch, on how Birch was able to disguise himself as a native laborer, how he "spoke Chinese so perfectly that the natives all thought he was a Chinese from another province."[30] Via his ability to "become" Chinese through language or costume, Birch adapted to the point where he could stay in the field with the Chinese Army. His example supposedly showed Asian counterparts that Americans were able to benevolently meet them on their level. "John Birch proved that he could get along on exactly the same rations, and live continuously under the same conditions that they did, and still fight and work twenty hours a day," Welch wrote. By learning to eat, fight, and live like them, Birch enjoyed the support and "sincere friendship" of Chinese soldiers and civilians alike.[31]

His intent to depict Birch as a compassionate savior figure was obvious, but Welch revealed some of his own unflattering stereotypes about the Chinese. Similar to views held by Americans in the nineteenth century, Welch presumed that the Chinese were able to live on a substandard diet and in cramped quarters. The high degree of admiration he used to describe Birch's ability to exist in the same conditions revealed just how poor the author believed those circumstances to be. Perhaps more importantly, a pointed illustration of Birch's camaraderie with the Chinese placed the protagonist in direct contrast with liberal Protestant YMCA missionaries who chose to live segregated from the very people they tried to convert. Many of those missionaries' sons became the State Department's ill-fated "China Hands."[32]

Albeit brief in years, Birch's life apparently contained everything any patriotic citizen needed to know about the nature and goals of global communism. As the book's tagline read, "In the story of one American boy, the ordeal of his age." Welch placed particular significance on the timing of the Birch killing. Armistice had been declared just ten days prior to the American captain's last mission. Despite Birch's alleged gifts of prophecy, he had no reason to believe that CCP troops, who had united with the United States against the Japanese, would harm him. The fact that the Communists killed— apparently without provocation—an American who was still formally their ally indicated Stalin and Mao's plans to subvert all diplomatic relationships in their quest for world domination. Or so Welch claimed. So great was his belief in the power of his own theories, he requested advance readers to avoid letting the manuscript fall out of their hands, lest "Communists or their sympathizers spike the book in any way, through knowing about it or its contents in advance."[33]

If MacArthur's dismissal had aroused the former vice president of the National Confectioners Association to investigate the influence of communism in American foreign and domestic policy, the research and writing of Birch's biography awakened him to the importance of China in the race between good and evil, faith and atheism: "John Birch, as fine a young man as America has ever produced, was born in Asia and also died in Asia. Perhaps the fact is symbolic of the great interest in America was already taking and must now continue to take in that continent."[34] Because of Birch, Welch's perception of Asia had significantly evolved. His loyalties still placed the United States before all other nations, but he was now concerned for both parties in the US-China relationship.

Embracing Chiang Kai-shek

Welch's prior ambivalence toward the Guomindang consequently transitioned into ardent support. He soon argued that military and financial aid to the Chinese Nationalist government on Taiwan should cornerstone US East Asia policy. He also threw himself into promoting Chiang, whose government proved a willing partner. After learning that *May God Forgive Us* had been translated into Chinese and was being used by the Guomindang Education Department, Welch traveled to Taiwan in 1955 to gather information for a brief biography of Chiang. As "an earnest anti-Communist and friend of

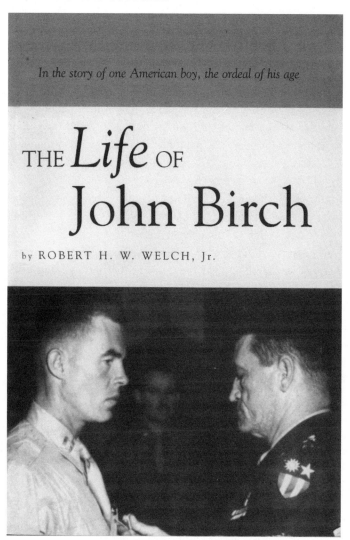

In the story of one American boy, the ordeal of his age

THE *Life* OF
John Birch

by ROBERT H. W. WELCH, Jr.

FIGURE 4.1. Book cover, *The Life of John Birch* by Robert H. W. Welch Jr. (Appleton, WI: John Birch Society).

Free China," Welch experienced the welcome for which General and Madame Chiang were famous. His trip included visits to designated farms, a military parade, and tea with Soong Mei-ling. He was also granted time with high-ranking officials, including Vice President Chen Cheng and Defense Minister Yu Ta-wei. Welch wrote, "The kindness and hospitality with which [I] was received, and the opportunities given [me] to see and do so much in so comparatively short a time, need to be mentioned, even at the regrettable expense of making [me] sound a lot more than [I] was, or [am]."[35]

Chiang made certain to leave a good impression. "May you join other lone voices crying in the wilderness until you become a chorus which cannot be silenced," he wrote to Welch shortly after.[36] The latter came away enthralled, his desire to defend Nationalist China's past and present amplified even further. He wrote a worshipful article that chronicled Chiang's life in its entirety and published it in his political magazine, *One Man's Opinion*. The story comprised the entire May 1957 edition, giving Chiang and the Guomindang what amounted to a propaganda pamphlet.[37] Welch later combined it and the earlier MacArthur text into one volume endowed with the title *Again, May God Forgive Us.*

With the end of the Chinese civil war nearly ten years past, the passage of time meant the reading public might have forgotten Chiang's contributions to the United States. Welch strenuously attempted to render Chiang relatable to Americans, starting with the Chinese leader's ideological and spiritual principles. Because he shared popular Western spiritual and moral values, Chiang was therefore deserving of American assistance in his campaign to take back mainland China. Welch described Chiang's boyhood on a small farm, during which his subject ostensibly learned the value of land and hard work. He contended that such lifelong virtues of Jeffersonian republicanism allowed Chiang to cherish democratic values similar to those of Americans.[38] This was also a way to counter accusations that Chiang only represented an elite, wealthy segment of Chinese society and was out of touch with the common peasant.

Chiang's Christianity was the other highlighted trait. Welch described it as "a wholehearted consecration that has never wavered." Unlike the Communists who had driven him into exile, the leader of Free China was neither an atheist nor a pagan. Like many Americans anxious about the Cold War future, Chiang used his faith as "an inspiration, a solace, and a guide" that kept his hopes for a democratic China alive.[39]

These claims about Chiang's biography were hardly novel. On the contrary, they were old news thanks to both Chinese and American public relations efforts. For example, Chiang had long recognized the value of his conversion to Methodism; he and his government had been using invocations of Christianity to court American sympathy since the Sino-Japanese War. Henry Luce had also been making similar arguments since the 1930s, and his audience was exponentially larger than Welch's due to the vast circulations of *Time* and *Life* magazines.[40] Nevertheless, in terms of narrating Chiang's story in correlation with conservative mobilization, quality over quantity ruled in favor of Welch. The readers who consumed texts like *One Man's Opinion* during the late 1950s and early 1960s were much more homogenous in their politics. If anything, titles like *Again, May God Forgive Us* showed how independent publishing afforded the freedom to appeal to a highly specific demographic.

To that end, Welch's presentation of Chiang as a conservative hero was evident in the unmistakable parallels he drew between the Chinese leader and John Birch. Both were ardent Christians who participated in the conversion process (Birch as a missionary, and Chiang as a soul who was saved).[41] The two men were meant to be effective anticommunists because of their spiritual beliefs. And like Birch, the very people who were supposed to aid Chiang had deceived him. In the latter's case, the culprit was Washington, DC. As staunch allies of the United States, "Chiang and his countrymen needed and *deserved* the help of America more than any other leader and his people, at any time the 170 years since we ourselves became a nation," Welch fumed. "Instead, he found the American government deserting him, deceiving him, betraying him, and aiding the Chinese Communists at every turn to take over his country." Whether deliberately or incompetently, liberal containment had failed to help, and that was why China was lost.[42]

Like many Asia Firsters, Welch argued that an allied China was integral to America's national security interests. He demanded changes in US policy to reflect that: It was tragic that Washington limited itself to gestures like the 1954 mutual defense treaty, leaving Chiang and his supporters frustrated by what they perceived as a lack of initiative on the part of the United States.[43] However, Welch invested wholeheartedly in the idea of Chiang as a figure beloved by his people, which led him to take extreme positions that had already been discarded by other conservative internationalists. He argued that the United States should spearhead Chiang's return to mainland China. Once the Chinese leader landed and was protected from immediate harm, daily uprisings would "merge and mushroom into effective and confident rebellion" against the Communist regime.[44] The Chinese were not the only ones who would arise. Welch also anticipated an emotional response from Americans.[45]

The dividing line of Guomindang capability led advocates of conservative internationalism down divergent paths that illustrated telling variations within the Asia First platform itself. Those who were doubtful abandoned Chiang as a legitimate answer to Mao and were silent on the topic of his restoration. Instead they turned inward, toward questions of executive power and the price of the nation's participation in collective security. Although Welch and those who shared his confidence in Chiang largely concurred with conservative officials' stances on the United Nations (UN) and other diplomatic issues, theirs was less an effort at laborious policy change than specific use of China as a reminder of communism's continued influence within the

United States—an argument that many GOP conservatives abandoned after McCarthyism died down. Both sides contributed to the right's development during the early Cold War, even if only one sustained that growth in the decades to come.

A Paul Revere for the Cold War

For its part, the Nationalist government proved extremely receptive to Welch's assessments. It purchased two thousand copies of *Again, May God Forgive Us* for distribution. Hollington K. Tong, Taiwan's ambassador to the United States, commended it as the "best short biography of President Chiang Kai-shek he had ever read."[46] Other China activists also sang praises. "More power to you," wrote an enthusiastic Kohlberg.[47] Such validation must have been gratifying to Welch, but he intended to reach an audience larger than the relatively small group of already convinced Chiang supporters. Both the Chiang and Birch biographies were case studies designed to illustrate a sweeping argument about faulty US Asia policy and internal deterioration. In other words, how liberalism had let down the nation and therefore the world.

Welch was a fervent admirer of Ralph Waldo Emerson, and throughout the latter half of the 1950s he styled himself as a scholar-philosopher with the power and the duty to awaken everyday citizens to the dangers of communism.[48] He believed there were roadblocks, however. For example, Welch was disappointed by the sales numbers of *May God Forgive Us*. Ignoring the fact that Regnery released multiple editions, including two printings in 1952 alone, he blamed reviewers who formed "a conspiracy of silence . . . for the purpose of smothering all books which seek to tell the truth about Communist infiltration of our government."[49] The only way to counter such discrimination was for him to create an alternative media outlet.

The monthly *One Man's Opinion* began publication in 1956. Its title reflected Welch's certainty that he stood as a solitary voice in a public sphere tainted by liberal bias. On the more practical side, the benefits of self-publication were obvious: articles could cover whatever he chose without editorial interference. More importantly, he could publish in the format of his choosing, "with either the informality of a letter to friends, or the careful language of a formal essay."[50] With its eclectic choice of writers and subjects, *One Man's Opinion* was styled as a voice for committed conservatism, the vision of one man with a message for all conservatives. Indeed, the magazine helped Welch to network among the right's boldface names, including Albert Wedemeyer (who contributed a piece on Communist China's possible admission to the UN called "Keep 'Em Out") and Kohlberg, whom Welch asked to advise on content.[51]

That message was what Welch called the "New Americanism," a sweeping antistatist manifesto that called for fundamental changes to the federal government. He outlined its foundations at Dickinson College's 1957 convocation. The federal state, he said, was a necessary evil that was usually more evil than necessary, as it "is always and inevitably an enemy of individual freedom."[52] At bottom, its sins were monetary: It was fiscally wasteful and wont to expand until it became economically totalitarian. The implications of such oppression radiated well beyond the financial sector. Big government "always has a tendency to squeeze out the middle class; to destroy or weaken the middle for the benefit of the top and the bottom."[53] Moreover, the best bulwark against further socialization, the free market, was being choked to death by an ever-increasing army of bureaucrats. "I am convinced America would be better off with a government of three hundred thousand officials and agents, every single one of them a thief, than a government of three million agents with every single one of them an honest, honorable, public servant," he contended, "*The increasing quantity of government, in all nations, has constituted the greatest tragedy of the twentieth century.*"[54]

All was not doom and gloom, however. Like his hero John Birch, Welch mitigated fatalism with hope. He described the New Americanism as a "positive, forward-looking philosophy; a design and example of social organization which boldly and confidently offers leadership along the hard but sure road to a better world."[55] Because it outlined concrete steps for betterment, it was supposed to offer conservatives an optimistic, proactive perspective on the future.

The revamping of US foreign policy would constitute one major reform. Unlike isolationist/neutralist movements of the past, like America First during the 1930s, the New Americanism balanced libertarian rhetoric with the demand for military buildup and active shows of force whenever and wherever necessary. Cuts to the welfare state did not mean cuts to the defense state. On the contrary, the former were necessary so that national security could withstand perils both foreign (external attack, threats to national interests around the world) and domestic (dependence on government provision bred citizens likely to sympathize with the communist cause).[56]

Moreover, a rigorous diplomacy and defense policy would allow the proper American ideology to reach all corners of the globe. Just as communism had an international reach, so, too, should American values. Any individual regardless of origin would be able to identify as "americanist"—note the lowercase "a"—if he or she subscribed to its political philosophy.[57] Welch appropriated "americanism" and strove to turn it into a global identity unfettered by geographic boundaries.

His magazine underwent a subsequent makeover. Welch spent a year tinkering with formula and format. When it was relaunched in February 1958, *One Man's Opinion* became *American Opinion*. The rebranding and expansion reflected Welch's increasing confidence in his ability to speak for an entire nation, or to claim his and other right-wing voices as the only ones that were capable of proper patriotism. The revamped publication joined the growing place that conservative magazines like *Plain Talk*, *Human Events*, and *National Review* were forging in the national public sphere. In fact, Welch was a fervent admirer of the latter. He served on organizational boards with William F. Buckley Jr. and had donated money to *National Review* when it was getting off the ground.[58] Buckley would later be noted for his critique of Welch's activities, but, during the 1950s, their relationship was more symbiotic than adversarial.[59]

On its own terms, *American Opinion* was perhaps best described as a stridently anticommunist *Reader's Digest*. Although Welch maintained editorial control, a stable of journalists and writers rounded out the feel of the magazine. Among the earliest articles were an exposition on "Why People Become Communists" and a yearlong series by Holmes Alexander called "How to Read the Federalist Papers."[60] Lee Edwards, who became a prominent historian of the American right, was another contributor.[61] Regular features included an analytical news summary, quotes from famous conservatives, historical profiles, foreign policy items, and cartoons. Bible colleges, evangelical seminaries, conservative publishing houses, and the Kwik Lok Corporation of Yakima, Washington (makers of reusable plastic package ties) comprised the bulk of advertisers. Such institutions represented sources of both financial backing and readership.

An earnest attempt to engage its audience on an ideological level signaled *American Opinion*'s lofty aspirations to move grassroots conservatism beyond single-issue politics. Via reportage and recommended reading, it attempted to bind all conservatives who sought knowledge about their country and their world. At the same time it crafted its own unique slant by promising to "avoid eggheadism and lay it out straight."[62] The January 1959 issue embodied such an approach. It consisted entirely of reviews of books recommended by the magazine's staff; dubbed "100 Steps to the Truth," these texts were presented as tools for "systematic study of the Communist time table for world conquest." Knowledge of the enemy was a prerequisite to combating socialism, and *American Opinion* Bookstore reading lists, complete with convenient order forms, were ready to help readers enhance their knowledge and buttress their beliefs.[63]

American Opinion offered ideas and analysis that resonated with conservatives of all types, from internationalists to antitax crusaders. As the mouthpiece for Welch's New Americanism, it attempted to address long-term problems via a comprehensive agenda with the goal of driving the grassroots right toward radical activism. The core of its mission was to raise awareness of the challenge global communism posed to Americans in their daily lives.

The Blue Book

Welch's impatience with the direction of the Cold War soon forced his considerable energies into the realm of militant political mobilization. He never forgot the MacArthur dismissal and continued to blame what he saw as a corrupt system of consensus. Since those days he had been conceptualizing a national group that would shake the foundations of the two-party system.[64] In December 1958 it was time to start work. Welch invited a small group of prominent businessmen to Indianapolis, explaining that the purpose of their visit would be revealed only after their arrival.[65]

After his eleven guests had gathered, Welch stood in front of them with a world map. He opened the meeting by sounding an alarm. The "simple, incontrovertible, and deadly" truth was that communism was steadily taking over the world. "[Y]ou have only a few more years before the country in which you live will become four separate provinces in a world-wide Communist dominion ruled by police-state methods from the Kremlin." With the fall of Eastern Europe and much of Asia, and with Western Europe in the advanced stages of "socialization," he calculated the Soviet plan for global conquest to be already two-thirds complete. The United States was the last stronghold of freedom, but its citizens were ignorant of the danger around them. To illuminate their precarious position, Welch offered a striking analogy: "We are living, in America today, in such a fool's paradise as the people of China lived in twenty years ago."[66]

Just as hope for the future rested with ordinary Americans, so, too, did the responsibility for their precarious position in the Cold War. Had citizens been more cognizant of communist influence within their own government during the 1940s, the defeat of their most valuable ally, Chiang Kai-shek, would never have occurred. Back then, China was "Fortress Asia"; it was the Kremlin's greatest acquisition and served as the geographic base from which the Soviet Union planned to conquer the Western world. As Lenin himself once stated, the "road to Paris" ran through Peking.[67] Welch presented the events of 1949 as proof of the long reach of subversive agents and ideas within the United States. He persistently referred to that year as what should have been a decisive moment in the battle against communism. Instead, blissfully ignorant citizens sat by as one betrayal after another took place.

Over the course of two days, Welch repeatedly used China to illustrate his anticommunist theories and arguments. So what was to be done? The answer came in plans for a new political organization that would combat what he saw as the nation's internal decay. He christened the newborn group after the individual who had awakened him to China's importance: John Birch. Shortly afterwards, the presentations he made in Indianapolis were compiled in the group's manifesto, *The Blue Book of the John Birch Society*, which became required "must reading" for anyone who wanted to join.[68]

His text reasoned that the Cold War was not the effect of communist aggression alone but rather a natural and perhaps predictable byproduct of degeneration. To explain the sorry state of affairs in which the United States found itself, one only needed to examine the fundamental patterns of advanced civilization. Welch's argument relied heavily on the work of Oswald Spengler, the interwar German historian-philosopher whose multivolume work, *The Decline of West*, charted the rise and fall of several world societies.[69] From the Middle East to classical Greece to China, Spengler offered a universal model of cultural degeneration.[70] The final stage was what he termed "aesthetic unity," in which citizens decadently rested on the laurels of development rather than striving for the innovation that had driven their society forward.[71]

Welch applied Spengler's theories to the mid-twentieth century in wholesale fashion. He contended that Western civilization's final stronghold was postwar America, itself in the throes of aesthetic unity. Welfare state collectivism threatened to destroy the American republic and throw open the door to domination by the "pseudo-civilization" of Soviet communism. Offsetting his emotionally charged delivery, Welch used a biological metaphor to illustrate the recurring collapse of self-reliance: "For collectivism destroys the value to the organism of the individual cells—that is, the individual human beings—without replacing them with new ones with new strength. The Roman Empire of the West, for instance, started dying from the cancer of collectivism from the time Diocletian imposed on it his New Deal."[72] By comparing the United States to the Roman Empire and vice versa, Welch imbued his antistatist, anticommunist argument with a sort of timelessness. This rhetorical maneuver impressed on would-be disciples concurrent senses of historicity, urgency, and finality, forcing them to consider the (significantly) broader implications of local and federal politics.

Although its author made protestations to the contrary ("There is certainly more Welch than there is Spengler in what follows"[73]), *The Blue Book*'s interpretation of postwar American government was essentially an addendum to *Decline of the West*. By aligning himself with Spengler's philosophy of history, Welch revealed serious aspirations toward intellectualism. He strove to emulate what H. Stuart Hughes described as Spengler's position as "historian, diagnostician, prophet" all in one.[74] Certainly the two shared a predilection for absolutes: Western civilization was undeniably in decline; barbarians were at the gate; and the inheritors of all civilization's advancements (Americans, in Welch's case), remained uneducated and easily fooled.

It was clear that Welch related to Spengler on a personal level. In *The Blue Book*, he spent considerable time railing against academia's dismissal of *Decline* vis-à-vis its praise for Arnold J. Toynbee's *A Study of History* (1934–54). Another multivolume work with a large-scale analysis of global history, Toynbee's book was, according to reviewers at the time, "an imposing achievement . . . with a majestic vision" and "a work of art."[75] Welch on the other hand considered it "half-baked nonsense."[76] He was convinced academics had denied Spengler recognition because his political beliefs did not mesh with theirs. Meanwhile *American Opinion* contended that Toynbee, who was the nephew of celebrated left-wing economic historian Arnold Toynbee, undeservedly enjoyed accolades and book sales. Here Welch was undoubtedly projecting his own life experiences. Academics and the mainstream media had largely ignored his book on the MacArthur dismissal (*May God Forgive Us*), whereas the liberal Richard Rovere and Arthur Schlesinger Jr. received much more attention and praise for their account in *The General and the President* (1951).[77]

In his eagerness to co-opt Spengler for the conservative cause, Welch overlooked certain aspects of the German scholar's career that hardly complemented the goal of saving American democracy from totalitarianism. Tellingly, he omitted the fact that Spengler's writings had served as an inspiration for Nazi fascism. Although Spengler himself disapproved of Hitler and the Third Reich because of their racism, his work nevertheless devalued the Weimar Republic and, as Danish scholar Adam Paulsen argues, "contributed to calling forth the empire with his vision."[78] Whether Welch was simply unaware of or deliberately ignored his idol's significance within German politics, the would-be scholar sidestepped those contexts altogether. In doing so he impressed his American readers with a sense of civilizational destiny without having to address *The Blue Book*'s problematic appropriation of *Decline of the West*.

Most significantly for American conservatism, by readily adopting the

Spengler model and inserting the United States within it, Welch demonstrated his acceptance of the fact that the nation's own fate was entwined with historical trends and developments around the world. The cultural pluralism of *Decline* articulated a perspective that factored each nation-civilization within a global schema; the book was transhistorically internationalist. Especially in someone so nationalistic, Welch's assumption that the United States had a responsibility to safeguard the world for *any* ideology showed how internationalism had become an accepted, popular worldview within the right. From congressional officials to the grassroots, the integral importance of foreign relations was not only recognized but also taken for granted. As Welch informed Chiang in 1955, he was primarily concerned with his own country, but thanks to what happened to China, he acknowledged that the United States' fate was tied to that of other nations.[79]

That did not mean conservative internationalism was uniform across the board. Welch's specific version had an evangelical fervor to it. In that regard, his embrace of Birch, a Baptist proselytizer, made perfect sense. "[T]he kind of life, of peaceful opportunity and responsibility, which John Birch wanted for his fellow Americans, and for his Chinese friends, and for all men of good will, is exactly the kind of life we should like to see possible everywhere," he wrote.[80]

The repeated references to China and past diplomatic wrongs in *The Blue Book* showed that Welch intended China to play a vital role in his plans. He used them whenever there was a critical historical point to make. At the same time, there were subtleties to his narrative that bespoke a take on East Asia that was more considered than, for example, Alfred Kohlberg's hopes for restoration. While support of the Guomindang was a given, as was demand for continued US aid, by the time *The Blue Book* was released Welch no longer advocated giving Chiang carte blanche. He seemed to realize that recapture of the Chinese mainland was unfeasible, and he privately expressed reservations about the Guomindang leader's practical capabilities, despite having lauded them to the skies in *Again, May God Forgive Us* just two years earlier.[81]

What Welch had in mind could be described as altogether more mercenary. He saw China's future role as a political mobilizer rather than an active participant in the Cold War. Instead of a dramatic change to the diplomatic status quo, or even the emphasis on finer points of executive power and foreign policy that Asia Firsters in Congress were making, Welch counted on the emotional weight of the 1949 "loss" to sustain popular anticommunism. The choice to name the group after John Birch illustrated how Welch presumptively relied on American orientalism. China provided important context for Birch's motivational life story, but it remained just that: context. Cast as an important episode in US-China relations, Birch's death nevertheless remained a firmly American story. The same held true for US foreign policy as a whole. China's fate, and thus its political symbolism, revealed the American condition, not the Chinese one. More mileage was to be gained from using China to foreshadow what lay in store for the United States if it did not go on the offensive against communism.

By the time of the inaugural John Birch Society (JBS) meeting, Welch's stance on China had achieved a balance between hero worship of Chiang and his earlier argument for unabashed national self-interest. The latter would be expressed via a popular foreign policy driven by citizens who understood that a free China depended on the United States, and how American national security needed a bulwark in East Asia. Therefore he still pushed for a foreign policy that increased aid to the Nationalists on Taiwan, but he only did so on behalf of middle-class Americans outside the tainted federal government (those unlike Dean Acheson, Alger Hiss, and Dwight Eisenhower), the demographic that he saw as the world's best hope against Soviet domination.

To Gather an Army

Corrective foreign policy would be founded on mass education and mobilization, and the ultimate objective was to teach and sway the voting public to the conservative frame of mind. Despite all the imagery of losing scoreboards and maps running red, the JBS's founder believed in the power of populist activism. In a departure from Spengler, who gloomily offered no remedy for decline, Welch hoped to use the nation's alleged deterioration to compel citizens to change the course of history: "To feel that we cannot win that struggle is a form of pessimism to which I, for one, shall never yield."[82] After all, the JBS was founded as a grassroots organization that could turn the tide of the Cold War in Western civilization's favor, beginning with grassroots mobilization and subsequent reform of national politics. Wielding the fate of China as concrete proof of what would happen to the United States if sufficient measures were not taken, Welch was confident he could bring about change.

He made it clear that the JBS was to function as a "body," not an organization: "An organization is a collection of individuals or groups held together more or less loosely and more or less temporarily by a common interest or common objective. A body, in the sense I am using it because it is the closest word to express my concept, is an organic entity."[83] A body was only as healthy as the sum of its parts. The JBS needed men and women willing to throw themselves into the fray—intellectually, financially, and politically: "Every bit of dedication to the cause is worthwhile."[84] If the JBS was a body, then Welch was its brain, training all parts for the Armageddon that Birch had prophesized in China.

The very choice of John Birch as figurehead signaled the scope of the JBS's purpose. Welch described its namesake as a brave, righteous, and dutiful missionary who actively tried to change the world in the name of freedom and Jesus Christ. As a World War II veteran, an anticommunist, and a youth, Birch possessed qualities relatable to the men and women his face and story were meant to attract. He represented the type of grassroots organization Welch wanted and what he expected from its members.

Through his status as an inspirational poster boy, the humble missionary became an exalted symbol whose exploits seemed lifted from the pages of contemporary fiction. Birch's comfort with the Chinese and their way of life undeniably paralleled the storyline of Father John X. Finian in *The Ugly American*, William J. Lederer and Eugene Burdick's best-selling 1958 novel about American intervention in Southeast Asia. Like Birch, Finian channeled his religious beliefs into a fervent anticommunism, and his ready assimilation into native life (via language, food, and grassroots activism) was integral to the success of his crusade.[85] Both characters were designed to vent frustration with the US government's course of policy. Both championed more effective ways of combatting the spread of communism in Asia.

Finian was not the only literary figure to whom Birch bore an uncanny resemblance. Welch's portrayal of the solider inadvertently transformed his subject into a figure bearing an undeniable, if ironic, resemblance to the fascist symbol of Comrade Ogilvy from George Orwell's *1984* (1949). The superhuman accomplishments of both Birch and Ogilvy—whether factual, embellished, or completely imagined—turned propaganda into politically usable history. After creating the fictional Ogilvy, Winston Smith (a clerk in the "Ministry of Truth" and the novel's doomed protagonist) is struck by how easy it is to revise the past to suit the present: "Comrade Ogilvy, unimagined an hour ago, was now a fact. It struck him as curious that you could create dead men but not living ones. Comrade Ogilvy, who had never existed in the present, now existed in the past, and when once the act of forgery was forgotten, he would exist just as authentically, and upon the same evidence as Charlemagne or Julius Caesar."[86]

Certainly Welch's version of Birch accomplished formidable feats as a conservative figurehead. The all-American boy killed by Chinese Communists, Birch encompassed both the domestic and international and therefore signified the heart of JBS doctrine: US citizens needed to consider what it meant to be American in relation to the global problem of communism.

A Sunbelt Recruiting Ground

Welch was a natural born salesman and he precisely identified the people who would be drawn to the JBS and why. Extensive travels from coast to coast for the family candy business familiarized him with the untapped political potential of the postwar middle-class.[87] This growing population was weaned on the Cold War economy and dotted the national landscape with suburban housing developments.[88] Nowhere did it expand as quickly as in the portion of the country now known as the "Sunbelt," an area that stretched from Virginia to Texas to its anchor, the Golden State.

Over the last twenty years, extensive study has been dedicated to the rapid growth of grassroots conservatism in the American West during the 1960s. Many scholars point to Southern California as the cradle of the "New Right."[89] With its influx of recent transplants, thriving evangelical culture, and strain of regional libertarianism, the Southland was possessed of a unique type of sociocultural alchemy, one that wove politics into the fabric of everyday life. As Lisa McGirr writes in her seminal 2001 study *Suburban Warriors*, this new California conservatism was a movement "fueled by the politics of anti-statism, virulent anticommunism, and strict normative conservatism." It was forged "at living room bridge clubs, at backyard barbecues, and at kitchen coffee klatches."[90] A booming economy and unprecedented growth were not enough to ease the concerns of residents discomfited by what they considered to be the decline of traditional America. In this milieu, men and women transformed their domestic spaces into centers of mobilization, while social events became indistinguishable from organizational meetings.

The worldview that Welch espoused through the JBS contributed greatly to the group's rapid growth in areas like Orange County, California. For the libertarian or the economically minded, Welch railed that government's responsibility was "not to provide security, but only to restrain the tyrant so that men might compete industrially in 'peaceful rivalry.'"[91] There was a cultural war to wage as well. John Rousselot, a former JBS Western states' director whose successful bid for a congressional seat in 1960 proved the increasing influence of Birchism in Southern California, distilled many conservatives' frustrations during an interview shortly after his win. He complained that "neo-Marxists"—many of whom were academics, doctors, and attorneys—enjoyed prestige, while conservatives who believed in "simple truths" like God and capitalism were denigrated as intellectually inferior.[92]

If fiscal and cultural conservatism were not enough, then spiritual faith, which Welch identified as the common denominator among Birchers, provided a trump card. Those who maintained their beliefs deserved praise. "I know that there are still millions of devout Catholics, fundamentalist Protestants, and faithful Jews in this country who still believe unquestioningly in the Divine," Welch wrote. "Let all of us thank whatever God we severally worship that there is so large a remnant of the really true believers still left. We honor them. . . . We admire them."[93] Religious devotion was understood to instill values of individual responsibility and morality that prevented practitioners from relying on the state for their welfare. By inference, those who took government assistance or supported New Deal concepts not only forfeited their self-determination but also could not be considered to be truly spiritual.

The secular nature of modern life allegedly meant religion and the freedom to practice it were under constant assault. Welch expected his faithful to be perturbed by the corrosion of morality and terrified at the prospect of atheistic communism's expansion. The JBS offered a haven for their religious zeal in a godless world. Moreover, it did not just promise a sanctuary but made "the moral salt of the earth" its foundation.

The one caveat was that potential members had to be *fundamentalist* practitioners of their respective religions. Liberal Christianity was not enough. Welch argued it was a lack of staunch spiritual devotion that had led the nation down the road of federal collectivism, opening itself to communist subversion, in the first place.[94] Although he professed to esteem a range of faiths, Welch's personal religious views and subsequent rhetoric favored "devout Catholics and fundamentalist Protestants." The JBS founder called them his "best friends and strongest supporters."[95] Esteem for Christianity's tenets overshadowed even the influence of the Enlightenment. "The reality and earnestness of Christian faith was the foundation of our ethics, and the substance of our consciences," he claimed. "When Voltaire said that if God did not exist we should have to invent him, it was a very blasphemous remark."[96]

The choice of John Birch as mascot for a Sunbelt-led conservatism was incredibly shrewd for a number of reasons, none more significant than how it managed to combine fundamentalist spiritualism with geopolitical concern over the Cold War in Asia. Recent history had shown postwar Southern California to be receptive to religious revival. Darren Dochuck has eloquently described how the success of Rev. Billy Graham—who, like Birch, was a Southern evangelical—bloomed first in the Los Angeles area and then on a national stage.[97] Ministers less well known than Graham also prepared the ground for the JBS. One example was Rev. James W. Fifield Jr. of the First Congregational Church in Los Angeles. In the mid-1930s, Fifield founded the Spiritual Mobilization movement, which has been described as "a religious version of the anti–New Deal Liberty League."[98] He considered religion to be a tool to ease social conflict and to promote what he identified as "the common good." During the early 1950s and debates about China and Korea, that common good was a rabid anticommunism that affirmed capitalism and religious faith. He and Welch both sat on the Board of Directors for the conservative Citizens' Foreign Relations Committee, a group that also included Bill Buckley, Albert Wedemeyer, and William J. Loeb, among others. After Fifield resigned from Spiritual Mobilization in 1959, he personally helped Welch to establish the JBS in California.[99]

Evangelical theology easily lent itself to anticommunist crusade, and the Birch backstory of militant missionary activity perfectly complemented what McGirr describes as "conservatives' messianic vision of the communist threat." Just as Soviet communism was bent on taking over the world, American citizens had to be prepared to go to "total war" to preserve their way of life and safeguarding national interests abroad; communist expansion and improper foreign policy were threats to both.[100] Thanks to the Korean War, an emphasis on unilateralism and military supremacy was a familiar conservative refrain. Yet, it could also be considered a large-scale version of the self-sufficient, Christian individualism that Birch had practiced in China.

The geographic and racial elements of Birch's conversion efforts mattered a great deal as well. China had long been a subject of interest for religious bodies and presses in the United States.[101] American missionary activity on the mainland proper may have come to a standstill after 1949, but church congregations and religious groups had a continuing interest in shaping China's future as part of wider efforts to reach out to the Third World. Conservative spiritual organizations like the Christian Anti-Communist Crusade and the Cardinal Mindszenty Foundation continued to regard mainland East Asia as a target for reform.[102] Their extensive efforts demonstrated that, to this burgeoning audience of conservatives, the China issue retained an important moral dimension. This side of Asia First was not just mere partisanship but an ongoing commitment to spiritual paternalism that arguably carried over from the previous century.

Deployment

JBS members were recruited as if they were soldiers. Told they were the ground troops battling for freedom around the world and that there was no cause more righteous, newcomers were instilled with a sense of combat: "We Are At War!" declared one leaflet, "The John Birch Society is dedicated to do its part to halt, weaken, rout, and eventually destroy the whole international

Communist Conspiracy."[103] The JBS army was willing to accept any conservative undeterred by directives such as, "We are expecting far more work and dedication, and far more sacrifice of other interests . . . than you ever thought of giving to any other organization which you joined or even considered joining."[104] The society was also militaristic in its organization. Members were grouped into platoon-like local chapters that formed regional companies.

As befitting Welch's emphasis on empowerment through self-education, knowledge was the weapon of choice. The society's most important function was teaching its members about the nature of communism. Only if properly informed would Birchers be aware of communism's influence and empowered to effectively combat it. To that end, chapter meetings often resembled instructive seminars in the tradition of nineteenth-century Populist schoolhouses. JBS reading rooms around the country also helped to disseminate necessary information. Similar to the Christian Science reading rooms, these would be stocked with approved literature and issues of *American Opinion*— texts that constituted a "complete education" in the field of anticommunism.[105]

The campaign to educate JBS members and the broader public was directly linked to conservatives' fears about communism in public school curricula during the early 1950s. According to one booklet from the National Council for American Education, "The Little Red Schoolhouse" was at the heart of a plot to target the nation's youth with propaganda in the guise of "progressive education." Right-wing activists mobilized to critique everything from textbook choices to faculty hires to pedagogical method within their local communities.[106] Welch simply expanded on that formula. Rather than being concerned with schoolchildren only, his group's educational mission encompassed all citizens living in an American society he saw as vulnerable to Cold War subversion.

Correspondingly, as the JBS increased its resources, its media outlets quickly grew to include a collection of speakers, radio programs, and films that supplemented chapter meetings and the *Blue Book*.[107] Members were provided with enough learning materials so they would not need to turn to other (i.e., "liberal") institutions for information. They read monographs with titles like *The Red Fog Over America, Know Your Enemy, Communism at Pearl Harbor*, and *Let's Take the Offensive: A Detailed Blueprint Showing What the Patriotic American Can Do to Win the Victory Over Communism*.[108] An entire industry of right-wing publishers flourished because of the JBS.[109] Intellectual and economic investment was the foundation of growth.

The JBS's outreach to the ordinary citizen disgruntled with Cold War America was undeniably populist, but its grassroots mobilization did cultivate a certain degree of exclusivity. The organization required members to adhere to an ideology that was more complex, sophisticated, and expansive than knee-jerk reaction. According to a former insider, one could remain a member of the group only by meeting certain epistemic requirements, and an ever-expanding syllabus of recommended readings was designed to promote rigorous scholarship. Birchers were supposed to be privileged students.[110]

Once members absorbed the founder's ideological message, they were expected to translate what they learned into political activism. Acting as an "educational army" they would engage in a variety of anticommunist pursuits. These ranged from censoring their local library to making sure every local fraternity house was stocked with the appropriate conservative periodicals. To keep busy at home, members wrote floods of letters to politicians, newspapers editors, television and radio executives, university officials, nonprofit organizations, and so on. These "powerful weapons" would create a conservative groundswell to slow the communist advance.[111] They might even replicate what Welch did with the letter that turned into *May God Forgive Us.* Through the use of wide variety of strategies, group members were encouraged to believe they could impact the lofty arena of foreign relations.

They did not have to look too far back for inspiration. In its organization and operations, the fledgling JBS borrowed tactics used by earlier supporters of Free China, particularly the "front" or lobby model that pushed for a single cause. Welch specifically cited Walter Judd's Committee of One Million as a successful organization to emulate. "It has helped a great deal in keeping Red China out [of the UN] so far," he said, "And, as is true in the case of all good fronts, well run, its influence has spilled over helpfully in many ways."[112] The JBS also borrowed the technique of the unflagging letter-writing campaign from another grassroots Asia Firster: Alfred Kohlberg. In fact, Kohlberg was directly involved in the group. Welch appointed the man behind the China Lobby to the JBS Council in November 1959 shortly after the latter formally joined the group as a member.[113]

Welch's twist was his push for an entire network of fronts—"little fronts, big fronts, temporary fronts, permanent fronts, all kinds of fronts"—that may have appeared remote from one other but were actually parts of the JBS "body," or network.[114] These groups formed a kaleidoscope of anticommunist activism, ranging from the "Impeach Earl Warren Committee" to the "Committee to Warn of the Arrival of Communist Merchandise."[115]

Unsurprisingly, one of the earliest and most prominent JBS fronts dealt with diplomacy. The purpose of the Committee Against Summit Entanglements (CASE) was to protest Nikita Khrushchev's 1959 visit to the United States and Eisenhower's willingness to meet with him. In light of its importance, Welch himself chaired CASE, and he asked conservative activists and leaders like Kohlberg, Buckley, Clarence Manion, Barry Goldwater, and Ludwig von Mises to sit on its board.[116] The fact that those men were not all JBS members was precisely the point. Fronts were meant to attract new associates as well as raise awareness.

By placing so high a premium on foreign affairs so early in the society's existence, Welch set an example that his supporters followed. It was not unusual for Birchers to be involved with the Committee of One Million or the Citizens Foreign Aid Committee. One JBS chapter in Ohio even established a committee to revive the Monroe Doctrine. That particular front achieved significant success. In 1965, it merged with Committee on Pan American Policy, a conglomeration that counted Buckley, Russell Kirk, William Knowland, Marvin Liebman (head of public relations for the Committee of One Million), and Henry Regnery as supporters.[117]

With a motto like "Less government, more responsibility, and—with God's help—a better world," the JBS had a large agenda, and a survey of its fronts reflects an overall emphasis on diversity.[118] Welch largely succeeded in making the group a grassroots body that addressed a broad range of issues. The readiness of *American Opinion* to publish pieces that tackled the subject of communism from any political, cultural, social, economic, or intellectual angle reflected that mission. In 1961 alone, the journal's contents ranged from Rosalie Gordon's diatribe against the Supreme Court ("Nine Men Against America") to "An Introduction to the Contemporary History of Latin America" by Revilo P. Oliver to a Kirk article on academia's silent majority.[119]

The diversity of fronts and topics was the inverse of Kohlberg's earlier attempts to deliberately create a monolithic façade for his cause. Whereas the China Lobby could easily be ridiculed as the project of a small number of zealots, Welch wanted his organization to have the power of numbers and therefore longevity. He made sure the JBS did not labor under the constraints of a single issue and instead followed a varied program within which support for Free China was just one of many bullet points. Given the array of concerns under the umbrella of anticommunism, Birchers would not become easily bored; prospective members had a great deal of autonomy in selecting their pet causes, whether foreign or domestic. Flexibility meant sustainability and there was but one common mission: total victory in the Cold War, on the ground and in government.

Although they studied how best to maximize freedom around the world, Birchers had to absolutely accept Welch as their leader. In this matter alone, they could not question the established order. "The men who join the John Birch Society during the next months or few years," Welch stated in his *Blue Book*, "are going to be doing so primarily because they believe in me and what

I am doing and are willing to accept my leadership. . . . [W]e are not going to be in the position of having the Society's work weakened by raging debates. We are not going to have factions developing on the two-sides-to-every-question theme." Members who wished to express differing viewpoints, or whose anticommunism was judged to be lacking, were to be expelled before they could factionalize the rest of the organization.[120] Loyalty to the anticommunist cause was made indistinguishable from personal fealty to Welch's leadership. When profiling the group for *National Review*, Buckley acridly explained that it was "dominated" by Welch who wielded "plenipotentiary powers within the organization."[121] Even friendly rivalry was not condoned.

Welch justified such extreme measures because he believed the nation and the world to be in dire peril. He oversaw practically every aspect of daily operations, from chairing the Executive Council to editing publications to coordinating local chapters.[122] Through the JBS monthly *Bulletin*, he proposed policies, evaluated current events, and outlined upcoming strategies and tactics "in the fight for a better world." To preserve some semblance of second- or third-party input, there was the Members Monthly Message Department. Using a standardized form, members sent their ideas, information, criticism and inquiries to Welch, who evaluated them during his lunch hour. Each message received a personalized response, but there was no recourse for the individual left unsatisfied.[123] The founder's decisions were final, and his stranglehold on the organization meant there was almost no opportunity for change at the top.

Onward and Upward?

One year after the Indianapolis meeting, Welch claimed JBS working chapters could be found from New Hampshire to New York, Michigan to South Carolina, with "home chapter" members in four states.[124] Rapid growth continued well into the 1960s as the group experienced stunning success in the Sunbelt. In 1963, when questioned about Richard Nixon's political future, Welch smugly responded that the former vice president was aware of his group's numerical power, implying that the outcome of the California gubernatorial race the previous year was the result of Nixon's disavowal of the JBS: "We have hundreds and hundreds of very prominent members in California who are known to be actively working in as members of the John Birch Society and make it clear."[125]

The JBS's rapid growth in the Sunbelt spoke volumes about the political climate of the Cold War. Historians of postwar conservatism in California have pointed out that anticommunism in the American West had as much to do with the defense economy as it did with Christian moralism or class resentment.[126] The results of the 1952 elections, which saw a wave of victories for vocal Korean War critics like Knowland and Goldwater, indicated that a hyperawareness of East Asia was also a contributing factor. It was no coincidence that an organization named after an American soldier killed in China, one that emphasized both foreign and domestic agendas, became a political force in places like Orange County.

The JBS clearly filled a niche that all the assurances of liberal consensus could not. Most critically, the Society offered a plan to stop the spread of communism while it accused Washington officials of idly, perhaps deliberately, fiddling as Rome burned. Would-be members were warned that both major political parties were compromised by communism (witness the bipartisan Senate censure of Joseph McCarthy), and the only way to achieve personal liberty was to join.

Nevertheless, Birchers remained haunted by the specter of a perfectly coordinated, Soviet conspiracy to take over the world.[127] Little had changed since Welch had outlined his predictions in 1958:

> Basic Communist strategy for conquest of the world, as laid out thirty-five years ago and relentlessly followed ever since, consisted of three steps: (1) Take eastern Europe; (2) next take the masses of Asia; (3) then take the rest of the world, including the United States. The Communists complete their first step in 1950; the second step is now about three-fourths accomplished; and they have gone at least one-fourth of the way towards carrying out their third step. Which means that the Communist have now covered about two-thirds of the total distance to their final goal of world-wide dominion. And the momentum and the speed of their progress are steadily increasing.[128]

Subsequent editions of *American Opinion*'s annual "scoreboard" issue failed to show any advancement of the anticommunist cause. The score remained virtually the same year after year, with the globe perpetually teetering on the brink of a communist majority.[129] There was a psychological strategy behind the unchanging numbers. The scoreboard was both a scare tactic and a call to arms. Communism's territory needed to be exaggerated, but its growth also had to be frozen to preserve hope for rollback. The United States, the beacon of republican free enterprise, could still make a difference. Vigilance, militancy, and spiritual faith could yet save the world. If nothing else, the JBS supplied members with constancy in "a world gone crazy." But to remind his followers of what had already been lost, Welch featured Chiang Kai-shek on the cover of the 1966 scoreboard edition.

Tools like the scoreboard marked a two-dimensional understanding of diplomacy that prevented the organization's ideas from evolving with the constantly shifting circumstances of the Cold War. For example, when discussing the trajectory of the Vietnam conflict, Welch proposed that Chiang be allowed to contribute half a million troops. He still asserted that Guomindang soldiers were "the best trained and the most knowledgeable troops in the world for fighting Communist guerillas in Asia, and their whole ambition in life [was] to have a chance to do so."[130] In 1972, when Nixon discussed rapprochement with the People's Republic of China (PRC), *American Opinion* still insisted that the "American man on the street" would condemn the president for his disloyalty.[131]

From its earliest years, the JBS was a political topic that elicited strong reactions. "Fascist, secret, un-American, extremist, anti-Semitic, racist, even Communist" were adjectives often used to describe it. Even one of its most prominent recruiters admitted as much.[132] The organization's message and methods threatened to divide the American right against itself. Some prominent conservatives saw the group as a roadblock to the right's legitimacy and roundly criticized Welch's ideas.[133] However, even then they sought some way to salvage conservative Republicanism's connection to JBS members. As Barry Goldwater told a *New York Times* reporter and Bill Buckley, "[T]he best thing Bob Welch could do at the present moment would be to resign his leadership of the Birch Society, and failing that, the Birch Society should disband and reorganize under another name."[134]

But even if Welch's JBS did not represent the whole of the postwar right, it magnified demographic and political shifts that made Asia First a logical fit for a conservative movement distinctly oriented toward the Pacific Rim. The JBS was both a product and progenitor of political trends that bore the influence of conflicts in China, Korea, and Vietnam. For Birchers, the fate of China was an origin story of the nation's failings on both the international and home fronts. Their leader peddled fear and a plan for militant action at the same time, and out of his cautionary tale of East Asia grew an anticommunist, anti-statist worldview that appealed to thousands of Americans.

While the JBS became best known for its doomed "Impeach Earl Warren" campaign, conspiracy theories, and opposition to curtailment of property rights and increased taxation, it consistently framed those domestic matters within a scope of global anticommunism and styled itself as a sort of foreign policy watchdog organization. "Do you know why there is a John Birch Society?," Welch asked Michigan gubernatorial candidate George Romney in 1962. He proceeded to list over four dozen nations—from Albania to Mongolia to Yemen—that were governed by what he considered dictatorial rule, as well as few that were supposedly in peril.[135] All of them were indicators of a global battle being lost. JBS members' fierce commitment to international anticommunism could help turn the tide; it also reflected the considerable consideration their group gave to what they saw as the United States' exceptional position in the world. John Rousselot, the Bircher and congressman from California, swore "eternal vigilance" to making the JBS motto a reality.[136]

Acceptance as a legitimate political force remained elusive, regardless of self-righteousness and large membership rolls. As the mid-1960s approached, the moments when the JBS featured prominently on the national radar were almost uniformly negative: for example, the controversy surrounding Bob Dylan's performance of "Talkin' John Birch Paranoid Blues" on the Ed Sullivan Show in May 1963.[137] Or, immediately after the assassination of John F. Kennedy, when theories that the shooter was a Bircher seemed within the realm of possibility.[138] The release of *The Politician*, Welch's inflammatory profile of Eisenhower, that same year further illuminated the JBS's antagonistic and radical theories about communism in American government. Yet, until the mid-1960s, the group remained relatively obscure to most Americans and irredeemably extremist when considered at all. As Dylan half-facetiously put it, members were nonsensical paranoids who looked for communists everywhere (even in chimneys and toilet bowls) and believed Abraham Lincoln and Betsy Ross were Russian agents.[139]

That was all subject to change in 1964, after Welch's strategy to capture the Republican Party for "true" conservatism achieved a major victory with the nomination of Goldwater for president, even if the senator himself declined affiliation with the JBS. The United States (and the right as a whole) was forced to acknowledge the power of grassroots conservatism and, with it, a militant foreign relations ethos for which the "loss" of China resonated everywhere in the Cold War world.

5

The New Normal: Asia First Realpolitik

[handwritten annotations: Practicality over idealism → I have to deal w/ PRC; No more nationalist.]

During the early 1960s, grassroots groups like the John Birch Society (JBS) grew in numbers and confidence, while conservative politicians continued to wage battle on moderate liberalism in Washington. With civil rights, regional electoral changes, and foreign affairs fueling conservatism's mobilization, the timing appeared increasingly ripe for the right to advance as a political movement. Meanwhile, the situation in East and Southeast Asia grew tenser. An ideological rift between the Soviet Union and China revealed itself to the entire world, upending established preconceptions about the dynamic between the two nations as well as the delicate balance of the entire Cold War. Chinese intervention in Vietnam and ensuing questions about its objectives made the lack of an articulate US China policy all the more glaring.

With the emergence of the People's Republic of China (PRC) as a power in its own right, its intentions seemed all the more alarming for their unknowability. During an August 1963 press conference, Pres. John F. Kennedy summarized what the PRC looked like from the perspective of American leadership: "[W]eak countries around it, 700 million people, a Stalinist internal regime, and nuclear powers, and a government determined on war as a means of bringing about its ultimate success." Kennedy warned that the United States faced "potentially a more dangerous situation than any we faced since the end of the second war." Even when the Soviet Union acted aggressively, as with the invasion of South Korea, it used proxies and limited its intervention. The same could not be said for China; its unpredictability was what made it so threatening.[1]

Sen. Barry Goldwater was the standard-bearer for the American right during that time. As the 1964 Republican nominee for president, he had an unprecedented opportunity to cement midcentury conservatism as a proactive philosophy that addressed the nation's global concerns. In April, Goldwater listed foreign policy first among major campaign issues.[2] James Burnham confidently wrote in the *National Review* that a Goldwater foreign policy would be "positive and dynamic: affirming both the ideals and the strength of our country" and ensure that "we, not the new barbarians, will master whatever wave the future may send."[3]

Committed military intervention, defense buildup, and American unilateralism overseas were at the core of the campaign's foreign policy message. They were lessons imparted by Asia First; demands for victory by all available means had been part of conservative internationalism since the Korean War. The senator's stated willingness to develop and use strategic atomic weapons in Southeast Asia made perfect sense along those lines, and like Robert Taft and William Knowland before him, Goldwater used events in Asia to shape his critique of US foreign policy and linked diplomatic setbacks to failures in federal government. From a developmental perspective, his foreign policy platform represented an apex for conservative internationalism.

The campaign itself was an uphill fight, however. Not only did Goldwater face an incumbent president, but presenting the right's brand of anticommunism as a solid foundation on which to base US foreign policy during a time of heightened intervention was no small task. Conservative internationalism may have become a commonplace notion, but its early associations with the recklessness of McCarthyism and the China Lobby still lingered. Liberals painted the right as an extremist bloc with a recent history of witch hunts and paranoia, unfit to lead the country and the world. Rifts within the conservative movement itself also presented significant hurdles. One example was the divide between William F. Buckley Jr.'s push for conservative intellectualism and the extremist beliefs of the JBS. While Buckley and *National Review* strove to present the right as a mainstream political option with a cerebral edge, their efforts clashed with the "popular front" methods that Robert Welch advocated and which left the entire movement vulnerable to ridicule.[4]

Goldwater's approach to Asia was a vital reason why his candidacy was able to unite conservatism's factions under the GOP banner. Indeed, the role of Asia in the 1964 California Republican primary, which clinched his party nomination, should be considered a major factor alongside postwar migration patterns and regional antistatism. The senator highlighted defense as a centerpiece of his presidential campaign, reemphasizing points that Asia First officials had made during the 1950s. His reputation as an ideologue in turn attracted grassroots factions like the JBS who were firmly pro–Free China but sometimes eyed the GOP as an entity that diluted militant conservatism.

Extensive study has been devoted to Goldwater's place within the conservative movement, with previous scholars uniformly acknowledging how the senator's presidential nomination influenced the right's growth for years afterward.[5] However, there has been little analysis devoted to his approach to issues like overseas intervention and collective security. This chapter takes the opportunity to do so, for the build-up to the 1964 race spotlighted the changing contours of conservative foreign policy during what was, for all intents and purposes, a wartime election. An examination of the senator's positions on US-Asia relations reveals the centrality of global anticommunism, foreign policy, and the Pacific Rim in the development of this rightwing icon.

At the same time, the history of Goldwater's relationship with China and East Asia proved a great deal more emblematic than exceptional. As he demonstrated, conservative internationalism's continued approach to China combined ideological rigidity with a flexibility born of Cold War realities. For Asia First, the early 1960s into the normalization of US-China relations during the late 1970s was a phase of both change and stasis. On one hand, it underwent significant revisions at the hands of Cold War triangulation and a recalibrated Taiwan policy. On the other, even as the Sino-Soviet split forced a readjustment of common definitions of "global communism," escalation and continued intervention in Vietnam reinforced preexisting notions about China's intentions in Southeast Asia.

The result was a conditional sort of realpolitik that was more sophisticated and less reactionary than initially credited. Later approaches to Communist China and Taiwan during the uneven advance to official US-PRC relations showed the new normal for conservatism—a legitimate internationalism that complemented its domestic stances and could adapt to changes in global affairs.

The China Connection

Given his Sunbelt home state (Arizona) and the context in which he first entered national politics (the Korean War), Goldwater was poised to usher Asia First into this later phase. Like many of his contemporaries, his initial encounter with East Asia came during World War II. As a first lieutenant in the Air Corps, he helped establish a new flight school in Yuma, Arizona, where he supervised pilot training on subjects like aerial gunnery and twin-engine instruction. Among his students were pilots from the Nationalist Chinese Air Force who were in the United States to gain flight experience and learn updated combat techniques that they would use against the Japanese. A group portrait taken in 1942 shows Goldwater proudly beaming with a cohort of his Chinese trainees (figure 5.1). Upon arriving at the India-China-Burma front

FIGURE 5.1. Barry Goldwater (*middle row, far left*) with Chinese Nationalist airmen, February 1942, Barry Goldwater Negative No. 89118, Barry M. Goldwater Papers, Arizona State University Libraries.

as a service pilot in 1944, Goldwater was pleased to find that many of the Guomindang pilots had been students at Yuma and Luke Field. While abroad he continued to train Chinese pilots to use the American aircraft that arrived as part of the China aid package approved by Franklin Roosevelt.

In his memoirs, Goldwater described how wartime work with the Nationalist armed forces caused him to form a positive opinion of what China, as an ally fighting against totalitarianism, could do if given appropriate support from the United States. That impression would color his attitude toward US-China relations for the rest of his life, and Asia would continue to shape his politics.[6] The Korean War, for example, was the catalyst that led Goldwater into public life. With this conflict in the Pacific, he sensed a decline in the public's willingness to automatically support US foreign policy: "As the Korean War dragged on, more and more of the people I talked with in Arizona expressed dissatisfaction with the national government. They didn't like the no-win war we were fighting in Korea. They objected to the giveaways of the Marshall Plan."[7] Goldwater himself believed that mere containment was no way to win, and, like the Asia First leaders already in office, he interpreted Douglas MacArthur's dismissal as a "signal that our country was unwilling to win in Korea and uphold our Asian commitments."[8] Troubled by the course of American policy, Goldwater decided to run for the US Senate in 1952.[9] It was a decision that made him part of what have been dubbed the postwar "G.I. rebellion" campaigns that featured reform candidates who were also veterans.[10]

Given conventional odds, Goldwater appeared to have no chance of winning. His opponent, Earnest McFarland, was the Senate majority leader and one of the most powerful men in Washington. However, postwar migration had diluted Arizona's traditional Democratic base, war in the Pacific once again demanded American lives and finances, and the roots of a nascent conservative movement were taking hold.

Past and present developments in East Asia provided vital context for Goldwater's critique of his opponent and the Truman presidency to which McFarland was closely tied. Asking voters to choose between "fear and faith," he cast Democrats as the progenitors of a corrupt system that badly needed to be reformed.[11] Like other Republicans running for office that year, Goldwater invoked the loss of China: "I believed the whole complex apparatus which had led us into what, in my opinion, amounted to a betrayal of the Nationalist forces of mainland China had been a tremendous concession to the communists and needed to be investigated," he recalled.[12] In the words of Goldwater's publicity team, a vote for Goldwater was a counter against corruption and an affirmation of "those moral principles which have made this nation the greatest citadel of freedom in the history of civilization."[13]

According to that calculus, the ongoing war in Korea was the most immediate evidence of the liberalism that threatened the "citadel" America had built, and McFarland made a grave error on that score shortly before election. During an unguarded moment, he described the Korean War as "cheap," explaining that the conflict was relatively inexpensive: for every American casualty, nine Chinese were killed. Goldwater pounced, challenging McFarland to find "a single mother or father who counts our casualties as cheap—who'd be willing to exchange the life of one American boy for the nine Communists, or 900 Red Communists, or 9,000,000 Communists." This election, he asserted, was an opportunity for Arizonans to assert their desire for integrity in government; the choice was between "good over evil, truth over falsehood, and peace over war." Thanks to the Pacific Cold War, McFarland's imprudence, and his own ability to capitalize on an opponent's error, Goldwater narrowly won with just over 51 percent of the vote, entering the US Senate as part of the GOP's national resurgence.[14]

The learning curve for a novice senator was steep. Some of his new constituents subscribed to a die-hard antistatism that had nothing but disdain for the federal government. "I am praying for a storm of skunk shit to fall over

Washington, D.C., and I sincerely hope that it centers around the Finance Committee of the United States Senate," wrote one irate Arizonan.[15] From the new senator's perspective, the average working man was hard-pressed on all sides, his basic freedoms swiftly eroded by the welfare state and the threat of communism. Conservatism was the only ideology that effectively addressed all those concerns.[16] Goldwater immersed himself in the domestic issues with which he became synonymous: open shop labor, lower taxes, and curtailing the federal government's reach into American daily life. He became close with Taft and served on the highly visible Labor and Public Welfare Committee at the latter's behest.[17] According to campaign manager Stephen Shadegg, Goldwater's efforts on behalf of "right to work" even elicited death threats from Jimmy Hoffa.[18]

When it came to foreign policy, the junior senator took his cues from Asia Firsters, especially Knowland and Styles Bridges. These mentors impressed on their colleague the importance of offering a conservative alternative to liberal containment. While he had no desire to emulate his California colleague's abrasive style, Goldwater admired the forthrightness Knowland brought to public office: "We were good friends. He was a man of great intelligence, strong philosophical conviction, devoted to the nation's welfare."[19] The two forged a particularly close relationship in which the freshman senator, a quick study, was regularly exposed to the majority leader's stewardship of GOP foreign policy at a critical time for conservative internationalism.

Conscience's Cold War

With many key conservative officials retired, defeated, or deceased by the end of the 1958 elections, Goldwater became the Republican right's brightest hope. His duties as chairman of the Senatorial Campaign Committee included stumping for GOP candidates across the country. Along the way, he became a familiar face to grassroots organizations that added to his future political capital.[20] "Out of a good deal of wreckage, Barry Goldwater's election stands as one of the few firm, solid items," wrote one supporter from Chicago. "At this moment he is a rallying point for those who wish to preserve our form of Government and our economic and social stability."[21] National media outlets took notice. The *Los Angeles Times* asked the new face of Republican conservatism to write a thrice-weekly political column called "How Do You Stand, Sir?" Within a year, it was syndicated and began to appear in one hundred forty newspapers.[22]

But the text that arguably made Goldwater a household name was somebody else's brainchild. Radio commentator and lecturer Clarence Manion began an early campaign to draft the senator as a presidential candidate for 1960. After obtaining Goldwater's somewhat reluctant approval, Manion tapped Brent Bozell (conservative journalist and Bill Buckley's brother-in-law) to ghostwrite a political manifesto. Essentially a piece of campaign literature, *The Conscience of a Conservative* was released in June 1960 with Goldwater's name on the cover and his photograph on the back.[23]

Largely marketed through word of mouth, the book became a phenomenon; in 1979, Goldwater estimated some 3.5 million copies had been sold.[24] After only eight years in public office, his reputation was such that his name symbolized America's idea of what "conservative" meant.[25] "'Movement' was the proper word," journalist Teddy White wrote. "The wordless resentments, angers, frustrations, fears and hopes that were shaping this force were something new and had welled up long before Goldwater himself took his Presidential chances seriously."[26]

A simple and direct narrative voice that distilled the right's plethora of concerns into a rousing call to arms accounted for much of the book's appeal: "For the American Conservative, there is no difficulty in identifying the day's overriding political challenge: it is *to preserve and extend freedom.*"[27] Higher taxes, social welfare provision, expansion of the welfare state, abrogation of states' rights, liberal interpretations of the Constitution, and weak diplomacy—all were taken as symptoms of the disintegration of individual liberty in the United States.

Given the mounting degree of US intervention in Southeast Asia and the prospect of a Communist China with its own diplomatic agenda at the moment of publication, *Conscience*'s treatment of foreign policy deserves special attention. After nine chapters on domestic issues, it ended with a section called "The Soviet Menace": "We can establish the domestic conditions for maximizing freedom, along the lines I have indicated, and yet become slaves. We can do this by losing the Cold War to the Soviet Union."[28] Part historical synopsis, part policy proposal, it outlined the authority the right believed it could bring to diplomatic relations and how far conservative internationalism had come within a short period of time.

Notably, intervention was a given. Absolutely no references were made to previous phases of isolationism. By equating the position of the United States during the Cold War to the uncertain revolutionary period of the late eighteenth century, Goldwater's position on foreign affairs was presented in terms of keeping a wary eye on imperialism. The struggle against global communism was a fight to preserve freedom for a nation whose interests had expanded around the world.[29]

In terms of defense, *Conscience* maintained that the way for the United

States to properly protect itself while safeguarding its traditional values was through a continued build-up of nuclear weapons and unilateralism. When combined with prepared armed forces, intercontinental ballistic missiles (ICBMs) would allow the nation to meet any scenario.[30] Nuclear development was the "long-overdue answer" that had the potential to limit warfare and ensure that the United States remained competitive against the manpower of the Communist world.[31] Multilateral alliances were too defensive in nature and impinged on American sovereignty; foreign aid programs were unconstitutional; and the United Nations (UN) was "in part a Communist organization" that gave the Soviet Union veto power. The objective should be victory rather than mere containment, and the United States itself had to strive to be better, faster, and stronger than its opponents. At bottom, this was an issue of sovereignty. Goldwater took the position that the nation could rely only on itself and not on the cooperation of the global community.

Conservatives' lingering interpretation of the Korean War was readily apparent as the text drew parallels to that conflict and the emerging situation in Vietnam. Just as Harry Truman had refused to allow MacArthur to cross the Yalu during Korea, naysayers stymied the Department of Defense and the conservative minority that wanted to see peace in Southeast Asia on American terms. By not taking advantage of technological advances and using every weapon they could to end the Cold War, Washington officials again immorally prolonged a conflict that the United States could win outright. Korea had exemplified the shortcomings of the UN as an effective peacekeeping entity; its bylaws kept the US on a leash even as the organization gave an individual president the ability to take the country to war without congressional input.

In contrast, the defense plan Goldwater advocated ostensibly offered a model of preemptive self-reliance rather than perilous collective peacekeeping.[32] It had a literal cost, however. More research and more weapons of course meant more money spent. From Goldwater's perspective, the price of winning against an armed Soviet Union and an ascendant China would be high yet worth it: "Such a program costs money, but so long as the money is spent wisely and effectively, I would spend it. I am not in favor of economizing' on the nation's safety."[33] His words were a direct echo of Knowland's 1952 convention speech about building muscle and not fat in the defense state. However, whereas Knowland's idea of increased spending had sounded novel for the right in the early 1950s, by 1960 the notion of allowing broad exceptions in the name of national security was a point of pride and not a contradiction of antistatism.

Indeed, many of the specifics on foreign policy outlined in *Conscience* continued the struggle waged by Knowland and other Asia Firsters against expansion of executive power and the UN during the 1950s.[34] The text described the UN as an overblown debating forum that allowed the airing of communist propaganda; moreover, as the organization's "fairy godfather," the United States was footing an expensive bill and burdening its taxpayers with no immediate, beneficial result. It argued that, in a situation as desperate as the struggle for global supremacy, there was no room for American officials ("UN Firsters") whose loyalty lay not with their country but with a diplomatic bureaucracy that legitimized and harbored communist aggression. Last but not least, the UN threatened "the unconstitutional surrender of U.S. sovereignty" and therefore the United States' freedom to act as it saw fit in the world.[35]

An insistence on nuclear build-up combined with harsh condemnation of both collective peacekeeping and foreign aid illuminated an inherent demand for unilateralism in foreign policy. Multilateral alliances, treaties, and other "understandings" were considered to be porous and unable to ensure national security. Moreover, should the Soviets or their affiliates be brought to the table, American officials were already put on the defensive by their agreement to negotiate with the enemy. Throwing money around was also not the answer: "Our Foreign Aid program, in sum, is not only ill-administered, but ill-conceived. It has not, in the majority of cases, made the free world stronger; it has made America weaker." By freely giving funding away without guarantee of results, the United States presumably created dependent welfare states around the world.[36]

Above all, the book underscored conservatives' long-standing global-domestic interpretation of the Cold War. It insisted that "unlimited power in Washington" was at least as dangerous as "the aggressive designs of Moscow." Even if the United States was able to eradicate foreign danger, the nation remained susceptible to destruction from domestic collectivism. Likewise, aggression from the Kremlin could never be stopped unless significant reform took place in Washington.[37] On the role of ordinary men and women, the text struck a tone similar to that of activist literature on the same subject. Citizens were a critical part of the equation; they needed to understand that their individual liberty had international ramifications and they needed to remain vigilant about the health of American democracy.[38]

Even if a literal interpretation of "Asia First" became less and less likely, a foreign relations ethos imparted by the initial push for Chiang's restoration still remained prominent. Unilateralism and the resources that allowed the United States to act the way it saw fit were key components, whereas technological advancements in the defense industry permitted conservatives to sustain their call for American self-sufficiency in foreign policy. The demand for defense proliferation worked on two levels: interiorly, to cure the nation's reluctance to embrace nuclear weapons as tools to end the Cold War; and exteriorly, to grant the United States the firepower it needed to talk and act tough when dealing with hostile nations. Conservatism's complaint was not that the United States was too involved with world affairs but that, when it was involved, its emissaries were either unwilling or ill equipped to bring conflict to swift, favorable resolution.

Public reception of Goldwater's strident positions was incredibly polarized. For those weary of containment, the message of "victory" in the national interest resonated deeply. It also elicited a great deal of cynicism among political opponents. *The Worker*, for example, discovered that the headquarters of Young Americans for Freedom (the youth organization founded by Buckley in 1960) was located at the same New York City address as Marvin Liebman Associates, the public relations firm retained by Walter Judd's Committee of One Million. A March 1961 article insinuated that "Goldwater's Youth Corps" and "the Chiang Kai-shek Lobby" were one and the same and that the proto-fascist JBS was also part of the conspiracy.[39] Suspicions that a sinister China Lobby was trying to unduly influence American policy still persisted, as if that were the only way the right could advance a foreign policy.

However, the very fact that Goldwater's philosophy of foreign relations responded to developments in Latin America, Africa, and Asia showed how conservatism, with the senator as its spokesperson, continued to adapt to postcolonial movements around the world.

China and the Third World

If *Conscience of a Conservative* provided a long glance at where GOP conservatism stood on a few key diplomatic issues, its sequel, *Why Not Victory?* (1962), was dedicated entirely to foreign policy. Goldwater again stressed tactical proliferation as a distasteful yet necessary resource to keep communist powers at bay. "Nations do not arm for war. They arm to keep themselves from war," he wrote.[40] The diplomatic contexts surrounding such a nuclear-centric strategy were made clearer in this new text: destabilization within the US-Soviet relationship, as well as the aftereffects of decolonization in the Third World, prompted its strident positions. In the wake of the Cuban Revolution and Bay of Pigs crisis, Goldwater invoked the spirit of the Monroe Doctrine as a basis for hemispheric defense against communist expansion disguised as native nationalism.[41]

Third Worldism was seen as a distinct threat to American interests, and it could be directly traced to China's increased diplomatic influence in the Pacific and beyond after the Bandung Conference. In 1960, Goldwater and Bozell had evoked fears of a menace originating from the Asian continent: "If all nuclear weapons suddenly ceased to exist, much of the world would immediately be laid open to conquest by masses of Russian and Chinese manpower."[42] Talk of disarmament played directly into one of communism's strengths—its sheer numbers. Images of Asia's swarming millions were vividly familiar to the American Pacific Rim, and they retained a rhetorical potency. Although the method of defense was different and the stakes higher, *Why Not Victory?* depicted the threat of Cold War Yellow Peril in much the same terms as nineteenth-century fears of Chinese immigration, and it predicted that, unless the United States chose to mount a resistance, fears of Asian invasion would be realized.

Such a heightened use of stereotypical, racialized imagery of a hostile China to advance a political agenda indicated a subtle though significant change in direction for Asia First. Conservative elites of the previous decade had emphasized China's democratic potential by describing its people as counterparts the American government was responsible for saving. In the 1960s, with a powerful PRC armed with nuclear weapons a distinct possibility, conservatives recast China as an adversary that was on par with the Soviet Union but even more difficult to understand. In a departure from previous Asia Firsters, Goldwater and his colleagues abandoned any pretense of humanitarianism by insisting national interest and security, rather than the democratic salvation of souls behind the Bamboo Curtain, were their primary motivations for a tough China policy.

The maturation of conservative internationalism vis-à-vis China was evident. Ideologues had finally arrived at an argument for fighting the Cold War that could appeal to a broad swath of conservative voters: national self-interest. The right acknowledged the importance of foreign policy and clearly abandoned doctrinaire isolationism, but that did not mean it forsook nationalism as a motivation for its diplomatic ethos. In 1950, voices on the right asserted that the condition of China reflected the condition of the United States itself. By the early 1960s, they had graduated to the idea that what was best for the United States was best for the world, and its officials should be able to exercise a free hand starting in the near future.

Why Not Victory? once again pointed to the UN as an obstacle to American unilateralism and China's admission as a perennial sticking point. "I have a proposal to make to meet this annual challenge," Goldwater wrote. "'[T]he government of the United States should declare that if the United Nations votes to admit Red China, our government will, from that moment until the action is revoked, suspend its political and financial support of the United Nations."[43]

Although the senator retained some of the old argument about potential Soviet gains, he also dealt with China in its own right, particularly its growing influence in the developing world. Despite reports of starvation and repression on the mainland, China's international influence grew stronger with each passing year. Its admission to the UN emerged as a real possibility.[44] Because of the long history of European imperialism and China's new stature as an anticolonial power, African republics were the UN bloc with which Goldwater was most concerned should the Chinese issue come to a vote. Those new nations were "still ignorant—let's face it—of the ways of the world" and could not be allowed to obstruct the course of US foreign policy. While decolonization represented an advance for global democracy, it had also created unpredictable allies. The senator cautioned that new African states needed to know "that the greatest colonialism ever developed, anywhere, is that of communism in China."[45] American policy under the Democrats simply was not strong enough to keep lesser nations in line and maintain China's exclusion from the UN.

Partisanship aside, Goldwater's words underscored real fears of Third World nationalism. His arguments pointed to the UN as a conduit for disaster wrought by *both* undeveloped states and communism. Nonwhite peoples would become firm anticommunist allies only if the US policy took a hard enough stand: "The true friends of international peace and freedom everywhere, including millions upon millions of Asiatics, will look upon us with gratitude and confidence."[46] Blurring the line between leadership and paternalism, Goldwater insisted America should teach more naive countries that their interests aligned with those of the United States, the original beacon of anticolonialism.

The senator did not omit Taiwan from his analysis. While a "swarm" of refugees from the PRC fled oppression, "By contrast, Formosa's economy is thriving, land redistribution has brought a wide ownership of property, and the morale of its armed forces is at an all-time high."[47] Taiwan was proof of what developing nations were capable of if their governments fully aligned with the West: prosperity, individual self-reliance, and a strong partnership with the United States. Such attributes brought the alleged decline of "civilization" in the PRC into sharp contrast, and Goldwater implied that these attributes were proof that Taiwan deserved to represent China in the UN. If such a worthy country were to be replaced, the political and moral effects would be devastating to world peace.

Aftermath

As *Conscience* became a national bestseller, Goldwater was transformed from regional politician into a contender in the upcoming presidential race.[48] To his supporters, he represented the first conservative candidate who spoke with equal authority on issues global and domestic. He could soothe Americans "apprehensive about the encroachment of federal authority in their everyday lives" and also "lead the country back to the days when Uncle Sam walked unchallenged and foreign alliances were taboo."[49]

The timing was ideal, for the various branches of the right—from Cold Warriors to tax warriors to antifluoridation warriors—were coalescing into a genuine political movement that drew from a deep well of social and cultural ferment. Not only did conservatives have the will to institute reform in Washington, their impulses were supported by an emerging prevalence of ideas (articulated by *National Review*) and political culture (magnified by the JBS). Even if total agreement between factions was impossible, the rift between Buckley and Welch remained a case in point, most shared the objective of national power.

As the subject of the draft effort, Goldwater's long-standing goal was not to destroy the GOP but to recapture it. That meant an internal power struggle against Eastern moderates like Nelson Rockefeller and George Romney, as well as convincing his supporters that the GOP was their natural home base.[50] At the 1960 convention, Goldwater urged fellow conservatives to tow the party line: "[F]or Conservatives there exists no other alternative to Nixon. This is true whether they be 'Taft Republicans' or 'Jeffersonian Democrats.'"[51] That gesture of loyalty nonetheless did not mean consensus. His very presence at the podium served notice that conservatives were an integral part of the Republican organization and the GOP needed their voting power.[52] Meanwhile, young, conservative politicians were shaking up the hierarchy, jolting liberal and moderate "do-nothings" from complacency.[53] One candidate expressed his exuberance about conservatism's prospects, despite having lost his own bid for Congress in 1962: "I am encouraged about the future from everything I hear," he wrote Goldwater after Election Day.[54]

After 1960, grassroots organizations mobilized in earnest for the next campaign for the White House. In a remarkable display of ability and coordination, groups from Connecticut to Ohio to California began laying the groundwork for a presidential candidacy.[55] They had *Conscience* translated into German, Spanish, and Italian, to attract immigrant voters; investigated Rockefeller's tactics in New Hampshire; and refined the right's platform by consulting with conservative intellectuals.[56] Activists across the country galvanized to get out the vote for a candidate who was "the wave of the future . . . young, dynamic, and alive."[57] The Arizona senator, according to Phyllis Schlafly, "combined the integrity of Robert Taft with the glamour of Dwight Eisenhower."[58] George Sokolsky described him as "unspoiled by Park Avenue sophistication," a man untainted by the cynicism that marked the East Coast establishment.[59] Goldwater's regionalism set him apart from Washington politics as usual, particularly the capitol's traditional diplomatic focus on Europe.

Therefore, it was to be reasonably expected that a commitment to security in the Pacific would inform a Goldwater administration's approach to foreign policy. Campaign advisors touted the nominee's expertise in foreign affairs and marketed his platform toward conservatives eager to see one of their own take a decisive stand.[60] The senator's tough talk on communism and Vietnam certainly fulfilled their expectations. Schlafly's *A Choice Not an Echo* illuminated the degree to which grassroots activists valued foreign relations. A call for aggressive action in international affairs and denunciation of what the author labeled "America Last" foreign policy underscored the whole text. It amplified the demand for diplomatic self-sufficiency. If elected, Schlafly wrote, Goldwater would "let the Soviet system collapse of its own internal weaknesses . . . curtail the foreign giveaway programs, as well as the level of Federal spending."[61] As president he would place the United States' needs above all else and carry conservative mores of fiscal thrift, individuality, and sovereignty into the diplomatic realm.[62] Albert Wedemeyer, a member of the Asia First vanguard, also gave an enthusiastic endorsement.[63]

Even if Goldwater personally did not agree with all of those voices on every single issue (he once remarked of Schlafly, "She's so conservative she makes me look like a socialist"[64]), he conceded that grassroots activists, even the radical ones, were a key component of his base. Public display of internal dissent could splinter the fragile alliance that had coalesced around his candidacy and jeopardize conservatism's quest for national relevance.[65]

1964

Whatever their political persuasion, all presidential candidates had to face the uncertainty of China after the deep ideological split between the Soviet Union and the PRC came to light in the summer of 1963. From an American perspective, the prospect of a China that was close to nuclear armament but unregulated by the Soviet Union was not an opportunity for triangulation so much as a likely disaster. A close Sino-Soviet working relationship had suggested at least the possibility of mitigation while US-Soviet relations improved after the Cuban Missile Crisis.

In her commencement address at St. John's University that June, Clare Boothe Luce outlined the confusion wrought by what she called a destabilizing "crisis" between two Communist allies. The Soviets and the Chinese were still in agreement on their shared objective of achieving Communism's global domination, Luce asserted. Where they differed was on "how to bury us the fastest." Khrushchev did not accept nuclear war as inevitable; Mao insisted peaceful coexistence betrayed global Marxism.[66] Luce saw an unbridled China as a greater threat than the Soviet Union, just as Kennedy had the previous summer. But as a longtime Asia Firster who was the cochairman of the National Citizens Committee for Goldwater, she offered an even starker analysis: China used cynical charges of racism to discredit Soviet leadership in a communist world whose majority population was not white. Mao, like Genghis Khan, sought to bury Moscow and then conquer the West, and he would wield a nuclear bomb to do so.[67]

Luce deftly used a host of imageries to portray the dangers of a China at odds with the Soviet Union. Her language often called to mind the racialized fears of Yellow Peril that surfaced after the Russo-Japanese War. In her summation, she used gendered terms to illustrate the predicament the United States faced. "Mother China" was the nation to fear. "[N]othing—short of nuclear annihilation—can stop her from breeding by the end of this decade a billion children. And we must not deceive ourselves, it will take the Chinese time, but they will find the means of creating a nuclear arsenal sooner or later."

Given its harsh language, the address ended on a rather surprising note. With China making military interventions in Southeast Asia, moving steadily closer to nuclear capability, and increasingly prestigious in the Third World, whoever won the White House would have to rethink Asia policy in order to halt Chinese expansionism and avoid World War III. Withdrawal from Vietnam remained off the table, but the time had come to "go over Mao's head." The next president would do well to appeal directly to the Chinese people with trade and food aid. It had worked with Russians—why not China?[68] According to Luce, Mother China could be wooed and won.

Her proposal proved to be one of the more progressive suggestions on what do to about China. The candidate himself still clung to the standard narrative of the 1950s: "The sell-out of freedom was on our minds. Hiss had been part of the US delegation at Yalta. We were also concerned about the fall of Chiang Kai-shek. Despite his faults, Chiang was more faithful to the cause of liberty than Mao Tse-tung," Goldwater recalled.[69] He continued to champion the development and use of nuclear weapons as November drew closer. Unless the United States was willing to match Communist states' motivation and protect itself and its national interests, democracy would presumably be lost: "Free world and US security are indeed indivisible."[70] A hesitancy to explore all available means, he proclaimed, was tantamount to cowardice. Even worse, it was a sign of weakness both the Soviet Union and China could exploit. Goldwater remained consistent even within his private correspondence. After the passage of a new nuclear-test ban treaty, he wrote to close friend Bill Saufley: "In my own opinion this could well be the opening wedge to disastrous negotiations with the enemy, which could result in our losing the war or becoming a part of their system."[71]

Such confident, sweeping assertions contrasted sharply with Goldwater's inconsistencies on how exactly he would manage China through diplomatic channels. An increasingly indefinite stance on the UN was a case in point. Whereas he had sounded absolutist two years prior, recent developments in East and Southeast Asia had apparently forced a reevaluation. Goldwater vacillated between describing the UN as a valuable forum and denouncing the rules that made discussion among nations possible. One morning he said the United States should withdraw from the UN if the latter admitted Red China; at the next stop he declared that the United States should remain in the organization. Goldwater's position was no clearer on paper. In six pages of *Where I Stand*, the companion text to his campaign, he made declarations and exceptions to the point where the reader might wonder exactly what American participation in the UN would entail during his administration.[72] The one real constant was his refusal "to recognize Red China, even though it 'exists.'"[73] Flexibility in diplomatic affairs was an admirable virtue, but fluctuation between absolutes easily translated as recklessness.

Goldwater walked a tightrope when discussing diplomacy as his party's nominee. Any nuances within his foreign policy platform were crowded out, despite his own insistence that the nation's foreign policy should be a "clear statement of our interests, a vision of the sort of world in which nations like ours can live."[74] A belief in the country's right and ability to act to protect its own interests was a solid ideological stance. Armament was an expression of self-reliance and self-defense.[75] However, translating ideas about morality and national interest–as–world interest into reassuring policy positions proved difficult. Average voters were hard-pressed to distinguish what a Goldwater foreign policy plan would entail beyond nuclear stockpiling.

For better or worse, the senator retained his vision of the role he wanted defense technology to play in the future. From his perspective the possession of powerful arms had both figurative and literal uses. "What would this world be like, if Communism ever pulled even or ahead of us in nuclear capability?," he asked a California audience. In *Where I Stand*, the answer was clear: "We *need* the missiles. But we need tomorrow's missiles as well as yesterday's."[76] Perhaps to soften that stance, he offered the hope that American technological dominance would provoke ordinary people behind the Iron and Bamboo Curtains to abandon their leaders.[77] If given the chance, Goldwater planned to deploy nuclear resources as prudently as he knew how. Throughout his campaign, he strenuously advocated their careful, tactical use and development and not their exponential production.

Nonetheless, his immovability on the subject of negotiation with Communist states, China's successful detonation of an atomic bomb in October, and the extremist reputation of his supporters meant Goldwater appeared overly willing to use nuclear weapons. Opponents happily furthered that supposition. For all his attempts to clarify his position on what types of weapons he favored, why, and where, he was unable to overcome the image of trigger-happy cowboy.[78] "[N]o man ever began a Presidential effort more deeply wounded by his own nomination, suffering more insurmountable handicaps. And then it must be added that he made the worst of them," wrote Teddy White in his campaign postmortem.[79] The circumstances surrounding Goldwater's often imprudent remarks were enough to escalate even a passing utterance into the realm of frightening possibility. As a political issue, the ongoing situation in Vietnam was therefore a decidedly mixed bag for the campaign. Detractors and supporters could interpret the senator's stance as either the ravings of a man determined to take the world over the nuclear brink or as a show of determination to end waste overseas.

Whatever the response, Goldwater clearly used Vietnam as a magnifying lens for the shortcomings of containment policy. He was dismayed by the Democratic administration's unwillingness to classify the protracted conflict in Southeast Asia as war. From the very outset, he invoked Vietnam as the latest example of liberals' missteps: "Yesterday it was Korea. Today it is Vietnam. We are at war with Vietnam—yet the President who is the Commander in Chief of our forces refuses to say whether or not the objective is victory."[80] If the United States was at war—and Goldwater was assured that it was—Pres. Lyndon Johnson and Sec. of Defense Robert McNamara were at fault for not fighting to win. American officials should use all troops, equipment, and arms it would take to ensure the outcome was victory. "Peace in Asia depends on our strength," Goldwater affirmed. "Nowhere in the world today is there a clearer road to *peace through strength* than in Vietnam."[81]

In addition to drawing a direct line from MacArthur and Korea to Southeast Asia, those words clearly evoked the broader idea of the United States as the sole guardian of democracy in the Pacific. By classifying Vietnam intervention as yet another armed engagement with Mao's China, Goldwater drew on fifteen years of conservative angst about the relationship between the United States and Asian communism. "Like or not," he warned, "Communist-inspired events around the world have placed this nation in a conservative position."[82] Now, the United States once again had the chance to prove itself on a "major battlefield," where a US victory would strike a critical blow against a Chinese proxy and perhaps guarantee regional stability.[83] In sum, citizens could either cast ballots to finish the conflict quickly and decisively or remain in the holding pattern of containment.

The voters attracted to the senator's message were a more diverse group than one might assume, for his campaign mindfully cultivated an ethnic voting bloc that had been widely categorized as electorally apathetic.[84] The Cold War in Asia and the Nationalist-Communist divide demonstrated how some factions of the Chinese American diaspora were, in fact, very engaged when it came to foreign policy and politics. The established merchant class that dominated Chinatown benevolent associations and community political life was firmly in the Guomindang camp.[85] As one of the most voluble politicians in support of Taiwan, Goldwater benefitted from their endorsement. The result, as this group of Chinese American "Goldwater Girls" demonstrates, was a support base that included at least some urban minorities in addition to white suburbanites.

Although his resoluteness won Goldwater admirers, it also did much to obscure the nuances that were in fact present within his assessment of Cold War alliances. Whereas Asia Firsters through the 1950s had believed Chinese communism to be a mere offshoot of Soviet ideology, the senator in fact took into account the discord between the Soviet Union, China, and North Vietnam.[86] The problem was that advocacy of "victory" using all possible means overshadowed the more subtle components of his proposals, making it appear as if a President Goldwater would be the one to bring the entire world into nuclear warfare. The Sino-Soviet split revised previous assumptions about the Soviet "monolith," with significant consequences for the American public's receptiveness to seemingly one-dimensional Asia First anticommunism. Voters overall proved less open to the kind of alarmist rhetoric that swept Republicans to power during the Korean War election of 1952. If Ho Chi Minh was not another Kim Il-Sung, then Goldwater's foreign policy plan was ill suited to deal with this new Asian conflict, a miscalculation reflected by his emphasis on technological weaponry and discouragement of humanitarian aid.

Paired with his increasingly strident line on foreign policy, Goldwater's refusal to exclude radical activists from the conservative movement proved fatal to his candidacy. His association, however reluctant, with certain grassroots groups clearly took a toll on public opinion. His supporters were often

FIGURE 5.2. Kem K. Lee, [Goldwater Girls in Chinatown, San Francisco, 1964], Kem K. Lee Photographs and Other Materials, AAS ARC 2006/1, Ethnic Studies Library, University of California, Berkeley, Box 40, Fol. 25.

portrayed as "kooks, extremists, know-nothings, dopes, John Birchers, lunatics, Neanderthal types."[87] Upon hearing the GOP convention results, sports star Jackie Robinson reportedly remarked, "Now I know what it feels like to be a Jew under Hitler."[88] A somewhat hesitant figurehead, Goldwater framed his long-shot candidacy as the act of a political martyr: "Someone had to rally the conservatives, take over the Republican Party, and turn the direction of the GOP around," he recalled. "There was no one to do it but me."[89] If the American right lost the election, as he anticipated it would, wresting control of the GOP from the me-too moderates would be an excellent consolation prize.[90] However, the magnitude of the Republican defeat—52 to 486 electoral votes—meant that the right's supremacy within the party was hardly assured, and the struggle between conservatives and GOP moderates continued well after the election.[91]

The reasons behind Goldwater's loss to Johnson have been well chronicled. They ranged from his inability to satisfactorily address the civil rights movement to public fears of his plans for national security to Republican factionalism.[92] In his own words, he had been typecast as "a fascist, a racist, a trigger-happy warmonger, a nuclear madman, and the candidate who couldn't win."[93] Even some of his closest advisors wrote him off.[94] After such a blow, fundamental questions about the future of conservative internationalism arose. Was there still a place for Asia First within the right and the GOP as a whole? What role could it continue to play with potential gains to be made in the wake of a Sino-Soviet split?

Mission: Taiwan

The answers varied widely in tone if not in substance. In the House, Rep. John Ashbrook (R-OH) devoted an address to the cabal of intellectuals, journalists, and politicians that he claimed was working to overturn nonrecognition of "one of the most revolutionary and violent dictatorships the world has ever known." Resorting to the language of the 1950s, he called them the "Red China Lobby."[95] Walter Judd's 1967 Christmas letter cautioned against a divided nation as "Chinese masses" threatened to enter the war.[96] Bill Buckley took a somewhat more measured approach on his television program *Firing Line*. During a debate with Brandeis professor Max Lerner, Buckley asserted the United States should stand firm in its position on not letting China into the UN. It was "extremely risky" to depart from a long-standing policy simply because "somebody has discovered that the Soviet Union happens to be less noisy the last couple of years." Moreover there was still a strategic advantage to supporting Taiwan: "[I]t has to do with holding up some light of hope." After all, Buckley reminded the audience, there was precedent for American support of governments exiled by dictatorship—de Gaulle's France during World War II, for example.[97] Even at this juncture, the mere suggestion of a "two Chinas" policy was unacceptable. Despite what Democrats and moderate Republicans suggested, Buckley claimed any recognition of the PRC, through either UN or US channels, would be a disastrous erosion of Taiwan's status.[98]

Meanwhile, thanks to an Arizona law that dictated he could not hold on to his Senate seat while running for president, Goldwater became a private citizen for the first time since the Korean War. The period after the election found him slightly mellowed. On *Meet the Press* in June 1965, he stated that, while China was a nuclear danger, the United States should not "willy-nilly" use atomic weapons there or in Vietnam even if China entered the conflict.

"In other words, don't use a twelve gauge shotgun to kill a target that one BB will work on." For Southeast Asia, he outlined a plan that strongly resembled Taft's proposals for the Korean War: rather than ground troops, air power that spared no strategic target north of the 17th parallel.[99]

Despite adjustments in his other foreign policy positions, Goldwater still did what he could to ensure that American commitment to Taiwan did not abate. A pivotal visit to the island in 1967 cemented this pattern. Goldwater had been eager to meet Chiang Kai-shek, and he expressed that wish to various military and State Department officials. In fact, he had tried contacting Soong Mei-ling when she was in the United States but had little luck.[100] The trip was to be part fact-finding mission, part vacation with his wife Peggy. Before embarking, he studied recent State Department bulletins and extensive background reports on each country he was going to visit. Judging from the thick file of information he amassed, the recent history of US defense commitments in the Pacific was of particular interest.

During the 1950s, spurred on by the conflict in Korea, the State Department had increased its efforts in the Pacific. A flurry of negotiations yielded agreements with the Philippines, Japan, South Korea, Thailand, and, of course, the 1954 mutual defense treaty with Taiwan. The Senate Committee on Foreign Relations supported this new direction: "It (the committee) fully appreciates that acceptance of these additional obligations commits the United States to a course of action over a vast expanse of the Pacific. Yet these risks are consistent with our own highest interests."[101] Noble words aside, the interests of American corporations (ranging from IBM to Singer Sewing to Proctor & Gamble) that profited from the island's ready labor supply and large consumer market underpinned continued US assistance to Taiwan.[102] After his trip, Goldwater planned to report back to American citizens "hungry for actual on-the-ground opinions of that part of the world."[103]

While in Taiwan, the Goldwaters received the type of welcome one would expect for the most favored foreign visitors or diplomats. Their carefully orchestrated itinerary seemed more appropriate for a head of state than an ex-senator at somewhat loose ends. It included military parades, a dinner with the Chiangs, and formal receptions.[104] Yet, the pomp and circumstance made sense in consideration of Goldwater's status as an influential Asia First conservative who had come close to the White House. He and Peggy were even presented with pilot wings signifying honorable membership in the Third Tactical Wing of the Chinese Air Force, a highly personal tribute to Goldwater's contributions during World War II.[105]

Goldwater returned home deeply moved by the experience. Three days on Taiwan convinced him American failures in Asia had forced an honorable and noble man from leading the way for democracy in the Pacific. "We will never forget our stay in your country or forget all that you are doing for your people," he wrote to his hosts soon after returning home. "When one visits with people like the Chinese, that is the Free Chinese, one comes away with a great feeling of encouragement about this whole world and what man can do with it if man will only realize his mistakes and resolve never to repeat them."[106] Their time together was brief, but Chiang obviously made a deep impression on Goldwater, and the latter's enthusiasm for the Nationalist leader did not abate over time. The pair exchanged gifts, birthday wishes, and extravagant compliments.[107]

The 1967 trip marked the beginning of Goldwater's deeply personal support of Taiwan. At the beginning of his career, he had followed, not led, the Asia First initiative. Now, he was determined to realize its objectives as best he could. Recovery of the mainland was of course impossible; therefore, protection of Taiwanese independence via unambiguous US policy became the primary objective. Goldwater received letters from prominent Chinese businessmen and civic leaders who encouraged him to maintain his position as a friend of the "Free Chinese." Chu Ching-tong, president of the National Federation of Certified Public Accountants, praised his contribution to "the protection of human rights and the Free World as a whole." Chu added that saving mainland China from communism also meant saving the globe from nuclear warfare, a connection the American politician would "certainly" understand.[108]

Meanwhile, conservatives of the JBS maintained unalloyed faith in Chiang's abilities, this time buttressed by the quagmire in Southeast Asia. Their interpretation of the war—that American officials lacked the will to win, outside organizations (the UN and SEATO) confused who was actually fighting the war, etc. etc.—evoked a sense of déjà vu in Robert Welch. "This is just the same old road show enacted in Korea . . . the same plot, the same management, and a very similar cast," he wrote.[109] And again, Chiang had a role to play but was being prevented from doing so: "Why, when we are asking for troops to help us from all other allies we can get, do we not ask Chiang Kai-shek to send over his half a million men?," asked Welch in 1967.[110] He took the refusal to unleash Chiang as a sure sign of subversion on the part of the Johnson administration, which was "consciously and deliberately" murdering US troops "to serve Communist purposes."[111] If Vietnam had to be fought, and Welch was not sure it was entirely necessary in the first place, Chiang and his troops should be deployed. Doing so would give the Taiwanese an opportunity to fight their moral enemies and reduce the expenditure of American lives.

Clearly, Taiwan still elicited strong emotions across the Asia First spectrum. Although they differed as to whether it would be militarily active or more symbolic, conservative leaders still believed Taiwan had a vital part to play in US Asia strategy, and any suggested changes to the island's diplomatic status would meet with a volley of responses from the right.

Divisions over Détente

The push for China policy revision came to a sudden head at the end of the decade, and with it, another round of politicization. Early in 1968, the Tet Offensive demonstrated the inability of existing US policy to contain Asian communism. By year's end, the Soviet invasion of Czechoslovakia and Chinese Premiere Zhou Enlai's denunciation of the brutal suppression made a US-PRC alliance seem all the more possible, and desirable, to members of both parties. For example, Arthur Goldberg—former secretary of labor, Supreme Court justice, and ambassador to the UN—voiced his support for seating both the PRC and Taiwan in the UN.[112] On the other side of the aisle, Nelson Rockefeller tried to use China to score political points. While the State Department tried but failed to reopen diplomatic talks with the PRC, he openly called for "contact and communication" with China as a way to highlight what the GOP presented as the Johnson administration's ineffectualness.[113]

All these contexts favored Richard Nixon, whose new White House had an opportunity to dramatically revise Asia policy. Further Sino-Soviet strife in the spring of 1969 represented the ideal moment to make possibility a reality. In April Sec. of State William Rogers announced a "two Chinas" policy that formally recognized the existence of the mainland Chinese government as a permanent entity. Just a few months later, in July, the president outlined the "Nixon Doctrine" regarding expectations for allies' contributions in the Cold War: The United States "cannot—and will not—conceive all the plans, design all the programs, execute all the decisions and undertake all the defense of the free nations of the world." The doctrine's first application would be Vietnamization of the ongoing war.

With its overhaul, the Nixon administration made a calculated decision to capitalize on two concurrent trends: demand for an end to firsthand American intervention in Southeast Asia and the public's growing receptiveness to dialogue with the PRC. "Losing" Vietnam was a probability, but the US stood to "win" the prize of diplomatic relations with Mao and China. Excitement over the latter would certainly help negate political blowback over another military loss in the Pacific.[114] Nixon had been contemplating such a strategy for some time, at least since his 1967 *Foreign Affairs* piece "Asia Policy

After Viet Nam," which urged US policy to seize an "extraordinary set of opportunities" that lay beyond Vietnam.[115]

Change proved dramatic and swift. Easing of travel and trade restrictions
and an end to US patrols of the Taiwan Strait were the opening salvo. Ping-
pong diplomacy, an end to the trade embargo, and the announcement of
Nixon's impending trip to Beijing all occurred within a span of four months
in 1971. But the real test of a two-Chinas policy came down to the admission
of the PRC into the UN and whether or not PRC membership would impact
Taiwan's standing within the international community. Even while stating the
end of the United States' opposition to the PRC's seating, the administration
expressed its support of Taiwan as a continuing member nation.[116] Its wishes
went unheeded. After a week of debate, the General Assembly voted on October 25 to admit the PRC and expel Taiwan, despite American officials' attempts to marshal a majority in favor of dual representation.

For Asia Firsters, this turn of events was a waking nightmare, the realization of long-standing fears about the UN's inability to fulfill its objectives of
peaceful stability.[117] In sum, the incident exemplified the workings of "world
government" through which Communist and small, left-leaning states could
leverage undue control.[118] Conservatives saw PRC admission as a direct threat
to the independence of Taiwan, a longtime American ally, because it legitimized the mainland government as a state fit to partake in collective peacekeeping.

Moreover, the outcome of the vote directly countered the push by Nixon,
Rogers, and George H. W. Bush, ambassador to the UN, for dual representation. This setback (on a position that was unacceptable to begin with) raised
old dreads of UN infringement on national sovereignty.[119] To mitigate "a hu-
miliating defeat," Walter Judd decided to reorganize the Committee of One
Million Against the Admission of Communist China to the United Nations
into the Committee for a Free China.[120] Bill Buckley also characterized the UN
vote as "a humiliation" and pointed an accusing finger at the president: Nixon
had not defended Taiwan aggressively enough and, in fact, had created the
conditions for a shift in the General Assembly with his plans to visit Beijing.
China developments called into question the president's ability to safeguard
conservative interests in general. Although the president was the presumptive
nominee in 1972, he needed to be reminded of the "vast, and slightly sullen
constituency to his right that needs a little sustenance."[121]

Other prominent conservatives aired their opinions in January during a
Firing Line special on PBS called "American Conservatives Confront 1972." In
addition to Buckley, the episode's crowded panel included California governor Ronald Reagan, Clare Luce, Sen. James Buckley (R-NY, and Bill's brother),

economist Milton Friedman, John Ashbrook, and J. Daniel Mahoney (founder, Conservative Party of New York State). Their discussion began and ended with US-China relations. Luce commended Nixon for exploiting the Sino-Soviet split in service of the national interest. Reagan agreed: Rapprochement was neither a formal recognition of the PRC nor an American withdrawal from the mutual security pact with Taiwan, and Nixon knew what he was doing. The Buckley brothers, Ashbrook, and Mahoney strenuously objected, contending that the administration should have anticipated the ripple effect of détente, including Taiwan's UN expulsion. It could be difficult to discern between realpolitik and "ideological sentimentalism," Bill Buckley cautioned. Which one was this new direction on China? Friedman responded with "realpolitik" and a vote of confidence in the president's diplomatic experience, but he then quickly deferred to others on the panel.[122] Harmony on the issue proved elusive as the conversation weighed the balance between principle and strategy, and short-term setbacks and long-term gains.

Goldwater's voice was missing from that particular debate, but there was little doubt about where he stood on the matter. Party loyalty clearly colored his early comments in favor of the Republican president's China policy, and he still believed Taiwan's status would not suffer any further damage. At a GOP event in Atlanta, he declared the impending visit was not a "cozying up to Red China." Goldwater, who was back in the Senate representing Arizona after a successful 1968 campaign, instead staked a position that in hindsight sounds overly trusting, if not naive. He credited the president for attempting to discover information about a growing military power and lauded Nixon for "playing the big power game the way a nation of our importance ought to play it."

As for the American right, Goldwater believed conservatives upset with détente as a general principle had to get over themselves. His impatience was palpable: "We cannot afford to the let the old ideas about Red China keep us from opening channels of communication so that we can try and find out something about what this bandit nation is up to." Unlike Buckley, Goldwater did not hold Nixon or even the PRC responsible for China's admittance to the UN. The idiosyncrasy of world organizations in general was the real culprit. Taiwan's expulsion was "a disgrace," but it was "water over the dam." Conservatives had to stomach reality and support their president in his efforts to preserve American power in a shifting Cold War world, as well as against the impending election challenge from Democrats.[123]

Such support for rapprochement with the very government that had been Asia First internationalism's bogeyman for over twenty years was surprising, especially coming from someone who had advocated for Chiang Kai-shek in the past. Goldwater took rounds of personal criticism from constituents who objected to Nixon's accommodation of China. One letter to the *Arizona Republic* accused the senator of ignoring how the new policy impacted Taiwan and "legitimize[d] the criminal government that enslaves the people of China." According to the irate voter, the senator no longer deserved the title "Mr. Conservative" for such acquiescence.[124]

Public addresses such as the Atlanta speech could be deceiving. Goldwater did indeed have qualms about the upcoming China visit (his use of the term "bandit nation" was lifted straight from Guomindang terminology). He was also not entirely at ease with the administration—its secrecy and distance from congressional Republicans complicated dealings with the White House. Although strained at times, a pragmatic working relationship still endured. Nixon and national security advisor Henry Kissinger made gestures of consultation with Goldwater about China. The senator accepted explanations that the PRC was still regarded as an enemy, but the 1972 Beijing trip could help end the Vietnam War and triangulation would hasten world peace. Both Nixon and Rogers had promised Taiwanese independence was not at stake.[125] Finally, common partisan bonds trumped any lingering reservations. Goldwater, a loyal GOP soldier, firmly believed conservatives had to unite behind the president on foreign policy. Nixon's Republicanism meant he should receive the benefit of the doubt. So, while the president met with Mao, toasted Zhou, and posed at the Great Wall, Goldwater continued to act the team player back home.

At least until any specifics from the trip emerged, assuaging apprehension on the right was perhaps less daunting than it looked at first. Most prominent conservatives were resigned, however grudgingly, to a two-Chinas policy. After sparring, they had agreed that Taiwan needed to remain protected by American diplomacy and defense resources. In fact, it was the president's quick avowal of Taiwan's independence that swayed figures like Goldwater and Reagan to his side.[126] Even Buckley acknowledged the necessity of realpolitik insofar as it was waged with ideological fortitude and not acquiescence to Communist demands.[127] As long as US policy clearly provided for *two* Chinas and moved slowly on any formal recognition of the PRC, a tenuous truce existed between conservatives who condemned the results of Nixon's China outreach and those who cautiously condoned it.

The Shanghai Communiqué, released on the last day of the state visit, soon upended any unified response to détente with China. The joint statement's words regarding the PRC as the sole legal government of China, Taiwan as a part of China, and the US government's pledge not to dispute that position caused major backlash from conservatives who saw it as a betrayal of an ally, as well as a significant faction of the president's own party.[128] Buckley flatly lambasted Nixon on television: "I desire the liberation of the Chinese people from their current slave masters."[129] There was speculation about the statement's potential impact on US trade with Taiwan and Japan, Japan's future armament decisions, and a boost for unruly Third World nationalism.[130] The potential implications for Taiwanese sovereignty were just as troubling. If the communiqué was used as precedent for a formal downgrading of defense agreements with the ROC, it left the island diplomatically alienated or even susceptible to reincorporation into the mainland. Goldwater struggled to decide between support for the presidential office and his misgivings about the future of Taiwan. With some reluctance, he chose the former and got an earful from Buckley.[131]

Interlude

Such variable responses to Nixon's China policy showed how the president threw off balance political factions across the spectrum. For the right, even a symbolic opening of the door was fraught with a slew of partisan, historical, and diplomatic meanings. With so many competing impulses, conservatives whose political development had been forged in Asia First internationalism understandably reacted in mixed ways as they weighed different aspects of détente. Given all the bickering, it was easy to overlook the level of unity on realpolitik that they actually did achieve. Their loyalty to Chiang Kai-shek did not preclude them from acknowledging the necessity of a two-Chinas policy, but it did make them vigorously oppose any further erosion of Taiwan's international standing.

Conservatives' relative flexibility on China was further underscored by their absolutist reaction to Watergate. For Goldwater, who had campaigned for Nixon and vouched for him during détente, the president's lies, not to mention damage to the GOP, amounted to personal duplicity. Days after the White House refused to turn in tape recordings to the Senate investigating committee, the senator described Nixon as "sinking further and further into the line of disrespect, disbelief and uselessness."[132] Shortly before the resignation, Goldwater privately remarked, "You can only be lied to so often, and it's time to take a stand that we want out."[133]

Coming from "the conscience of the right," those words reflected conservatives' weariness with a president whose actions had tested them beyond their limits. Détente with the PRC was perhaps understandable, but the Watergate scandal was unforgivable. The incident exacerbated the long-standing issues that had existed between the right wing of the GOP and Nixon since the 1950s. True, the then-congressman had launched his national political career as a rabid anticommunist. However, rather than align himself with the Taft wing of the party, he angled to be vice president under the moderate Eisenhower shortly afterward.[134] His foolhardy run for the California governor's seat in 1962, which featured a bruising primary campaign against the ultraconservative Joe Shell, had further estranged him from the growing Sunbelt movement. Calling his opponent "a loser," Shell declared that a sizeable portion of the state's GOP organization would refuse to work for the "liberal" Nixon if the former vice president won the nomination. It was a prediction that held true.[135]

Doubts about Nixon's conservative credentials still lingered over ten years later and prevented already disbelieving right-wing leaders from coming to his defense during Watergate. When Buckley lamented in July 1974 that one could not take pride or have confidence in an executive like Nixon, he also meant that the soon to be ex-president was hardly a true conservative to begin with.[136] Despite the president's self-victimization at the "hands of the liberal establishment," he and the right stood far apart on key ideological fronts.[137]

On the most basic level, Watergate clearly demonstrated Nixon's lack of respect for the principle of federal balance of power. Conservatives and liberals alike could point to his administration as an "imperial presidency" that resisted any oversight, congressional or public, with the controversial justification of "executive privilege."[138] Such an attitude clashed with the GOP right's long-standing platform of constitutional originalism, and it contributed to conservatives' eventual disavowal of Nixon as any credit to their party. Years later, Goldwater told Harry Riesener of CBS News, "Mr. Nixon hurt the Republican Party and he hurt America . . . I've never gotten over it."[139]

Whatever the damage done at home, the scandal did result in one foreign policy development that was undeniably positive from an Asia First perspective. In her analysis of US-China-Taiwan relations, Nancy Tucker states that Watergate rendered rapid normalization with the PRC "impossible."[140] The political fall-out was simply too great for even Nixon's considerable diplomatic achievements to overcome.

After Nixon's resignation, Goldwater continued to advocate for Taiwan however he could. It was a difficult time for him as a conservative, for he questioned the commitment of the GOP, as led by Gerald Ford, to creating a party in which the right had an integral place.[141] The new president's commitment to preserving strong US-Taiwan relations was also in question, especially since Ford retained much of the old administration's foreign policy team, the most important signal of continuity being Kissinger as secretary of state. During the transition, Kissinger had worked assiduously to assure Chinese officials that the path to normalization would not change just because Nixon was no longer in the White House. Mere hours after being sworn into office, Ford, presumably upon Kissinger's advice, wrote a personal letter to Mao declaring, "[N]o policy has higher priority."[142]

Ford's decision to send Sec. of Agriculture Earl Butz instead of Vice President Rockefeller to Chiang Kai-shek's funeral in April 1975 typified Goldwater's frustrations with the moderate Republican leadership. The senator was infuriated by the slight. He denounced the gesture as more than simple disrespect—its thoughtlessness was surely a precursor to formal recognition of the PRC and the abandonment of Taiwan. He created such a furor of criticism that Rockefeller ultimately led the American delegation—which included Goldwater, Judd, Sen. Hiram Fong (R-HI), and Claire Chennault's widow Anna—to Taipei.[143]

By that time, the goodwill toward China that rapprochement had built was dissolving, while mainstream media began to question why normalization was not proceeding apace.[144] Within the conservative base, the funeral episode clearly touched a nerve and illuminated lingering unease about an ambiguous China and Taiwan policy. Notes and letters from those who appreciated the stand Goldwater took flooded his office. "Chinese people will never forget what you have done for them," wrote Sister Agnes U. Higgins from a convent in Chanhua. An administrator from a Taiwanese girls' school praised Goldwater for his "way in pursuing democracy and freedom."[145] Given the near-simultaneous invasion of South Vietnam by the North, other correspondents framed the commotion surrounding Chiang's funeral as the most recent example of American failure in the entire Asia Pacific. "Our foreign policy is shambles," wrote Moses Long, a California businessman based in Taiwan. He sounded a refrain familiar to Asia Firsters: "Everything we do is done for expediency and not based on moral principles. We are so wishy washy our friends do not know where they stand. . . . We are treating the Chinese Communists like friends in the name of détente when we know full well they are the ones creating all the trouble in the Far East. We are just deluding ourselves."[146] Kissinger meanwhile informed Ford that the collapse of Saigon made any drastic changes in Taiwan policy that "implied abandonment of yet another ally" impossible.[147]

Although the defeat of South Vietnam was complete and Kissinger's shepherding of US foreign policy still boded ill for their cause, Taiwan supporters continued to find hope in Goldwater. According to one Baptist missionary, "[Y]ou spoke up and our hearts were lifted . . . It is probably too late for Vietnam, but perhaps we can awaken from our slumber and strengthen our support of the Republic of China." Others urged the senator to run for the White House again; some even volunteered their services straightaway.[148]

At the very least, the hubbub over Chiang's memorial service renewed Goldwater and conservatism's reputations as steadfast friends of Taiwan. Even if affinity for the Guomindang was on the wane—some months after the funeral Buckley remarkably attributed Chiang's downfall in the civil war to internal corruption rather than inadequate American support—the Asia First impulse to protect Taiwan remained intact.[149] For his part, Goldwater threatened to retract his 1976 campaign endorsement of Ford in favor of the upstart Ronald Reagan if reports of the administration's plans to recognize the PRC after the election were accurate. When the senator demanded to know the truth about the future of US-Taiwan relations, Kissinger soothed "Taiwan's staunchest supporter in Washington" by telling him what he wanted to hear. However, the sincerity of the secretary of state's placating words was questionable at best. He did the same with Huang Zen, the head of the PRC's liaison office in Washington, who was just as anxious but obviously hoping for the opposite policy outcome.[150]

The Not-So-Curious Case of *Goldwater v. Carter*

With the rise of the evangelical "Moral Majority" and issues like the Equal Rights Amendment, domestic preoccupations dominated conservatism's agenda by the end of the 1970s. With a few exceptions, foreign policy took a backseat to social morality and school busing. However, Pres. Jimmy Carter's December 1978 announcement of plans not to renew the mutual defense pact with the ROC once again brought US-Taiwan-China relations to the fore of conservative consciousness and reinvigorated the right's devotion to Taiwan security.

The president's statement that to normalize relations with China was to recognize simple reality elicited vehement responses.[151] Sen. Bob Dole (R-KS) predicted that allowing the treaty to expire would damage "the reputation of our nation within the world community" and global stability would be undermined. Bill Buckley dismissed the presumption that human rights reform would take place in China because of normalization as "romantic." The Carter administration was "long on TV, short on strategy," lamented George F. Will. Inadvertently echoing the title of Robert Welch's tome on MacArthur and Chiang, Pat Buchanan asked, "In the name of God, why?"[152]

No critic, however, was as aggressive as Goldwater. "I submit there is nothing either simple or realistic in what the President has done in the name of peace," he retorted. The dissolution of the mutual defense treaty was an act of betrayal comparable to the Japanese attack on Pearl Harbor, and Carter's speech would be remembered as "ten minutes that lived in infamy." This was no mere reshuffling of diplomatic priorities. It was the obliteration of an entire nation: "He is saying that Taiwan has no right to exist."[153]

Such words were furious and harsh, but they were perhaps to be expected since the topic was Taiwan's international status and the target was a liberal Democrat. The senator had also been critical of Carter since the 1976 campaign, and the then-candidate's foreign policy inexperience was what Goldwater found most concerning. "I see Mr. Carter's future and I don't believe in it," he told the GOP convention that year. "This country, the United States, has never lived in an era of so much promise in the field of peace. And I don't want to see it destroyed by a man and men who know absolutely nothing about foreign policy."[154] Normalization simply confirmed Goldwater's early suspicions about the administration's diplomatic naïveté.

Regardless of what the right thought about his greenness, Carter had a committed vision for how he wanted to shape US foreign policy. A growing number of scholars argue that Carter's vision was simply ahead of its time and suffered from the contexts of the Iran hostage crisis and a national recession.[155] Douglas Brinkley has characterized Carter's approach as "a post-Cold War policy before the Cold War was over."[156] After all, it was his White House—and not Nixon's or Ford's—that managed to achieve normalization with the PRC.

Significant factors worked in Carter's favor. The PRC was still a willing diplomatic partner, since its officials were eager, if not impatient, to establish diplomatic ties as part of a drive to open up to the West to achieve modernization.[157] Just as importantly, the political climate within the United States seemed conducive to another shift in China policy. The passage of time since Nixon's Beijing trip and the incremental changes wrought by his and Ford's administrations laid the groundwork for American voters to ultimately accept the concessions necessary to make the new relationship materialize. Deng Xiaoping's 1979 cross-country tour of the United States, a public relations success, demonstrated the change in attitude toward Communist China.[158] Finally, as a Democrat, Carter was also able to avoid the intraparty divisions that had plagued his Republican predecessors and still lingered within the GOP.[159] True, there were disagreements between Sec. of State Cyrus Vance and Zbigniew Brzezinski, the national security advisor, on how best to interpret China's place in the larger Cold War. Yet, unlike the previous two presidents, Carter was able to choose which route to take and publically act accordingly.[160] The combination of all those conditions allowed his administration to announce that the United States was able to meet outright the PRC's stipulations for a formal relationship, the most vital of which was the termination of any official US presence on Taiwan.[161]

Even as all these changes occurred, Asia First continued to challenge liberals, moderates, and other conservatives who saw potential ties to the PRC as anti-Soviet measures. The recurring issue of Taiwan's sovereignty and what protections, if any, it would receive from the United States reignited Asia First conservatives' dedication to ROC independence. For his part, Goldwater was determined to vigorously preserve it regardless of the forces aligned against his goal.

No one could one accuse him of inaction even during this latter phase of his public service. He zeroed in on the mutual defense treaty's termination and launched a campaign to dispute it by sponsoring a Senate resolution amendment and writing open letters to colleagues.[162] "The issue is not a partisan one. It is not a vote of confidence in the President," he wrote, "It is an up or down vote on the Senate's historical treaty power."[163] The usual legislative channels were not his only recourse, and Goldwater did not hesitate to simultaneously use extraordinary measures. In June, he, nine other senators, and sixteen members of the House took the president to federal court.

Filed with the US District Court in June 1979, the civil suit *Goldwater v. Carter* was a mix of both past and present for Asia First conservatism. Foundational to the plaintiffs' case was the argument that the president's refusal to renew the mutual defense agreement amounted to illegal abrogation of a treaty. They alleged that Carter's unilateral decision to end the agreement "impaired their legislative right to be consulted and to vote on treaty termination."[164] Once again, US-China relations were the catalyst for renewed debate surrounding balance of power in foreign policy.

In many ways, the case strongly echoed previous anti-Yalta positions and efforts like the Bricker Amendment. *Goldwater v. Carter* also illustrated how conservatives still used the domestic stage as a platform to address their diplomatic concerns.[165] On the other hand, the case differed from earlier Asia First legislative initiatives in a number of respects. The lawsuit focused on whether or not a president had the unilateral power to *end* a foreign treaty that had been ratified by two-thirds of the US Senate. Moreover, unlike in preceding decades, the angle of anticommunism entered the discussion only obliquely.[166]

Suing the president was an unpleasant business, and Goldwater's chances of winning were slim. Nevertheless, he was willing to lose in order to prove a moral point. From his standpoint, the Constitution itself was at stake, and "as an American, I felt it had to be done."[167] Morality, or "decency, which the President has very obviously forgotten, or never understood," had to be preserved.[168] The suit was also intended as a diplomatic gesture to show the people of Taiwan that not all American leaders agreed with Carter's foreign relations agenda. Domestic politics were not forgotten, either. In an address at the Heritage Foundation, J. Terry Emerson, plaintiffs' lead counsel, described the debate over the mutual defense treaty as a "war" for public opinion, the outcome of which would "determine whether the people, through their chosen representatives in Congress, remain supreme, or whether the Executive gains position of imperial dominance based on expediency of the moment."[169]

Dismissed without prejudice in district court in October 1979, *Goldwater v. Carter* was quickly sent to the US Court of Appeals the following month. It eventually reached the US Supreme Court, which reviewed the case via writ of *certiorari*, without oral arguments, in December 1979. The court declined jurisdiction over the matter explaining it was "not ripe for judicial review." The majority opinion written by Justice Lewis Powell argued that questions of presidential power could, and should, be addressed through congressional avenues and not through the court system. It would be embarrassing for the three branches of government to contradict one another by reaching conflicting resolutions. The court voted to dismiss by a vote of 6 to 3.[170]

Technically, those results represented a legal defeat for Goldwater. Yet, the court's dismissal was not an endorsement of presidential unilateralism. The justices expressly left the matter open for resolution by the executive and legislative branches. Even if the constitutional question of power in foreign policy remained ambiguous, by the time the Supreme Court made its decision, the immediate issue of protection for Taiwan had come to a resolution. As the case made its way through the legal system, the pro-ROC faction in Congress reasserted its voice in a more conventional manner by passing the Taiwan Relations Act (TRA) in April 1979.

An effort to preserve flexible US-Taiwan relations, despite the end of official diplomatic ties, the TRA's preamble forcefully reasserted American commercial, cultural, and security interests in Taiwan.[171] Defying Carter, legislators specifically stated that the island required US support to maintain its security and they "refus[ed] to entrust the island's future to the goodwill of Washington or Beijing."[172] It was the type of safeguard Asia Firsters had not thought to demand from Nixon in 1972. In terms of specific protections, the TRA provided an option for future arms sales to the island should Taiwan's security come under duress.[173] The final vote count—339 to 59 in the House and 85 to 4 in the Senate—showed an overwhelming degree of support for an explicit commitment to Taiwan. Given those numbers, a reluctant Carter was forced to sign off on the legislation rather than risk an embarrassing veto override.[174] Although a diplomatic sea change was well underway, and despite Goldwater's ultimate loss in court, the TRA proved a measure of continued support for the island. At the very least, it represented the type of legislative mitigation in US-China-Taiwan relations that conservatives had long sought.

As this chapter has shown, Goldwater's relationship with Taiwan was a hallmark of his conservatism. At the end of his public career, one political cartoon depicted him in a wheelchair with the Chinese Nationalist flag draped over his lap.[175] In the senator's own words, the friendship felt between Americans and the "Free Chinese" would endure, despite the efforts of certain US officials, for diplomacy was an issue that mattered, and belonged, to all citizens.[176]

Indeed, he was among the last conservative politicians who consistently used Asia to cement the right's turn toward an original internationalism. The dawn of the Reagan era signified adjustment in the tenor and direction of American conservatism as the ethical justification for interventionist anticommunism was replaced by a moral commitment of another kind. Social and cultural issues became priorities for the next version of the New Right, and Goldwater found little in common those objectives. He considered the so-called Moral Majority impudent and overreaching: "Just who do they think they are? . . . I will fight them every step of the way if they try to dictate their moral convictions to all Americans in the name of conservatism."[177] The fundamental question of what a government should and should not do created a generation gap between conservative cohorts. An older antistatism concerned with national character, but reluctant to police citizens' everyday lives, clashed with this newer impulse to legislate social morality.

While the use of government to dictate family values may have appeared to clash with the libertarian spirit of Goldwater conservatism, the two actually held much in common. For instance, both looked to federal channels to intervene in what they saw as a decline in morality. In the case of Asia First internationalism, that meant the restoration of a special friendship between the United States and Free China via defense of Taiwan's interests as America's own.

During his time as a political leader, Goldwater strove to facilitate the right's move away from literal antistatism. Much of his impetus derived from the struggle against Soviet and Asian communism, which taught conservatives of the 1950s and 1960s to embrace federal interventionism as a tool to shape both domestic and foreign policy. With the latter, the shift that Asia First imparted became patently obvious to the entire nation during Goldwater's run for president in 1964. His platform featured a marked commitment to overseas intervention unencumbered by multinational organizations like the UN and fueled by a growing defense state. With lessons learned from 1949 China and the Korean War, conservatives extended the Asia First critique to the conflict in Vietnam.

Despite its immediate application to Southeast Asia, "Why not Victory?" was not a static slogan. By the 1970s a sort of realpolitik came to the fore as a strategy for winning the Cold War, and it replaced an earlier refusal to deal with the PRC. But this new normal for conservative internationalism hardly included Carter's version of US-China normalization. Relations with Beijing were acceptable only as long as Taiwan was independent and granted a consistent level of diplomatic recognition. Led by Goldwater, conservative officials at the end of the decade revived the saliency of Asia First in the face of normalization. They proved willing to defy executive prerogative by simultaneously using legislative means and more unconventional channels in order to safeguard a traditional alliance. The episode represented just the latest chapter of conservatism's development into a political force that helped to shape the nation's role in the wider world. That it stemmed from the fraught narrative of US-China relations seemed apropos.

When postwar conservatism reached an apogee with Ronald Reagan's administration during the 1980s, how the US-China-Taiwan issue would fare came into question. If Asia First had proven to be a useful tool to express opposition to consensus moderation, particularly against the White House, what would happen when the president himself was a Republican conservative and the right no longer needed to invoke China as it had in the past? Well into the 1980s, the political legacy of the Cold War in East Asia was still evolving.

Conclusion

After the formal normalization of relations between the United States and the People's Republic of China (PRC), Open Door politics ceased to become as clear-cut. Major shifts in East Asia policy and the US-Taiwan bond resulted from an overhaul of Cold War strategy, but leadership and status changes on the American right contributed as well. Certainly, Ronald Reagan's victory in the 1980 presidential election was an unprecedented apex for postwar conservatism. With his election came a renewed emphasis on laissez-faire capitalism, a reduced welfare state, and an evangelical moralism. On the diplomatic front, the White House championed a foreign policy that used aggressive public rhetoric tempered by a healthy measure of practical realpolitik.[1]

Reagan's personal stance on the China-Taiwan issue was deeply conflicted as he attempted to navigate the tug of war that existed among Asia First conservatism, the often-contradictory recommendations of his advisors, and his own pragmatic desire to win at home and in the Cold War. The lead-up to the 1980 election provided an early glimpse of internal turmoil. During the 1970s, the former governor of California had established himself as a vocal supporter of Taiwan. Living up to that reputation, Reagan criticized Jimmy Carter's Asia policy early in the campaign and even expressed a desire for the restoration of an official relationship with Taiwan. His words raised hopes that, if he won the White House, the island would again find a protector in the United States.[2]

The timing was terrible from an electoral perspective. Reagan appeared out of date and out of touch, and the diplomatic fallout from China could undermine any authority he claimed on foreign policy. Seeking to contain any damage, his campaign team hurriedly dispatched George H. W. Bush to Beijing to reassure PRC officials that a Reagan presidency would not fundamentally alter the trajectory of US Asia policy. Under some pressure from advisors, Reagan read a public statement that essentially promised to leave Carter's accomplishments intact. He was bound to make more compromises soon after inauguration day, for the political balance he was required to strike mitigated what his rhetoric on the campaign trail had suggested. Alexander Haig's appointment as head of the State Department, an attempt to appease moderates, proved that point early on.[3] Clearly the White House was not going to stick with the straightforward Asia First line Reagan had voiced on his road to the White House.

Haig presided over a foreign-policy apparatus that was intensely divided on the subject of China. In one camp stood the secretary of state, who, like Henry Kissinger, viewed the PRC as an important ally and firmly believed in continuing the course toward a full US-China partnership.[4] In the other, "hawks" like Paul Wolfowitz (director of policy planning at the State Department) theorized that the PRC's strategic importance had been grossly overestimated. Wolfowitz believed that too many points had been conceded to the PRC in the rush to achieve rapprochement. According to his calculus, China's precarious position with the Soviet Union meant that it needed an alliance with the United States more than vice versa; the United States could therefore afford to leverage Chinese demands accordingly, without entirely deserting Taiwan.[5]

Such factionalism led to a particularly confusing and fraught two years in US-China-Taiwan affairs.[6] At the heart of the debate was the provision of weapons and defense technology to Taiwan. By the summer of 1982, it appeared Haig's perspective had won. In a joint communiqué with the PRC, the United States promised to freeze arms sales to the island at existing levels to demonstrate its commitment to a new alliance.[7]

Then again, promises made in the open were not the entire story. The previous month, Reagan offered Taiwan a list of six confidential reassurances that essentially protected the status quo.[8] He also dictated a secret memo to the National Security Council on how he interpreted the agreement with China: The United States would restrict arms sales only as long as the balance of power between China and Taiwan was preserved. In the event of increased Chinese military capability, American aid to the ROC remained very much a possibility.[9]

Soon after the communiqué was announced, personnel changes in Washington suggested that a more public shift in East Asia policy was imminent. Haig resigned from office, and George Shultz took his place. The new secretary of state's views on China's strategic significance were much more aligned with those held by Wolfowitz; in fact, Shultz appointed the latter as assistant secretary of state for East Asian affairs. As James Mann points out, the stance they shared provided common ground between pro-Taiwan conservatives and those who prioritized winning the Cold War against the Soviet Union.[10] By forcing China's hand without sacrificing its own interests, the United States could continue its mission to emerge as the victorious superpower. To that end, Schultz and Wolfowitz (along with other influential officials like Richard Armitage and Gaston Sigur) reoriented American focus away from the PRC toward a "pan-Asian" strategy.[11] Conservative Taiwan supporters could hardly be blamed if such administrative comings and goings revived their aspirations for a strong bond with the island.

They were to be sorely disappointed. The change in diplomatic focus actually favored strong relations with Japan and did little to elevate Taiwan's status. In fact, what has been deemed a "golden age" in US-China relations began shortly after. Historian Nancy Tucker notes, "Reagan did not significantly change Taiwan's place in the world. He employed rhetoric and symbols, not conviction or plans for action."[12] This period of meaningful collaboration between the United States and the PRC—which saw cooperation between intelligence agencies, unprecedented educational exchange, and robust trade—lasted from 1983 until the end of Reagan's presidency.[13]

A number of compelling factors explain why the pendulum swung toward a close partnership with the nation that Reagan had strongly criticized just a few years earlier. Shifts in Chinese domestic politics were vital, for they resulted in a push for Westernization, which in turn led to a PRC foreign policy strategy that was more accommodating toward the United States.[14] For example, a shared desire to gain an upper hand against the Soviet Union in Afghanistan produced an intelligence partnership that underlined diplomatic demonstrations of friendship, such as Premier Zhao Ziyang and Reagan's respective head-of-state visits to Washington and Beijing in 1984.[15] Another element was the reawakened desire for an economic Open Door, this time with both sides hoping to prosper from trade with one another. By 1989, almost six billion dollars in goods were exported from the United States to China per annum, while China benefitted from a flow of new technology.[16] From a domestic political angle, the growth of financial opportunity in Asia paralleled Reagan's promotion of free-market practices as a cornerstone of conservative—nay, national—values.[17] Even as the Reagan administration's lasting approach to the PRC was a product of the Cold War, in many respects it was also a prescient example of the new world order that would emerge after 1991.[18]

The age of détente clearly meant a more elastic approach to former enemy states as the traditional lines of anticommunism became blurred. At the same time, the divide between conservatives regarding an alliance with China grew increasingly sharp, despite shared opinions on other issues like national security and definitively ending the Cold War. Whereas neoliberal Reaganites saw attractive economic and geopolitical advantages, the pro-Taiwan bloc regarded recent developments with wary concern. The latter were what Prof. Donald Zagoria called the "ideological school, or one could say the more principled school" that rejected unpredictable totalitarian states as "unfit" partners for the United States.[19]

For the first time conservatives were in the awkward position of demanding "Asia First" from fellow members of the right. Previously, the call for equal prioritization of the Pacific in US foreign policy was a tactic used in opposition to Democrats and Republican moderates. Now Reagan, who had realized conservatives' quest for national power, headed an administration that showed more interest in using accelerated relations with China and little public consideration for Taiwan as justifiable means to a Soviet end. Asia Firsters had a choice. They could either fall in line with realpolitik after normalization or voice their objections on moral grounds and risk being sidelined as the Republican Party moved forward.

Barry Goldwater, for one, stood firm on the subject of Taiwan. On his way to China in 1984, Reagan met Goldwater in Hawaii as the latter was returning from his own trip to Taipei. During their confrontation, the senator expressed his misgivings about a presidential visit to the PRC in no uncertain terms. Reagan later recalled that nothing he said could sway Goldwater's opinion.[20] The passage of time only saw the senator immoveable in his resolve. In 1991, he reiterated his conviction using familiar terms of Asia First orientalism: "People ask me why I have always been a friend of the Republic of China," he told an audience in Taiwan. "The answer is simple. I am loyal to Free China because it has always been loyal to the American people and to American principles."[21]

His words were a throwback to the 1950s and early 1960s, when the early Cold War provided a much more rigid framework for conservatives to process developments around the world. Its stricter, at times absolutist, contexts at home and abroad effectively acted as an incubator in which to develop a proactive anticommunism that could fight the same enemy as containment but in a manner distinctive to the right.

Because of the two-fronted battle they fought with Democrats as well as moderates within the GOP during that period, postwar conservatives' choice of China as a signature foreign policy issue was easy to understand in strictly mercenary terms. A symbolic subject with wide appeal, it fulfilled a diversity of needs. Most basically, China was geographically distinct from the Democratic foreign policy that had experienced a great deal of success in Western Europe and Japan. Since American intervention in the late 1940s proved fruitless in China and the Chinese civil war wound down to its inevitable conclusion, the Republican right seized its opportunity. Conservatives characterized the inevitable "loss" of China in 1949 as proof of how moderate consensus and its offspring, bipartisan foreign policy, had failed the United States and its ally, the Nationalist Guomindang government.

Asia First conservatives mobilized in a variety of ways. Officials in Washington used their positions to raise awareness with speeches in the Senate and the House, by proposing and debating legislation, and using their party leadership positions to cement the GOP's commitment to Asia during election cycles. They most often used China to illustrate imbalances of power in US foreign policy making, a focus that was the product of their own institutional positions in Congress and their tense relationships with presidents of both parties.

That top-down approach complemented the simultaneous mobilization of Asia First activists, whose extrastate campaigns to raise awareness of the Nationalist cause comprised an early model for rightwing mobilization on the grassroots level. While often incendiary and plainly inaccurate when it came to piecing together the narrative of US-China relations, their efforts were nevertheless effective among a growing audience of citizens troubled by the trajectory of American foreign policy. With a common interest in Pacific affairs and a growing electoral base in regions like the Sunbelt West, conservative elites and activists forged a working relationship that featured the Cold War in Asia as a unifying interest. Its leaders may have been loath to acknowledge it outright, but conservatism reaped a multitude of benefits from the American estrangement from mainland China. By politicizing the subject for much of the postwar period, they gained votes, an undeniable voice within the GOP, and, eventually, national power.

Of course, the central irony of conservatism's appropriation of the China issue was that it made only a minor impact on practicable East Asia policy. Because conservatives wanted to reestablish their ideology and worldview as a genuine alternative to liberalism, the way forward involved more domestic action than actual diplomacy. "All that can be wisely concluded is that essentially noninterventionist elements in the Republican Party have shown themselves to be somewhat less noninterventionist toward Asia than toward Europe," one scholar dryly noted at the time.[22] Nevertheless, Asia First's value lay in a stance made virtually unassailable by the continued existence of the PRC and conflicts like the wars in Korea and Southeast Asia.

Political motivations were a large part of Asia First internationalism, but there were other, equally important dimensions at play. As the previous chapters have shown, a particular form of orientalism motivated many Asia Firsters to revise their ideology on behalf of "Free China" and a broader internationalism. Historical, if not historically based, it cast (1) the United States as guardian of China's fate and (2) China as a barometer of the health of America's democratic government. However narcissistic, those tenets were also inherently internationalist. They compelled even old-guard conservatives to join in constructing an original foreign policy that was a potent combination of the traditional and the modern.

Another factor to consider was the deeply personal, emotional element to Asia First, indicated by the ferocity with which key conservatives clung to China. From the China Lobby and the John Birch Society to legislative efforts by officials like William Knowland and Barry Goldwater, conservatives who supported the ideal of a special US-China relationship often sustained their belief in the cause via China's connection to their own experiences. Fealty to Chiang Kai-shek sustained Alfred Kohlberg; for Robert Welch, China was vital to raising his anticommunist citizen army; and Knowland's and Goldwater's regional roots prompted them to battle for a Pacific focus within American Cold War strategy. Although China meant different things to different conservatives, its storyline of loyalty betrayed and preventable error fused conservative factions together under the banner of a Free China that supposedly once was. That in turn translated into a vision for what the United States should be, for its own people and to the world.

After the Reagan era and the end of the Cold War, China's legacy within American conservatism lacked direction without the singular unifier of strict anticommunism. The 2012 presidential campaign provided ample evidence of that continuing ambiguity. In a video released online during the GOP primaries, anonymous supporters of the libertarian Ron Paul accused former US ambassador to China and moderate candidate Jon Huntsman of being a "Manchurian Candidate." With hackneyed Asiatic music playing in the background, Huntsman's service abroad and ability to speak Mandarin were presented as evidence of un-American, even Maoist, values.[23] Meanwhile, former governor of Massachusetts and eventual party nominee Mitt Romney appeared to switch positions according to electoral need. After a bruising primary season during which his conservative credentials were regularly questioned, Romney's statements noticeably tacked rightward. From healthcare to defense, his former moderation rapidly faded from view. The subject of China was no different. During his second debate with President Barack Obama, Romney repeatedly made the PRC a foreign scapegoat for the national recession: It was a "currency manipulator" that was "stealing our intellectual property," and he vowed to "crack down" if elected.[24] At the final debate six days later he softened his stance somewhat, asserting that a "responsible" China could be an effective diplomatic and trading partner. He refrained from elaborating how economic toughness would impact the US-China alliance.[25] Over the course of a few months Romney ran the gamut on China, Reagan-like détente on one end and hard-line Asia First conservatism on the other.

Within a Republican Party heavily swayed by a very vocal and increasingly radicalized conservative wing, China continues to play an array of roles. These range from communist Yellow Peril to geopolitical collaborator, and none remain fixed for very long. Today, the right appears at least reconciled to the existence of the PRC. Like their liberal counterparts, conservative leaders must take into account China's status as a global superpower if they are to effectively address developments in Asia and beyond. Nevertheless, political compartmentalization still lingers. The 2012 campaign demonstrated how the old story of undue Chinese interference in the United States' well-being plainly remains a rhetorical touchstone, and it tempted more than one candidate vying for the rightwing approval necessary to capture a Republican presidency.

Despite such paradoxes, the lasting impacts of the Cold War in East Asia have been numerous. The right and Republicanism as a whole underwent fundamental transformations. A large defense state; antipathy toward the United Nations and collective peacekeeping; and an argument for selective, unilateral military action became major hallmarks of conservatism's approach to foreign policy. In sum, the wing of the GOP that was once considered isolationist achieved a lasting political platform that addressed the nation's globally expansive interests.[26] The drive toward a specifically conservative brand of internationalism was Asia First's most important legacy, and it is one that continues to mold perceptions—both positive and negative—of American power.

Notes

Introduction

1. David M. Oshinsky, *A Conspiracy So Immense: The World of Joe McCarthy* (New York: Free Press, 1983), 485.

2. "What Next for McCarthy After Vote on Censure?" (reprint), *Congressional Report* 3, no. 4 (December 1954): 2, Dean G. Acheson Papers, Harry S. Truman Library, Independence (hereafter cited as Acheson Papers), Box 86, Fol. "McCarthy, Joseph—Corr., 1953–1954."

3. Marilyn B. Young, *The Rhetoric of Empire: American China Policy, 1895–1901* (Cambridge, MA: Harvard University Press, 1969); Richard Madsen, *China and the American Dream: A Moral Inquiry* (Berkeley: University of California Press, 1995), 81–82; and Warren I. Cohen, *America's Response to China: A History of Sino-American Relations* (New York: Columbia University Press, 2010), 29–114.

4. "What Next for McCarthy After Vote on Censure?," 2.

5. Rick Perlstein, *Before the Storm: Barry Goldwater and the Unmaking of the American Consensus* (New York: Hill and Wang, 2001), xv.

6. Examples include Daniel T. Rodgers, *Atlantic Crossings: Social Politics in a Progressive Age* (Cambridge: Belknap Press, 1998); Alan Dawley, *Changing the World: American Progressives in War and Revolution* (Princeton: Princeton University Press, 2003); Thomas J. Knock, *To End All Wars: Woodrow Wilson and the Quest for a New World Order* (New York: Oxford University Press, 1992); John Milton Cooper Jr., ed., *Reconsidering Woodrow Wilson: Progressivism, Internationalism, War, and Peace* (Baltimore: Johns Hopkins University Press, 2008); Robert A. Divine, *Second Chance: The Triumph of Internationalism in America* (New York: Atheneum, 1967); Wayne S. Cole, *Roosevelt and the Isolationists, 1932–1945* (Lincoln: University of Nebraska Press, 1983); and Melvyn P. Leffler, *A Preponderance of Power: National Security, the Truman Administration, and the Cold War* (Stanford: Stanford University Press, 1992).

7. Christopher McKnight Nichols, *Promise and Peril: America at the Dawn of a Global Age* (Cambridge, MA: Harvard University Press, 2011).

8. "U.S. Government Aid to China," prepared by the Clearing Office for Foreign Transactions (of the US Government), Office of Business Economics, Department of Commerce, 26 January 1950, William F. Knowland Papers, Bancroft Library, UC Berkeley, BANC MSS 75/97 c (hereafter cited as WFK Papers), Carton 277. Figures generated by the State Department showed that the United States gave over \$1.5 billion in aid to China during World War II, an amount

that was overshadowed, however, by the tens of billions it granted European countries via the Lend-Lease Act of 1941.

9. Clarence Kelland to Robert A. Taft, 11 February 1949, Robert A. Taft Papers, Library of Congress, Washington, DC (hereafter cited as RAT Papers), Box 911, Fol. "1949—Political: Republican." See also David Farber, *The Rise and Fall of Modern American Conservatism: A Short History* (Princeton: Princeton University Press, 2010), 19.

10. David Halberstam, *The Fifties* (New York: Fawcett Columbine, 1993), 4–5.

11. Robert Divine, *Foreign Policy and U.S. Presidential Elections, Vol. 1: 1940–1948* (New York: New Viewpoints, 1974).

12. Arthur H. Vandenberg Jr., ed., *The Private Papers of Senator Vandenberg* (Boston: Houghton Mifflin, 1952), 126–420, 461–579; Eric F. Goldman, *The Crucial Decade—And After: America, 1945–1960* (New York: Vintage, 1960), 29–30; and Michael W. Miles, *The Odyssey of the American Right* (New York: Oxford University Press, 1980), 120.

13. These included Homer Ferguson (MI), Kenneth Wherry (NB), Wallace White (ME), Styles Bridges (NH), John Bricker (OH), and William Jenner (IN). William F. Knowland (CA) and Joseph McCarthy (WI) also won their first elections that year.

14. Michael Hogan, *A Cross of Iron: Harry S. Truman and the Origins of the National Security State, 1945–1954* (New York: Cambridge University Press, 1998), 69–118.

15. Arthur M. Schlesinger Jr., *The Vital Center: The Politics of Freedom* (New Brunswick: Transaction Publishers, 1998), 31 (emphasis added).

16. Robert R. McCormick to Robert A. Taft, 3 June 1948, RAT Papers, Box 899, Fol. "Senators, Correspondence, 1948." See also Halberstam, *The Fifties*, 214–18.

17. George Sokolsky, "Our Foreign Policy," Weekly Sunday Broadcast Over ABC Stations, 13 November 1949, RAT Papers, Box 506.

18. Jerome L. Himmelstein, *To the Right: The Transformation of American Conservatism* (Berkeley: University of California Press, 1990), 31–32.

19. As Sen. Robert Taft stated, "Only Congress may regulate commerce with foreign nations. Only Congress may declare war. Only Congress may raise and support armies and provide for and maintain a navy, although the President is commander in chief when they are raised or provided." Robert A. Taft, "The New Deal and the Republican Program" (speech delivered to the National Republican Club of New York, 18 March 1939), reprinted in Robert A. Taft, *A Republican Program: Speeches and Broadcasts* (Cleveland: David S. Ingalls, 1939) 7. See also Thomas Verner Smith and Robert A. Taft, *Foundations of Democracy: A Series of Debates by T. V. Smith and Robert A. Taft* (New York: Alfred A. Knopf, 1939), 14–20.

20. Vandenberg, *Private Papers of Senator Vandenberg*, 519–20, 522.

21. Senate Foreign Relations Committee, "S. 1063, A Bill to Provide Economic, Financial and Other Aid to China, Friday, March 18, 1949," p. 49, Harry S. Truman Papers, President's Secretary's Files, Truman Presidential Library, China Lobby Subseries, Box 139, Fol. "China Lobby, General."

22. Goldman, *Crucial Decade*, 121–23.

23. Lisa McGirr, *Suburban Warriors: The Origins of the New American Right* (Princeton: Princeton University Press, 2001), 147–86; and Kurt Schuparra, *Triumph of the Right: The Rise of the California Conservative Movement, 1945–1966* (Armonk: M. E. Sharpe, 1998), 3–41.

24. E. J. Kahn Jr., *The China Hands: America's Foreign Service Officers and What Befell Them* (New York: Penguin Books, 1976); Gary May, *China Scapegoat!: The Diplomatic Ordeal of John Carter Vincent* (Washington, DC: New Republic Books, 1979); Robert P. Newman, *Owen Lattimore and the "Loss" of China* (Berkeley: University of California Press, 1992); and Nancy Bern-

kopf Tucker, *The China Threat: Memories, Myths, Realities in the 1950s* (New York: Columbia University Press, 2012).

25. Robert A. Divine, *Since 1945: Politics and Diplomacy in Recent American History* (New York: Alfred A. Knopf, 1985), 53; Gordon H. Chang, *Friends and Enemies: The United States, China, and the Soviet Union, 1948–1972* (Stanford: Stanford University Press, 1990), 49–50, 60; Robert E. Herzstein, *Henry R. Luce, Time, and the American Crusade in Asia* (New York: Cambridge University Press, 2005); and Cohen, *America's Response to China*, 179–83.

26. "The Knowland Story," *U.S. News & World Report*, 24 December 1954, 37.

27. Douglas T. Miller and Marion Nowak, *The Fifties: The Way We Really Were* (New York: Doubleday, 1977), 239–40.

28. Patrick Allitt, *Conservative Intellectuals and Conservative Politics in America* (Ithaca: Cornell University Press, 1993), 158–65; Donald Critchlow, *The Conservative Ascendancy: How the GOP Right Made Political History* (Cambridge, MA: Harvard University Press, 2007), 7–8, 13–18; Jennifer Burns, *Goddess of the Market: Ayn Rand and the American Right* (New York: Oxford University Press, 2009); and Geoffrey Kabaservice, *Rule and Ruin: The Downfall of Moderation and the Destruction of the Republican Party: From Eisenhower to the Tea Party* (New York: Oxford University Press, 2012), 16–17.

29. Tucker, *China Threat*, 25–29.

30. Ross Y. Koen, *The China Lobby in American Politics* (New York: Octagon Books, 1960); Stanley D. Bachrack, *The Committee of One Million: "China Lobby" Politics, 1953–1971* (New York: Columbia University Press, 1976); and Nancy Bernkopf Tucker, "Taiwan Expendable? Nixon and Kissinger go to China," *Journal of American History* 92, no. 1 (2005): 111, 118.

31. Koen, *China Lobby in American Politics*, 56–57.

32. Recent work that has employed orientalism as a central theme varies widely in both subject matter and geographic scope. Examples include Anthony Lee, *Picturing Chinatown: Art and Orientalism in San Francisco* (Berkeley: University of California Press, 2001); Christina Klein, *Cold War Orientalism: Asia in the Middlebrow Imagination, 1945–1961* (Berkeley: University of California Press, 2003); Colleen Lye, *America's Asia: Racial Form and American Literature, 1893–1945* (Princeton: Princeton University Press, 2005); and Douglas Little, *American Orientalism: The United States and the Middle East since 1945* (Chapel Hill: University of North Carolina Press, 2008).

33. Edward W. Said, *Orientalism* (New York: Vintage Books, 1978), 1.

34. Akira Iriye, *Across the Pacific: An Inner History of American-East Asian Relations* (Chicago: Imprint Publications, 1992), 3–110; Jane Hunter, *The Gospel of Gentility: American Women Missionaries in Turn-of-the-Century China* (New Haven: Yale University Press, 1984), 174–228; James Reed, *The Missionary Mind and American East Asia Policy, 1911–1915* (Cambridge, MA: Harvard University Press, 1983); Michael Schaller, *The U.S. Crusade in China, 1938–1945* (New York: Columbia University Press, 1979), 1–16; Delber L. McKee, *Chinese Exclusion versus the Open Door, 1900–1906: Clashes Over China Policy in the Roosevelt Era* (Detroit: Wayne State University Press, 1977), 9–27; T. Christopher Jespersen, *American Images of China, 1931–1949* (Stanford: Stanford University Press, 1999); Lye, *America's Asia;* and James Mann, *The China Fantasy: How Our Leaders Explain Away Chinese Repression* (New York: Viking, 2007).

35. Iriye, *Across the Pacific*, 7.

36. Quoted in Goldman, *Crucial Decade*, 116.

37. Robeson Taj P. Frazier, "Thunder in the East: China, Exiled Crusaders, and the Unevenness of Black Internationalism," *American Quarterly* 63, no. 4 (2011): 929–53.

38. Klein, *Cold War Orientalism*, 9, 23.

39. Madsen, *China and the American Dream*, 28, 40–42, 52–54.

40. Herzstein, *Henry R. Luce*, 100–111; and Patricia Neils, *China Images in the Life and Times of Henry Luce* (New York: Rowman & Littlefield, 1990), 84–217.

41. Chiang Kai-shek, "Bonds Between China and America," 10 May 1941, reprinted in Chiang Kai-shek, *The Collected Wartime Messages of Generalissimo Chiang Kai-shek, 1937–1945: Compiled by Chinese Ministry of Information* (New York: John Day, 1946), 587.

42. Chiang to Franklin Roosevelt, "All We Are and All We Have," 8 December 1941, reprinted in Chiang, *Collected Wartime Messages*, 640.

43. John Paton Davies Jr., *China Hand: An Autobiography* (Philadelphia: University of Pennsylvania Press, 2012), 45, 147–54.

44. 77th Congress, 1st sess., H.R. Doc. No. 458, *Summary of Past Policy, and of More Immediate Events, in Relation to the Pacific Area: Message from the President of the United States Transmitting a Summary of the Past Policy of this Country in Relation to the Pacific Area and of the More Immediate Events Leading Up to This Japanese Onslaught Upon Our Forces and Territory* (Washington, DC: US Government Printing Office, 1941), Huntington Library and Archives (call no. 606355); "Exclusion Repeal is Law," *New York Times*, 17 December 1943; and Jonathan Spence, *To Change China: Western Advisors in China, 1620–1960* (Boston: Little, Brown, 1969), 253.

45. Cohen, *America's Response to China*, 124–26.

46. William P. Bundy, "Dictators and American Foreign Policy," *Foreign Affairs* 54, no. 1 (1975): 54; and Nancy Bernkopf Tucker, *Patterns in the Dust: Chinese-American Relations and the Recognition Controversy, 1949–1950* (New York: Columbia University Press, 1983), 10. Historians of interwar China have extensively discussed the authoritarian tendencies of Guomindang factions, as well as Chiang himself. For example, see W. F. Elkins, "'Fascism' in China: The Blue Shirts Society, 1932–1937," *Science & Society* 33, no. 4 (1969): 426–33; and Frederic E. Wakeman, *Policing Shanghai, 1927–1937* (Berkeley: University of California Press, 1995).

47. Dulles quoted in David F. Schmitz, *Thank God They're On Our Side: The United States and Right-Wing Dictatorships, 1921–1965* (Chapel Hill: University of North Carolina Press, 1999), 184.

48. Michael J. Hogan, *A Cross of Iron: Harry S. Truman and the Origins of the National Security State, 1945–1954* (New York: Cambridge University Press, 1998), 139–54; and Clarence E. Wunderlin, *Robert A. Taft: Ideas, Tradition, and Party in U.S. Foreign Policy* (Lanham: Rowman & Littlefield, 2005), 131–32.

Chapter 1

1. Tsuyoshi Hasegawa, *Racing the Enemy: Stalin, Truman, and the Surrender of Japan* (Cambridge, MA: Harvard University Press, 2006).

2. "Manchurian Manifesto," *New York Times*, 15 May 1946, Harold Joyce Noble Papers, Bancroft Library, UC Berkeley, BANC MSS Z-Z 147 (hereafter cited as Noble Papers), Box 1, Fol. 3; John B. Powell, "Letter to the Editor," *New York Times*, 17 May 1946; and Stanley D. Bachrack, *The Committee of One Million: "China Lobby" Politics, 1953–1971* (New York: Columbia University Press, 1976), 31.

3. Clarence E. Wunderlin, *Robert A. Taft: Ideas, Tradition, and Party in U.S. Foreign Policy* (Lanham: Rowman & Littlefield, 2005), 33–64; and David Farber, *The Rise and Fall of Modern American Conservatism: A Short History* (Princeton: Princeton University Press, 2010), 25.

4. Patrick Allitt, *The Conservatives: Ideas and Personalities Throughout American History* (New Haven: Yale University Press, 2009), 155–57.

5. H. L. Mencken, *The Diary of H.L. Mencken*, ed. Charles A Fecher (New York: Vintage Books, 1991), 137.

6. John Paul Armstrong, "Senator Taft and American Foreign Policy" (PhD diss., University of Chicago, 1953), 1; and William F. Buckley Jr., *Up from Liberalism* (New York: McDowell, Obolensky, 1959), 60.

7. Quoted in Eric F. Goldman, *The Crucial Decade—And After: America, 1945–1960* (New York: Vintage, 1960), 54.

8. Goldman, *Crucial Decade*, 28, 132, 164–65, 289.

9. Russell Kirk and James McClellan, *The Political Principles of Robert A. Taft* (New York: Fleet Press, 1967), 99–100.

10. Ibid., 158–59.

11. Christopher McKnight Nichols, *Promise and Peril: America at the Dawn of a Global Age* (Cambridge, MA: Harvard University Press, 2011), 332; and Wunderlin, *Robert A. Taft*, 4–6. See also Jerome L. Himmelstein, *To the Right: The Transformation of American Conservatism* (Berkeley: University of California Press, 1990), 35–37.

12. Robert A. Taft, "The Republican Party," *Fortune*, April 1949, 114 and 116.

13. Kirk and McClellan, *Political Principles of Robert A. Taft*, 101–5; and John F. Kennedy, *Profiles in Courage* (New York: Harper & Brothers, 1955), 193–205.

14. John Paton Davies Jr., *China Hand: An Autobiography* (Philadelphia: University of Pennsylvania Press, 2012), 294.

15. *U.S. News & World Report*, 10 January 1950, 19.

16. William Stueck, "The Marshall and Wedemeyer Missions: A Quadrilateral Perspective," in *Sino-American Relations, 1945–1955: A Joint Reassessment of a Critical Decade*, ed. Harry Harding and Yian Ming (Wilmington: Scholarly Resources, 1989), 101–2.

17. "Marshall in China," *Washington Post*, 16 September 1950; and E. J. Kahn Jr., *The China Hands: America's Foreign Service Officers and What Befell Them* (New York: Penguin Books, 1976), 184–92; and Robert Griffith, *The Politics of Fear: Joseph R. McCarthy and the Senate* (Amherst: University of Massachusetts Press, 1987), 133–35.

18. Lee Dai-Ming and Choy Jun-ke to Chiang, 30 September 1947, Robert A. Taft Papers, Library of Congress, Washington, DC (hereafter cited as RAT Papers), Box 506.

19. "Summary Report of Vice President Wallace's Visit to China," 10 July 1944, George M. Elsey Papers, Harry S. Truman Library (hereafter cited as Elsey Papers), Box 59, Fol. "Foreign Relations—China."

20. Richard B. Scandrett Jr. to Robert A. Taft, 25 April 1949, RAT Papers, Box 506; and Taft to William J. Kostka, 19 January 1946, Clarence E. Wunderlin, ed., *The Papers of Robert A. Taft, Volume 3: 1945–1948* (Kent: Kent State University Press, 1997), 123.

21. Arthur H. Vandenberg Jr., ed., *The Private Papers of Senator Vandenberg* (Boston: Houghton Mifflin, 1952), 519–45; and Henry P. Fletcher, "China and Bipartisanism," *Human Events*, 14 December 1949 (reprint), 3, RAT Papers, Box 917.

22. Lowell Mellett, "On the Other Hand: Reckless Politics Seen in Attacks by Taft, Dewey on China Policy," 28 February 1948, RAT Papers, Box 506, Fol. "China, 1945–1949."

23. Robert A. Taft, "Speech to Economic Club of Detroit," 23 February 1948, Wunderlin, *Papers of Robert A. Taft*, 3:404.

24. Ibid., 408.

25. Ibid., 409.

26. Robert McCormick's newspaper, the conservative *Chicago Tribune*, prematurely printed

a front page that incorrectly declared Dewey the winner and thus contributed to one of the most indelible images in American political history. "Dewey Defeats Truman," *Chicago Tribune*, 3 November 1948.

27. Transcript of "Meet the Press," 7 January 1949, RAT Papers, Box 911.

28. Davies, *China Hand: An Autobiography*, 291.

29. Vandenberg quoted in Goldman, *Crucial Decade*, 132.

30. Henry P. Fletcher, "China and Bipartisanism," *Human Events*, 14 December 1949, enclosed in Henry P. Fletcher to Robert A. Taft, 27 December 1950, RAT Papers, Box 917.

31. Department of State, "Daily Summary of Opinion Developments," 8 August 1945, 2, Elsey Papers, Box 59, Fol. "Foreign Relations—China."

32. Sen. H. Alexander Smith, "Far Eastern Problems Facing the United States: Report of Visit to the Far East, September and October 1949," released November 1949, pp. 1–2, RAT Papers, Box 912.

33. Ibid., 10.

34. Ibid., 12.

35. Smith to US Senators, 6 December 1949, RAT Papers, Box 912.

36. Vandenberg, *Private Papers of Senator Vandenberg*, 519.

37. Taft to Smith, 19 December 1949, RAT Papers, Box 912.

38. Taft to Lewis Hoskins, 17 January 1950, RAT Papers, Box 917.

39. "Who Lost China!" *Washington Post*, 4 May 1950; and "No Time for Secret Diplomacy," *New Republic*, 16 January 1950 (reprint), Elsey Papers, Box 59, "Foreign Relations—China."

40. Douglas T. Miller and Marion Nowak, *The Fifties: The Way We Really Were* (New York: Doubleday, 1977), 28; and David M. Oshinsky, *A Conspiracy So Immense: The World of Joe McCarthy* (New York: Free Press, 1983), 100–102.

41. Acheson to Dr. I Ridgeway Trimble, 7 April 1959, Dean G. Acheson Papers, Harry S. Truman Library (hereafter cited as Acheson Papers), Box 89, Fol. "Democratic Advisory Council: Foreign Policy Pamphlet #3, 'How To Lose Friends and Influence: Mr. Dulles in a China Shop.'"

42. Dean Acheson, "American Policy Towards China—Statement Before a Joint Senate Committee," 4 June 1951, Acheson Papers, Box 134.

43. William S. Howe, "Memorandum for Senator Lodge and Republican Colleagues in Relation to Far Eastern Situation," pp. 9–10, RAT Papers, Box 727, Fol. "Neutrality—Far East."

44. "Speech of Robert A. Taft of Ohio in the Senate of the United States, January 11, 1950," RAT Papers, Box 296.

45. Ibid.

46. "Meet Your Congress," 22 April 1951, 8.

47. *Dayton Journal-Herald* (*OH*), 30 December 1949.

48. Ibid.

49. "No Political Gain Seen Now by GOP Stand on Formosa Policy," *Washington Evening Star*, 16 January 1950.

50. "Position on Formosa Leaves G.O.P. on 'Limb,'" *New York Times*, 15 January 1950.

51. Douglas MacArthur, "Memorandum on Formosa," 14 June 1950, p. 4, Elsey Papers, Box 59, Fol. "Foreign Relations—China."

52. Armstrong, "Senator Taft and American Foreign Policy," 3–4; and Wunderlin, *Robert A. Taft*, 33–43, 52–61.

53. Taft, *Republican Program*, 42.

54. Ibid., 26.

55. Goldman, *Crucial Decade*, 34.

56. "Address of U.S. Senator Robert A. Taft at Dinner of the Republican State Central Committee, Columbus, OH, July 31, 1947," William F. Knowland Papers, Bancroft Library, UC Berkeley, BANC MSS 75/97 c (hereafter cited as WFK Papers), Carton 269, Fol. "Corr.—Taft, Robert A."

57. The president's power to appoint delegates to the UN was of especial concern. Likewise, the Hiss conviction—and Hiss's presence at the Yalta conference—raised the specter of subversive executive appointees acting without oversight. Robert A. Taft to Lloyd Whitney, 27 March 1948, RAT Papers, Subject Files, Box 896, "1948—Foreign Policy"; and David Halberstam, *The Fifties* (New York: Fawcett Columbine, 1993), 16–17.

58. Koen, *China Lobby in American Politics*, 27–85; Keeley, *China Lobby Man*; and "Speech of Dr. V. K. Wellington Koo at the Luncheon Party Given in his Honor by the Governor of the State of New Jersey at Trenton, NJ, Thursday May 5. 1949" (press release), p. 4, William C. Bullitt Papers, Sterling Memorial Library MS 112, Yale University, Box 46, Fol. "Koo, 1947–1965."

59. "Republicans: Dynasty & Destiny," *Time*, 14 January 1957, 20; and Gayle B. Montgomery and James W. Johnson, *One Step from the White House: The Rise and Fall of Senator William F. Knowland* (Berkeley: University of California Press, 1998), 92.

60. "Address of U.S Senator Robert A. Taft at Dinner of the Republican State Central Committee, Columbus, OH, July 31, 1947," WFK Papers.

61. Herbert Hoover to William F. Knowland, 31 December 1949, WFK Papers, Carton 273, "Corr.—Special: Hoover, Herbert." At the time Douglas MacArthur was in charge of the Supreme Command of Allied Powers and headed the occupation of Japan.

62. Press release. "Bi-partisan Senate Groups Calls White Paper 'Alibi,' Urges More Aid for China," 22 August 1949, WFK Papers, Carton 242, "Corr.—Bridge, Styles (I)."

63. "M/C on Formosa (10/23/1950)," Acheson Papers, Box 77, Fol. "China."

64. Michael Schaller, "Securing the Great Crescent: Occupied Japan and the Origins of Containment in Southeast Asia," *Journal of American History* 69, no. 2 (1982): 392–414.

65. Michael Schaller, *Douglas MacArthur: The Far Eastern General* (New York: Oxford University Press, 1989), 183; and Wunderlin, *Robert A. Taft*, 156.

66. 81 Cong. Rec. 9320 (1950).

67. William Stueck, *Rethinking the Korean War: A New Diplomatic and Strategic History* (Princeton: Princeton University Press, 2002), 97.

68. Schaller, *Douglas MacArthur*, 191.

69. Press release by President Truman Announcing Military Assistance to Indochina, June 27, 1950, *Pentagon Papers, Gravel Edition, Vol. 1* (Boston: Beacon Press, 1971): 372–73; and Richard H. Rovere and Arthur Schlesinger Jr., *The General and the President, and the Future of American Foreign Policy* (New York: Farrar, Straus, and Young, 1951), 126.

70. Rovere and Schlesinger, *The General and the President*, 132–33; and Robert E. Herzstein, *Henry R. Luce, Time, and the American Crusade in Asia* (New York: Cambridge University Press, 2005), 58.

71. "Meet Your Congress," 22 April 1951, 3–4; and Rovere and Schlesinger, *The General and the President*, 169–71, 228–30

72. 81 Cong. Rec. 10823–25 (1950).

73. Stueck, *Rethinking the Korea War*, 119–20.

74. 82 Cong. Rec.—Appendix A420 (1951).

75. Halberstam, *The Fifties*, 56; and Oshinsky, *A Conspiracy So Immense*, 172.

76. Joseph Lang, "Don't Sell Yourself to Become a Slave of Government," enclosed in Paul W. Walter to I. Jack Martin, 25 April 1950, RAT Papers, Box 295.

77. James T. Patterson, *Mr. Republican: A Biography of Robert A. Taft* (Boston: Houghton Mifflin Co., 1972), 469.

78. Patterson, *Mr. Republican*, 477–78; and Schaller, *Douglas MacArthur*, 229.

79. 82 Cong. Rec. 56 (1951).

80. Herzstein, *Henry R. Luce*, 40.

81. 82 Cong. Rec. 60 (1951).

82. Quoted in Geoffrey Perret, *Old Soldiers Never Die: The Life of Douglas MacArthur* (New York: Random House, 1996), 567.

83. "Statement made by Senator William F. Knowland before the Joint Committee on Armed Service and Committee on Foreign Relations inquiring into the military situation in the Far East and the facts surrounding the release of General of the Army, Douglas MacArthur from his assignment on that area on Wednesday, May 16, 1951," p. 4, WFK Papers, Carton 260, "Corr.— MacArthur."

84. Typescript of General Douglas MacArthur, address to Congress, 19 April 1951, 10: http://www.loc.gov/exhibits/treasures/images/340010.jpg (accessed 6 March 2012).

85. Rovere and Schlesinger, *The General and the President*, 176, 191.

86. "Meet Your Congress," 22 April 1951, 12–13.

87. 82 Cong. Rec.—Appendix A2030–31 (1951); 82 Cong. Rec. S4462–76 (1951); and Bernard K. Duffy and Ronald H. Carpenter, *Douglas MacArthur: Warrior as Wordsmith* (Westport: Greenwood Press, 1997), 35.

88. US Senate, Committee on Armed Services and the Committee on Foreign Relations, *Military Situation in the Far East*, 82nd Congress, 1st sess. (May 1951), 42 and 68, excerpted in Lawrence S. Wittner, ed., *MacArthur* (Englewood Cliffs: Prentice-Hall, 1971), 52–53.

89. Ibid.

90. "Meet Your Congress," 22 April 1951, 8.

91. Rovere and Schlesinger, *The General and the President*, 191.

92. Miller and Nowak, *The Fifties*, 30–36; Oshinsky, *A Conspiracy So Immense*, 128–29; Griffith, *Politics of Fear*, 116, and 142–43; Harvey Klehr and Ronald Radosh, *The Amerasia Spy Case: Prelude to McCarthyism* (Chapel Hill: University of North Carolina Press, 1996); Ellen Schrecker, *Many Are the Crimes: McCarthyism in America* (Boston: Little, Brown, 1998); and Michael J. Ybarra, *Washington Gone Crazy: Senator Pat McCarran and the Great American Communist Hunt* (Hanover: Steerforth Press, 2004), 433–84.

93. Sen. Joseph McCarthy, "Speech Before National Convention of Young Republicans," 29 June 1951, RAT Papers, Box 619.

94. Charles F. Carroll to Joseph McCarthy, 17 December 1951, RAT Papers, Box 1064.

95. Truman to Acheson, 31 March 1950, Acheson Papers, Acheson-Truman Correspondence File, 1947–71, Box 161, Fol. "A-T Corr., 1947–52"; and Michael Paul Rogin, *The Intellectuals and McCarthy: The Radical Specter* (Cambridge: MIT Press, 1967).

96. "Tom" to Taft, 26 December 1951, RAT Papers, Box 975.

97. William S. White, *The Taft Story* (New York: Harper, 1954), 87. See also Goldman, *Crucial Decade*, 215; and Halberstam, *The Fifties*, 58.

98. Oshinsky, *A Conspiracy So Immense*, 133, 201–2; and Griffith, *Politics of Fear*, 189, 198.

99. Hoover to Robert A. Taft, 1951, RAT Papers, Box 975.

100. Sen. Robert A. Taft, "Reply to President Truman's Attack on Senate Investigation," 31 March 1950, RAT Papers, Box 917.

101. Taft to Benjamin S. Hubbell Jr., 17 August 1951, RAT Papers, Box 1064.

102. 82 Cong. Rec. 58 (1951).

103. Wunderlin, *Robert A. Taft*, 143.

104. Sen. Robert A. Taft, *A Foreign Policy for Americans* (Garden City: Doubleday, 1951), 5.

105. Taft, *A Foreign Policy*, 102. See also Sen. Robert A. Taft, "Why I Oppose Truman's Foreign Policy" [pamphlet] (Washington, DC: Taft Committee, 1952), 1; and Sen. Robert A. Taft, "A Realistic Defense and Foreign Policy" [pamphlet] (Washington, DC: Taft Committee, 1952), 3.

106. Armstrong, "Senator Taft and American Foreign Policy," 6–7.

107. Taft, *A Foreign Policy*, 84–87.

108. Ibid., 83.

109. Ibid., 89.

110. Ibid., 87.

111. "Can Taft Beat the Democrats?," American Forum of the air broadcast of 28 October 1951, between Sen. Robert Taft and Sen. Brien McMahon, RAT Papers, Box 1286.

112. Taft, *A Foreign Policy*, 111–13.

113. Ibid., 54–58.

114. Ibid., 111–13.

115. Ibid., 113.

116. Taft, *A Foreign Policy*, 75; and Taft, "A Realistic Defense and Foreign Policy," 4–5.

117. Michael J. Hogan, *A Cross of Iron: Harry S. Truman and the Origins of the National Security State, 1945–1954* (New York: Cambridge University Press, 1998), 119–58.

118. Taft, "A Realistic Defense and Foreign Policy," 7.

119. Taft, *A Foreign Policy*, 17, 65–66.

120. Robert A. Taft to Lou Guylay, 5 March 1952, RAT Papers, Box 1419.

121. MacArthur to Taft, 19 November 1951, RAT Papers, Box 1419

122. Arthur M. Schlesinger Jr., "The New Isolationism," *Atlantic* 189, no. 5 (1952): 34–38.

123. W. Reed West, "Senator Taft's Foreign Policy," *Atlantic* 189, no. 6 (1952): 50–52.

124. "Address of Senator Robert A. Taft to the Lincoln Republican Club, Denver, CO," 16 February 1952, RAT Papers, Box 1331; and transcript of 1 June 1952, broadcast by Robert Taft on NBC radio, RAT Papers, Box 1285.

125. Taft, *A Foreign Policy*, 6.

Chapter 2

1. 82 Cong. Rec. 7703 (1951).

2. George Elsey, "Memorandum on China Lobby," 8 June 1951, Theodore Tannenwald Jr. Papers, Box 4, Harry S. Truman Library, Independence.

3. 82 Cong. Rec. 6737–39 (1951); Max Ascoli, "Starting the Job," *The Reporter*, 15 April 1952, 2; Ross Y. Koen, *The China Lobby in American Politics* (New York: Octagon Books, 1973), 29; E. J. Kahn Jr., *The China Hands: America's Foreign Service Officers and What Befell Them* (New York: Penguin Books, 1976), 49; Stanley D. Bachrack, *The Committee of One Million: "China Lobby" Politics, 1953–1971* (New York: Columbia University Press, 1976), 3–9; Nancy Bernkopf Tucker, *Patterns in the Dust: Chinese-American Relations and the Recognition Controversy, 1949–1950* (New York: Columbia University Press, 1983), 80–99; and John Paton Davies Jr., *China Hand: An Autobiography* (Philadelphia: University of Pennsylvania Press, 2012), 293.

4. Koen, *China Lobby in American Politics*, 27–55.

5. Kahn, *China Hands*, 49.

6. Tucker, *Patterns in the Dust*, 75–76, 82–99.

7. Koen, *China Lobby in American Politics*, 29.

8. Warren I. Cohen, "Who's Afraid of Alfred Kohlberg?," *Reviews in American History* 3, no. 1 (1975): 119–20; *Oral History Interview with John S. Service*, 112–13; Bachrack, *Committee of One Million*, 167–72; and Nancy Bernkopf Tucker, *The China Threat: Memories, Myths, Realities in the 1950s* (New York: Columbia University Press, 2012), 168.

9. For examples, see Gordon H. Chang, *Friends and Enemies: The United States, China, and the Soviet Union, 1948–1972* (Stanford: Stanford University Press, 1990), 24; and Tucker, *China Threat*, 44, 57.

10. Robert E. Herzstein, *Henry R. Luce, Time, and the American Crusade in Asia* (New York: Cambridge University Press, 2005), 26.

11. Eric Hodgins quoted in T. Christopher Jespersen, *American Images of China, 1931–1949* (Stanford: Stanford University Press, 1999), 131.

12. *Time*, 3 January 1938, cover.

13. Jespersen, *American Images of China*, 131, 221.

14. Alan Brinkley, *The Publisher: Henry Luce and His American Century* (New York: Vintage Books, 2010), 335–37; and Patricia Neils, *China Images in the Life and Times of Henry Luce* (New York: Rowman & Littlefield, 1990), 153–217.

15. Lee Edwards, *Missionary For Freedom: The Life and Times of Walter Judd* (New York: Paragon House, 1990), 69–71.

16. Bachrack, *Committee of One Million*, 12–13

17. Rep. Walter H. Judd, *What is the Truth About China?: Speech of the Hon. Walter H. Judd of Minnesota in the House of Representatives, March 15, 1945* (Washington, DC: US Government Printing Office, 1945), Alfred Kohlberg Papers, Hoover Institution Archives, Stanford University (hereafter cited as Kohlberg Papers), Box 100.

18. Edwards, *Missionary For Freedom*, 112.

19. Michael Schaller, *The United States and China: Into the Twenty-First Century* (New York: Oxford University Press, 2002), 113; Bachrack, *Committee of One Million*, 37–38; and H. Bradford Westerfield, *Foreign Policy and Party Politics: Pearl Harbor to Korea* (New Haven: Yale University Press, 1955), 260.

20. Davies, *China Hand: An Autobiography*, 294.

21. *Oral History Interview with Dr. Walter H. Judd, conducted by Jerry N. Hess on 13 April 1970 in Washington, D.C.*, Harry S. Truman Library, Independence, 40. See also Ena Chao, "The China Bloc: Congress and the Making of Foreign Policy, 1947–1952" (PhD diss., University of North Carolina, 1992).

22. Edwards, *Missionary For Freedom*, 208.

23. *Oral History Interview with Dr. Walter H. Judd*, 44.

24. Schaller, *United States and China*, 113.

25. In 1970 Judd said, "I don't know except that doubtless people in the State Department gave him [Truman] the line that Judd's an old China hand, he's 'emotional' about Asia, he's a partisan of Chiang Kai-shek, he's an Asia-firster. These are the standard smears, or labels, which are used as substitutes for thought," in *Oral History Interview with Dr. Walter H. Judd*, 62. See also Kai Chung Kenneth Yung, "Personal Sympathy and National Interests: The Formation and Evolution of Congressman Walter H. Judd's Anti-Communism, 1925–1963" (MA thesis, University of Hong Kong, 2007).

26. *New York Post*, 15 July 1951; US Department of Commerce, "Alfred Kohlberg, Inc.," Harry S. Truman Papers, President's Secretary's Files, Box 139, Harry S. Truman Library; "The China Lobby: A Case Study," *Congressional Quarterly* 9, no. 25-A (1951): 939–40; and Kahn, *China Hands*, 49.

27. Alan Raucher, "The First Foreign Affairs Think Tanks," *American Quarterly* 30, no. 4 (1978): 496.

28. Alfred Kohlberg to IPR Trustees et al., 13 August 1945, Harold Joyce Noble Papers, Bancroft Library, UC Berkeley, BANC MSS Z-Z 147 (hereafter cited as Noble Papers), Box 1, Fol. 2. See also Statement from American Council, 19 December 1944, Noble Papers, Box 1, Fol. 1; and Raucher, "The First Foreign Affairs Think Tanks," 507.

29. Accounts of Kohlberg's conflict with the IPR differ. For a sympathetic perspective, see Joseph Keeley, *The China Lobby Man: The Story of Alfred Kohlberg* (New Rochelle: Arlington House, 1969), 79–94. For more critical analyses, see Koen, *China Lobby in American Politics*, 134–39; John N. Thomas, *The Institute of Pacific Relations: Asian Scholars and American Politics* (Seattle: University of Washington Press, 1974), 36–64; and Griffith, *Politics of Fear*, 123.

30. *Los Angeles Times*, 23 February 1951; Griffith, *Politics of Fear*, 64–65; David M. Oshinsky, *A Conspiracy So Immense: The World of Joe McCarthy* (New York: Free Press, 1983), 117–19; and Robert P. Newman, *Owen Lattimore and the "Loss" of China* (Berkeley: University of California Press, 1992), 142–43, 214, 219, 223.

31. Quoted in Keeley, *China Lobby Man*, 22.

32. Keeley, *China Lobby Man*, 24. See also Charles Wertenbaker, "The World of Alfred Kohlberg," *The Reporter*, 29 April 1952, 19–20.

33. Keeley, *China Lobby Man*, 37.

34. Wertenbaker, "World of Alfred Kohlberg," 20.

35. Committee for a Free Asia, Inc., "Questions and Answers" (San Francisco), Kohlberg Papers, Box 37.

36. Rep. Walter H. Judd, "What Should United States Policy in China Be?," 6 February 1950, Kohlberg Papers, Box 100.

37. Christina Klein, *Cold War Orientalism: Asia in the Middlebrow Imagination, 1945–1961* (Berkeley: University of California Press, 2003), 19–60.

38. *Oral History Interview with Dr. Walter H. Judd*, 23.

39. The Open Door Policy was mainly a rhetorical device and enforced by neither US foreign policy nor armed forces. Tang Tsou, *America's Failure in China* (Chicago: University of Chicago Press, 1963), 3–30.

40. Anthony Kubeck, *How the Far East Was Lost: American Policy and the Creation of Communist China, 1941–1948* (Chicago: Henry Regnery, 1963).

41. *How the Far East Was Lost: American Policy and the Creation of Communist China, 1941–1948*, review by F. C. Jones, *Pacific Affairs* 37, no. 2 (1964): 199.

42. Harold R. Isaacs, *Scratches on Our Minds: American Images of China and India* (Armonk: M. E. Sharpe, 1980), 67–70, 124–64; Jonathan Spence, *To Change China: Western Advisors in China, 1620–1960* (Boston: Little, Brown, 1969), 290–93; and Jespersen, *American Images of China*, 4–10, 172–82.

43. Henry R. Luce, "The American Century," *Life*, 17 February 1941, 61.

44. Ibid., 65.

45. *Oral History Interview with Dr. Walter H. Judd*, 13–21.

46. Ibid., 23.

47. Alfred Kohlberg, "The Monroe Doctrine: Hemispheric Defense Against Old World Aggression" (manuscript), Kohlberg Papers, Box 126; and Kohlberg to Herbert Brownell Jr., 28 June 1944, Kohlberg Papers, Box 53.

48. Dr. J. W. Decker, "China's Unity At Stake," *Christian Century*, 8 August 1945, 905, Kohlberg Papers, Box 94.

49. Judd, "What Should . . ."; "A Reprint of the Foreword to *Way of a Fighter, the Memories of Claire Lee Chennault, Major General, U.S.A. (Raet.) with Two Maps*" (New York: G. P. Putnam's Sons, 1949), Kohlberg Papers, Box 28.

50. Asia Firsters might have been chagrined to know that in 1944, Henry Wallace had also followed this "moral" line of reasoning regarding China's fate. The only difference between his rhetoric and theirs was the time frame. See Henry A. Wallace, *Our Job in the Pacific*, IPR Pamphlets No. 2 (New York: American Council, Institute of Pacific Relations, 1944), Huntington Library and Archives (call no. 445344).

51. Theodore H. White and Annalee Jacoby, *Thunder Out of China* (New York: William Slone Associates, 1946), 118-31; Sterling Seagrave, *The Soong Dynasty* (New York: Harper & Row, 1985), 390; and Barbara W. Tuchman, *Stilwell and the American Experience in China* (New York: Grove Press, 2001), 301-509.

52. Chiang abandoned Chen Jieru (also known as "Jennie") for Soong Mei-ling, denying the legality of their marriage and classifying her as a mere concubine. He was justifiably afraid of what her memoirs would have to say. Jonathan Fenby, *Chiang Kai-shek: China's Generalissimo and the Nation He Lost* (New York: Carroll & Graf Publishers, 2004), 45.

53. Alfred Kohlberg, "The Soviet-Chinese Pact," *China Monthly* (November 1945), Kohlberg Papers, Box 114; and Walter H. Judd, "Remarks on the State Department's White Paper" (1949), Kohlberg Papers, Box 100.

54. "Chiang's Own Plan: An Interview with Chiang Kai-shek," *U.S. News & World Report*, 15 December 1950, 17.

55. *State Department Duty in China, the McCarthy Era, and After, 1933-1977: Oral History Transcript / John Stewart Service; tape-recorded interview conducted in 1977-1978 by Rosemary Levenson for the Regional Oral History Office The Bancroft Library, University of California, Berkeley, California, 1981*, 225, BANC MSS 82/106 c.

56. Fenby, *Chiang Kai-shek*, 321; and Peter Gue Zarrow, *China in War and Revolution, 1895-1949* (New York: Routledge, 2005), 255-70.

57. Emily Hahn, *The Soong Sisters* (New York: Doubleday, Doran, 1941), 91-95; and Seagrave, *Soong Dynasty*, 139-41.

58. Fenby, *Chiang Kai-shek*, 321, 327-28; and Davies, *China Hand: An Autobiography*, 96.

59. Dewey quoted in Harry Thomas, *The First Lady of China: The Historic Wartime Visit of Mme. Chiang Kai-Shek to the United States in 1943* (New York: International Business Machines Corporation, 1943), Huntington Library and Archives (call no. 499084).

60. Fenby, *Chiang Kai-shek*, 327-28; Jespersen, *American Images of China*, 82-107; and Shirley Jennifer Lim, *A Feeling of Belonging: Asian American Women's Public Culture, 1930-1960* (New York: New York University Press, 2006), 82.

61. Mme Chiang, "The Power of Prayer," *Readers Digest*, August 1955, 57-58.

62. Frederic Wakeman Jr., "A Revisionist View of the Nanjing Decade: Confucian Fascism," *The China Quarterly*, no. 150, Special Issue: Reappraising Republican China (June 1997): 395-432; Chung Dooeum, *Elitist Fascism: Chiang Kai-shek's Blueshirts in 1930s China* (Burlington: Ashgate, 2000); Frederic Wakeman Jr., *Spymaster: Dai Li and the Chinese Secret Service* (Berkeley: University of California Press, 2003); and Margherita Zanasi, *Saving the Nation: Economic Modernity in Republican China* (Chicago: University of Chicago Press, 2006).

63. Seagrave, *Soong Dynasty*, 376-77, 384-91; and Karen J. Leong, *The China Mystique: Pearl S. Buck, Anna May Wong, Mayling Soong, and the Transformation of American Orientalism* (Berkeley: University of California Press, 2005), 106-154.

64. Westerfield, *Foreign Policy and Party Politics*, 264-66; Walter LaFeber, *The American*

Age: US Foreign Policy at Home and Abroad, Vol. 2 (New York: W. W. Norton, 1994), 279; and Ernest R. May, "1947–48: When Marshall Kept the U.S. Out of War in China," *Journal of Military History* 66, no. 4 (2002): 1003–10.

65. *Foreign Relations of the United States 1943: China* (Washington, DC: Government Printing Office, 1957), 769–87.

66. *New York Times*, 11 July 1958.

67. Philip Horton, "The China Lobby, Part II: VI. The Inner Circle," *The Reporter*, 29 April 1952, 5–7; and Koen, *China Lobby in American Politics*, 35.

68. Herzstein, *Henry R. Luce*, 79.

69. Kohlberg to Koo, 31 October 1949, Kohlberg Papers, Box 104.

70. Kohlberg to Koo, 29 December 1950 and 2 January 1952, Kohlberg Papers, Box 104.

71. Kohlberg to Mme Chiang, 27 November 1951, Kohlberg Papers, Box 28.

72. Kohlberg to Mme Chiang, 28 December 1959, Kohlberg Papers, Box 28.

73. Kohlberg to Mme Chiang, 13 December 1946, Kohlberg Papers, Box 28.

74. His biographer wrote that the mission on behalf of American Bureau for Medical Aid to China marked the beginning of Kohlberg's suspicions regarding US foreign policy on China; Keeley, *China Lobby Man*, 54–71. See also *Oral History Interview with John S. Service*, 195.

75. Bob Considine, "Chiang and the Chinese Puzzle," *Cosmopolitan*, October 1945, 26–27, 143–47, Kohlberg Papers, Box 28.

76. Colleen Lye, *America's Asia: Racial Form and American Literature, 1893–1945* (Princeton: Princeton University Press, 2005), 204–6, 240; and Leong, *China Mystique*, 12–56.

77. Buck to Kohlberg, 27 January 1945, Kohlberg Papers, Box 21.

78. Kohlberg to Buck, 30 April 1946, Kohlberg Papers, Box 21.

79. Buck to Kohlberg, 28 March 1947, Kohlberg Papers, Box 21.

80. Keeley, *China Lobby Man*, 233.

81. Mme Chiang to Kohlberg, 5 May 1947, Kohlberg Papers, Box 28.

82. Acheson to Kohlberg, 31 July 1946, Noble Papers, Box 1, Fol. 3.

83. Kohlberg to Chiang, 22 August 1949, Kohlberg Papers, Box 28.

84. Rep. Clare Boothe Luce to John B. Powell, 3 June 1946, Kohlberg Papers, Box 114; Alfred Kohlberg to Clare Boothe Luce, 4 June 1947, Kohlberg Papers, Box 114; and American China Policy Association, "Statement of Mrs. Clare Boothe Luce on her election as President of the American China Policy Association, Inc.," 23 October 1947, Kohlberg Papers, Box 114.

85. American China Policy Assoc., Inc., to Chairman of Resolutions Committee c/o National Democratic Committee, 12 June 1948, Kohlberg Papers, Box 53.

86. Judd to Kohlberg, 12 August 1948, Kohlberg Papers, Box 100.

87. Kohlberg to Judd, 1 October 1957, Kohlberg Papers, Box 100.

88. "Dewey's Talk Demanding US Help to China to Combat Communists," *New York Times*, 25 November 1947; transcript of speech given by Thomas Dewey on 12 February 1948, Kohlberg Papers, Box 53; transcript of speech given by Thomas Dewey on 1 April 1948, Kohlberg Papers, Box 53; and Robert Divine, *Foreign Policy and U.S. Presidential Elections, Vol. 1: 1940–1948* (New York: New Viewpoints, 1974), 223.

89. Kohlberg to Herbert Brownell, 6 July 1948, Kohlberg Papers, Box 53 (original emphasis).

90. Alfred Kohlberg, "Memorandum for 1949," 4, Kohlberg Papers, Box 53.

91. Alfred Kohlberg to Thomas Dewey, 26 March 1947, Kohlberg Papers, Box 53; and "The Truman-Wallace Red Pacific Versus the Open Door, Kohlberg Papers, Box 53, Fol. "Dewey Special Committee 1948 & Campaign Folder."

92. Kohlberg to Thomas Dewey, 9 February 1949, Kohlberg Papers, Box 53.

93. Divine, *Foreign Policy and Presidential Elections*, 189–90.

94. Kohlberg to Thomas Dewey, 17 March 1947, and Kohlberg to Arthur H. Vandenberg, 25 November 1947, Kohlberg Papers, Box 193; Kohlberg to Clare Boothe Luce, 19 November 1949, Kohlberg Papers, Box 114; and Kohlberg, "Does the Republican Party Contemplate Suicide?," 3 March 1950, Kohlberg Papers, Box 148.

95. Kohlberg to Joseph W. Martin Jr., 15 February 1951, Kohlberg Papers, Box 119; Kohlberg open letter to ACPA associates, 25 January 1950 and Kohlberg to Robert A. Taft, 17 May 1950, Kohlberg Papers, Box 169; and Kohlberg to Richard Nixon, 8 August 1950, Kohlberg Papers, Box, 136.

96. Jean Pegram to Kohlberg, 27 May 1950, Kohlberg Papers, Box 145; and Program for 28 January 1954 luncheon of New Jersey chapter, Kohlberg Papers, Box 145.

97. For representative examples of this correspondence, see Charles E. Scott [form letter], 30 March 1947, Kohlberg Papers, Box 126; Carol and Horace Dewey to "Friends," 18 June 1947, Kohlberg Papers, Box 126; "People's Court Dispenses Mock Justice," 20 February 1948 (bulletin from Jesuit Missions), Kohlberg Papers, Box 126; and Frank W. Rice to "Friends Across the Pacific," 23 September 1949, Kohlberg Papers, Box 145.

98. William H. Anderson to Kohlberg, 4 February 1947, Kohlberg Papers, Box 7; and Verne P. Kaub to Kohlberg, 20 July 1955, Kohlberg Papers, Box 7.

99. For an example, see Kohlberg to Walter Judd, 3 December 1948, Kohlberg Papers, Box 100.

100. Enclosure in William H. Anderson to Kohlberg, 17 August 1947, Kohlberg Papers, Box 7.

101. Frank T. Cartwright, "To Missionaries from China and to Chinese Christians now in the USA," 24 March 1949 (speech made before the Executive Committee of Board of Missions and Church Extension), enclosed in Frank T. Cartwright to Kohlberg, 31 March 1949, Kohlberg Papers, Box 33; J. W. Decker to Kohlberg, 3 June 1949, Kohlberg Papers, Box 94; and Kohlberg to Frank T. Cartwright and J. W. Decker, 15 June 1949, Kohlberg Papers, Box 94.

102. Kohlberg to Luce, 18 June 1945, Kohlberg Papers, Box 114; Kohlberg to Luce, 3 February 1948, Kohlberg Papers, Box 114; Luce to Kohlberg, 31 October 1951, Kohlberg Papers, Box 114; and Kohlberg to Luce, 13 November 1951, Kohlberg Papers, Box 114.

103. Kohlberg to Judd, 5 September 1955, Kohlberg Papers, Box 100; Judd to Kohlberg, 23 September 1955, Kohlberg Papers, Box 100; and Kohlberg to Judd, 27 September 1955, Kohlberg Papers, Box 100.

104. Kohlberg to Raymond Gram Swing, 31 July 1955, Noble Papers, Box 1, Fol. 2; and Cole, *America First*, 131–54. For a fictional narrative of the American Jewish perspective on Lindbergh, see Philip Roth, *The Plot Against America* (Boston: Houghton Mifflin, 2004).

105. Kohlberg to Hoover, 3 May 1950, Kohlberg Papers, Box 86; Keeley, *China Lobby Man*, 98–99.

106. Koen, *China Lobby in American Politics*, 221–29.

107. Kohlberg to Henry R. Luce, 13 November 1951, Kohlberg Papers, Box 114.

108. Koen, *China Lobby in American Politics*, 132–59, 195–211; Kahn, *China Hands*, 244–85; Newman, *Owen Lattimore*, 123–50, 207–86, 314–81, 472–94; and Ybarra, *Washington Gone Crazy*, 369–605.

109. Ernest R. May, "The China Hands in Perspective," in Paul Gordon Lauren, ed., *The China Hands' Legacy: Ethics and Diplomacy* (Boulder: Westview Press, 1987), 97–123.

110. Thomas, *Institute of Pacific Relations*, 49.

111. Kohlberg to Walter H. Judd, 29 April 1953, Kohlberg Papers, Box 100; "Speech of Alfred

Kohlberg, Nationalist Chairman, American Jewish League Against Communism, Inc., at dinner honoring Roy M. Cohn, Grand Ballroom, Hotel Astor, 28 July 1954, William F. Knowland Papers, Bancroft Library, UC Berkeley, BANC MSS 75/97 c (hereafter cited as WFK Papers), Carton 273, "Corr.—Special, "Kohlberg, Alfred, 1954."

112. For examples, see "The China Lobby: A Case Study," *Congressional Quarterly; New York Times*, 29 April 1952.

113. The pertinent excerpts from *The Reporter* are 15 April and 29 April 1952.

114. Charles Wertenbaker, "Voices in the Wilderness," *The Reporter*, 15 April 1952, 13.

115. Wertenbaker, "World of Alfred Kohlberg," 19–22.

116. Charles Wertenbaker, "The Legacy of T.V. Soong," *The Reporter*, 15 April 1952, 4–5.

117. Kathleen J. Frydl, *The Drug Wars in America, 1940–1973* (Cambridge: Cambridge University Press, 2013), 64.

118. Roger H. Davidson, "The Advent of the Modern Congress: The Legislative Reorganization Act of 1946," *Legislative Studies Quarterly* 15, no. 3 (1990): 363–65.

119. 82 Cong. Rec. 6736–37, 6770–87, 6795–804 (1952).

120. Alfred Kohlberg, "My China Lobby" [article submission to *American Mercury*, c. May 1952], Kohlberg Papers, Box 10; and Alfred Kohlberg, "I Am the China Lobby," *Facts Forum News*, May 1955, 22.

121. Kohlberg to *American Mercury* editors, 27 July 1953, Kohlberg Papers, Box 10.

122. Kohlberg Papers, Box 104; and Bachrack, *Committee of One Million*, 167–72.

123. William F. Buckley Jr., foreword to Keeley, *China Lobby Man*, xvii.

124. Rosemary Foot, *The Practice of Power: US Relations with China since 1949* (New York: Oxford University Press, 1995), 88.

125. Press release of address made by Rep. Joseph Martin at Lincoln Day Dinner of the Kings County Republican Committee, Brooklyn, 12 February 1951, Kohlberg Papers, Box 119.

126. The sheer volume of his personal correspondence is impressive. The collection of letters, memos, and handwritten notes fills 207 file boxes at the Hoover Institution Archives, Stanford University.

127. Buckley, foreword to Keeley, *China Lobby Man*, xvii.

128. Harold K. Thompson to *American Mercury* editors, 1 October 1953, Kohlberg Papers, Box 10.

129. H. L. Keenleyside to Kohlberg, 8 August 1949, Kohlberg Papers, Box 120. Kohlberg was not one to forget a snub. Two years later, he suggested that Sen. McCarran investigate Keenleyside's background and connection to Owen Lattimore. Kohlberg to Patrick McCarran, 18 October 1951, Kohlberg Papers, Box 120.

130. Keeley, *China Lobby Man*, 120.

131. Kohlberg to Herrymon Maurer, 4 June 1952, Kohlberg Papers, Box 120.

132. Bachrack, *Committee of One Million*, 32.

133. "Plain Talk," Gordon Hall and Grace Hoag Collection of Dissenting and Extremist Printed Propaganda, John Hay Library, Brown University, MS 76.23 (hereafter cited as Hall-Hoag Coll.).

134. Regnery to the editor of *Publishers' Weekly*, 19 February 1951, Kohlberg Papers, Box 148; and enclosure in Henry Regnery to Alfred Kohlberg, 2 March 1951, Kohlberg Papers, Box 148.

135. Regnery to Kohlberg, 19 September 1949, Kohlberg Papers, Box 147; and Regnery to Kohlberg, 13 March 1951, Kohlberg Papers, Box 147.

136. Regnery to Kohlberg, 2 March 1951, Kohlberg Papers, Box 147.

137. Kohlberg to Regnery, 20 March 1955, Kohlberg Papers, Box 147.

138. Kohlberg to Regnery, 20 March 1955, Kohlberg Papers, Box 147; and Regnery to Kohlberg, 27 September 1955, Kohlberg Papers, Box 147.

139. Kohlberg Papers, Box 86, Fol. "Hoover, Herbert."

140. Kohlberg to McCarran, 29 August 1952, Kohlberg Papers, Box 120.

141. William F. Buckley Jr., draft prospectus for "National Weekly" (c. August 1954), 1–5, Kohlberg Papers, Box 21 (original emphasis).

142. Buckley to Kohlberg, 7 December 1954, William F. Buckley Papers, Yale University Manuscripts and Archives, MS 576 (hereafter cited as Buckley Papers), Part I, Box 3; Buckley to Kohlberg, 14 April 1955, Buckley Papers, Part I, Box 3; and Kohlberg to Buckley, 26 April 1955, Buckley Papers, Part I, Box 3.

143. Kohlberg corresponded with Buckley and the National Review staff from 1955 to 1959, shortly before his death; Kohlberg Papers, Box 132.

144. William F. Buckley Jr., "Remarks at Testimonial Dinner for Alfred Kohlberg, Waldorf-Astoria Hotel, July 26, 1960," Kohlberg Papers, Box 21; and Keeley, China Lobby Man, xi–xx, 270. Buckley also served as a member of the Alfred Kohlberg Memorial Fund. See Marvin Liebman to staff and associates, memo, January 1961, Buckley Papers, Part I, Box 15.

145. See Kohlberg Papers, Box 169, Fol. "Taft, Robert A., Fol. 1 (1946–1951)."

146. "The Directors of this Association represent all American political views. The Association therefore cannot even by implication seem to take a partisan point of view politically." Helen Loomis (ACPA Secretary) to Directors of the ACPA, 5 December 1947, Kohlberg Papers, Box 53.

147. Kohlberg to J. W. Decker, 8 June 1949, Kohlberg Papers, Box 94.

148. Kohlberg to Thomas Dewey, 26 March 1947, Kohlberg Papers, Box 53.

149. Kohlberg to Martin, 15 February 1951, Kohlberg Papers, Box 119.

150. Kohlberg to Taft, 4 May 1951, Kohlberg Papers, Box 169.

151. Kohlberg to Hoover, 24 November 1950, Kohlberg Papers, Box 86.

152. "What Is Taft's Foreign Policy?" Plain Talk, April 1948; Radio Reports, Inc., broadcast excerpt of "Capitol Cloakroom," 3 July 1951; Robert A. Taft to Kohlberg, 5 November 1951, Kohlberg Papers, Box 169.

153. V. O. Key, Politics, Parties, and Pressure Groups (New York: Thomas Y. Crowell, 1952), 174.

Chapter 3

1. Kohlberg to MacArthur, 11 April 1951, Alfred Kohlberg Papers, Hoover Institution Archives, Stanford University (hereafter cited as Kohlberg Papers), Box 116.

2. Kohlberg to Nixon, 14 July 1952, Kohlberg Papers, Box 136; and Kohlberg to Nixon, 12 August 1952, Kohlberg Papers, Box 136.

3. Robert Taft, "Confidential: Memorandum on General Eisenhower" (1952), Robert A. Taft Papers, Library of Congress, Washington, DC (hereafter cited as RAT Papers), Box 1286.

4. Eisenhower to Taft, 18 March 1953, RAT Papers, Box 1286.

5. Kevin P. Phillips, The Emerging Republican Majority (New Rochelle: Arlington House, 1969), 412.

6. Marilynn S. Johnson, The Second Gold Rush: Oakland and the East Bay in World War II (Berkeley: University of California Press, 1996), 210; Phillips, Emerging Republican Majority, 443–44; Lisa McGirr, Suburban Warriors: The Origins of the New American Right (Princeton: Princeton University Press, 2001), 26–29; Matthew D. Lassiter, The Silent Majority: Suburban Politics in the Sunbelt South (Princeton: Princeton University Press, 2006), 10–11; and Eliza-

beth Tandy Chermer, "Sunbelt Boosterism: Industrial Recruitment, Economic Development, and Growth Politics in the Developing Sunbelt," in *Sunbelt Rising, The Politics of Place, Space and Region*, ed. Michelle Nickerson and Darren Dochuk (Philadelphia: University of Pennsylvania Press, 2011), 31–57.

7. Anonymous to William F. Knowland, 12 May 1949, William F. Knowland Papers, Bancroft Library, UC Berkeley, BANC MSS 75/97 c (hereafter cited as WFK Papers), Carton 272; Donald A. Armstrong to William F. Knowland, 16 July 1949, WFK Papers, Carton 272; Ed A. Borden to William F. Knowland, 21 November 1950, WFK Papers, Carton 272.

8. *World Affairs Council Bulletin of Northern California: China Conference Issue*, Vol. 4, No. 1 (January 1950), WFK Papers, Carton 277, Fol. "W.—Misc."

9. "What Should Be Our Policy in China?" *The American Forum of the Air*, 5 August 1949, 10, WFK Papers, Carton 299.

10. Estelle Knowland Johnson, "My Father as Senator, Campaigner, and Civic Leader" (interview by Ruth Teiser, 1979), in *Remembering William F. Knowland (1981)*, Regional Oral History Office, Bancroft Library, UC Berkeley, Governmental History Documental Project: Goodwin Knight/Edmund Brown Sr. Era.

11. Knowland served in the California State Legislature from 1933 to 1939; he was drafted into the Army in 1942 and served in the military until his special appointment to the US Senate in 1945. Gov. Earl Warren (an old family friend) selected the young war veteran to fill Hiram Johnson's seat.

12. Gayle B. Montgomery and James W. Johnson, *One Step from the White House: The Rise and Fall of Senator William F. Knowland* (Berkeley: University of California Press, 1998), 92–93.

13. Senator William F. Knowland, "The United States Should *Not* Recognize Communist China," *Journal of International Affairs* 11, no. 2 (1957): 168.

14. Hafner to William F. Knowland, 13 January 1950, WFK Papers, Carton 272, Fol. "Corr.—Special 'Ha-Hi.'"

15. Lippmann to Knowland, 21 September 1951, WFK Papers, Carton 272, Fol. "Corr.—Special "J-Li."

16. "The Knowland Story: Interview with Senator William F. Knowland," *U.S. News & World Report*, 24 December 1954, 36–37.

17. "Where Light Is Also Needed," *St. Louis Post-Dispatch*, May 3, 1951, Files of David D. Lloyd, Truman Presidential Library, Box 1, Fol. "China Lobby I"; *The Reporter*, April 15, 1952; *The Reporter*, April 29, 1952; and Kohlberg to Sen. Wayne Morse, 11 June 1951, WFK Papers, Carton 73, Fol. 3.

18. Montgomery and Johnson, *One Step from the White House*, 91.

19. Ibid., 87–88.

20. Nancy Bernkopf Tucker, *China Threat: Memories, Myths, and Realities in the 1950s* (New York: Columbia University Press, 2012), 164.

21. Alfred Kohlberg to Joseph P. McCarthy, 6 June 1950, WFK Papers, Carton 273, Fol. 1.

22. Keep to Knowland, 18 May 1951, WFK Papers, Carton 274, Fol. "MacArthur—Corr., Special, K-Mh."

23. Keep to Knowland, 21 May 1951, Fol. 4, WFK Papers, Carton 275.

24. Joseph Knowland to William F. Knowland, 11 April 1951, WFK Papers, Carton 275, Fol. 4.

25. Estelle Knowland Johnson, "My Father as Senator, Campaigner, and Civic Leader," 15; Montgomery and Johnson, *One Step from the White House*, 85.

26. "Welcome to Senator Knowland," *The Voice of Free China*, Press Opinion No. 714, CEC, 6 September 1953, WFK Papers, Carton 278.

27. Sen. H. Alexander Smith, "Far Eastern Problems Facing the United States: Report of visit to the Far East, September and October 1949," WFK Papers, Carton 273, Fol. "Kohlberg, Alfred (Sept. 1950-Dec. 1950)"; and Smith to Knowland, 17 May 1950, WFK Papers, Carton 273, Fol. "Kohlberg, Alfred (Sept. 1950-Dec. 1950)."

28. Choy to William F. Knowland, 9 April 1950, WFK Papers, Carton 273, Fol. "Newspapers, Chinese (in America)."

29. H. Kenaston Twitchell and Basil R. Entwhistle, "Report on Formosa," enclosed in H. Alexander Smith to William F. Knowland, 17 May 1950, WFK Papers, Carton 274, Fol. "Corr.—Special, 'Smith, H. Alexander.'" Both Smith and Knowland praised the report, and Knowland forwarded it to Herbert Hoover on 29 May 1950 and to CIA Director R. H. Hillenkoetter on 2 June 1950.

30. Anonymous, "Personal Observations on My Recent Trip to the East," WFK Papers, Carton 276, Fol. "Misc.—Knowland, Far East Trip" (I).

31. William F. Knowland, speech before GOP National Convention, 19 January 1952, 82 Cong. Rec.—Appendix A377–A380 (1952), WFK Papers, Carton 299.

32. William F. Knowland, Senator Knowland speech [sound recording], 21 August 1951, Bancroft Library, UC Berkeley, BANC CD 511.

33. Ibid.

34. Ibid.

35. McIntyre Faries, "California Republicans, 1934–1953," oral history interview by Amelia R. Fry and Elizabeth Kerby (Regional Oral History Office, Bancroft Library, UC Berkeley, 1973), 144.

36. William S. White, *The Taft Story* (New York: Harper, 1954), 259.

37. Because Taft was too ill to appear in person, his son read the speech in his stead. "Address by Robert A. Taft Before the National Council of Christians and Hews at Cincinnati, Ohio, May 26, 1953," Kohlberg Papers, Box 169.

38. There were two vacant seats, forty-seven Democrats, forty-six Republicans, and one independent (Wayne Morse of Oregon, who voted for Knowland's leadership). Montgomery and Johnson, *One Step from the White House*, 135.

39. Robert Caro, *The Years of Lyndon Johnson: Master of the Senate* (New York: Alfred A. Knopf, 2002); and Robert Dallek, *Lone Star Rising: Lyndon Johnson and His Times, 1908–1960* (New York: Oxford University Press, 1991), 351–592.

40. William F. Knowland, speech before Republican National Convention, 20 August 1956, WFK Papers, Carton 299.

41. Robert Welch, "Mr. Republican II: A Short Biography of Senator Knowland," *One Man's Opinion* 1, no. 2 (1956): 6.

42. Knowland, speech before Republican National Convention, 1956.

43. Stephen Shadegg, *Freedom Is in His Flight Plan* (New York: Fleet Publishing, 1962), 270; and Lee Edwards, *The Conservative Revolution* (New York: Free Press, 1999), 94.

44. Phillip A. Grant, "The Bricker Amendment Controversy," *Presidential Studies Quarterly* 15, no. 3 (1985): 572.

45. 82 Cong. Rec. 908 (1952); John W. Bricker to William F. Knowland, 18 February 1953, WFK Papers, Carton 242, Fol. "Bricker, John W."; John B. Whitton and J. Edward Fowler, "Bricker Amendment—Fallacies and Dangers," *American Journal of International Law* 48, no. 1 (1954): 24; Arthur H. Dean, "The Bricker Amendment and Authority over Foreign Affairs," *Foreign Affairs*, 32, no. 1 (1953): 2; and Mary L. Dudziak, "Brown as a Cold War Case," *Journal of American History* 91, no. 1 (2004): 33, 3n.

46. Duane Tananbaum, *The Bricker Amendment Controversy: A Test of Eisenhower's Political Leadership* (Ithaca: Cornell University Press, 1988), 49–53.

47. "Amending the Constitution to Prevent Abuse of the Treaty-Making Power: Statement of Senator John W. Bricker on the Floor of the United States Senate, March 13, 1953" (press release), p. 1, WFK Papers, Carton 242, Fol. "Bricker, John W."

48. "Amending the Constitution," 17; and Tananbaum, *Bricker Amendment Controversy*, 23.

49. Eric F. Goldman, *The Crucial Decade—And After: America, 1945–1960* (New York: Vintage, 1960), 258; and Cathal J. Nolan, "The Last Hurrah of Conservative Isolationism: Eisenhower, Congress, and the Bricker Amendment," *Presidential Studies Quarterly* 22, no. 2 (1992): 337–49.

50. Phillip A. Grant, "The Bricker Amendment Controversy," *Presidential Studies Quarterly* 15, no. 4 (1985): 574; and Tananbaum, *Bricker Amendment Controversy*, 80–94, 141–44.

51. "Ike Doesn't Want A Rubber-Stamp Congress," *U.S. News & World Report*, 24 July 1953 (reprint), *Congressional Report* 99, no. 12 (1953): A4528.

52. Tananbaum, *Bricker Amendment Controversy*, 179–81.

53. Dean, "Bricker Amendment and Authority over Foreign Affairs," 2; and Tananbaum, *Bricker Amendment Controversy*, 98, 109.

54. "Ike Doesn't Want A Rubber-Stamp Congress," A4529.

55. "Text of Knowland Talk on Policy Review," *New York Times*, 16 November 1954, Dean G. Acheson Papers, Harry S. Truman Library, Independence, Box 86, Fol. "Davies, John."

56. David M. Oshinsky, *A Conspiracy So Immense: The World of Joe McCarthy* (New York: Free Press, 1983), 475, 484–85, 492–94; and Robert Griffith, *The Politics of Fear: Joseph R. McCarthy and the Senate* (Amherst: University of Massachusetts Press, 1987), 270–317.

57. "Chances of War in '55," *U.S. News & World Report*, 24 December 1954, 17–19.

58. Gordon H. Chang, *Friends and Enemies: The United States, China, and the Soviet Union, 1948–1972* (Stanford: Stanford University Press, 1990), 117–18; and Richard C. Bush, *At Cross Purposes: US Taiwan Relations since 1942* (Armonk: M. E. Sharpe, 2004), 96–97.

59. Leonard H. D. Gordon, "United States Opposition to the Use of Force in the Taiwan Strait, 1954–1962," *Journal of American History* 72, no. 3 (1985): 638–39; and Nancy Bernkopf Tucker, ed., *China Confidential: American Diplomats and Sino-American Relations* (New York: Columbia University Press, 2001), 80–81.

60. George McTurnan Kahin and John W. Lewis, *The United States in Vietnam* (New York: Delta, 1967), 61; Marilyn B. Young, *The Vietnam Wars, 1945–1975* (New York: Harper Collins, 1991), 45–47; and George C. Herring, *America's Longest War: The United States and Vietnam, 1950–1975*, 4th ed. (New York: McGraw-Hill, 2002), 45–56.

61. Michael Schaller, *The United States and China: Into the Twenty-First Century* (New York: Oxford University Press, 2002), 148; and Chang, *Friends and Enemies*, 116.

62. "Prospects of War or Peace in the Formosa Area (From a News Conference Held by Secretary Dulles), 7 April 1955, WFK Papers, Carton 247, "Corr.—Dulles, John Foster (I); *Mutual Defense Treaty with China: Message from the President of the United States Transmitting a Mutual Defense Treaty between the United States of America and the Republic of China, Signed at Washington on December 2, 1954. 84th Congress, 1st Session, Executive A*, WFK Papers, Carton 150, Fol. "Committee on Foreign Relations, 1954–1956."

63. "Top Secret: Notes of a conversation between Foreign Minister George K.C. Yeh and Secretary of State John Foster Dulles, in which Ambassador Koo and Assistant Secretary of State Walter S. Robertson took part, 3:45 P.M., Wednesday, January 19, 1955, at the State Department," T'ang Wu Papers, Sterling Memorial Library MS 1435, Yale University (hereafter cited as T'ang

Wu Papers), Box 3, Fol. "Papers on US China Defense Treaty (1955), Part 1 of 3; and Gordon Chang. "To the Nuclear Brink: Eisenhower, Dulles, ad the Quemoy-Matsu Crisis," *International Security* 12, no. 4 (1988): 102–11.

64. Chang, "To the Nuclear Brink," 102–11; and Gordon H. Chang and He Di, "The Absence of War in the US-China Confrontation over Quemoy and Matsu in 1954–1955: Contingency, Luck, Deterrence," *American Historical Review* 98, no. 5 (1993): 1519.

65. "We Must Be Willing to Fight Now," *Collier's*, 1 October 1954, 24; and Montgomery and Johnson, *One Step from the White House*, 173, 185–87.

66. "Top Secret" (report on meeting between Sen. H. Alexander Smith and Foreign Minister George. K. C. Yeh on 3 February 1955), 1, 2, 4, T'ang Wu Papers, Box 3, Fol. "Papers on US China Defense Treaty (1955), Part 1 of 3."

67. "Address by Hon. William F. Knowland, of California, Before Indiana Republican Editorial Association, April 18, 1955," WFK Papers, Carton 299.

68. 84 Cong. Rec. 4284 (1955).

69. The Formosa Resolution also set a precedent for Eisenhower's approach to intervention in the Arab world and his 1957 Middle East Resolution, which would guide Lyndon Johnson's approach to the Gulf of Tonkin Resolution. Salim Yaqub, *Containing Arab Nationalism: The Eisenhower Doctrine and the Middle East* (Chapel Hill: University of North Carolina Press, 2004), 71, 90; and Brian VanDeMark, *Into the Quagmire: Lyndon Johnson and the Escalation of the Vietnam War* (New York: Oxford University Press, 1995), 78.

70. Tananbaum, *Bricker Amendment Controversy*, 25.

71. 84 Cong. Rec. 5205 (1955).

72. Nancy Bernkopf Tucker, *Strait Talk: United States Taiwan Relations and the Crisis with China* (Cambridge, MA: Harvard University Press, 2009), 17.

73. 83 Cong. Rec. 5115–17 (1953).

74. C. P. Fitzgerald, "East Asia after Bandung," *Far Eastern Survey* 24, no. 8 (1955): 113–19; George T. Yu, "China's Role in Africa," *Annals of the American Academy of Political and Social Science* 432, Africa in Transition (July 1977): 96–109; Chen Jian, "China and the Bandung Conference: Changing Perceptions and Representations," in *Bandung Revisited: A Conference's Legacy and Relevance for International Order*, ed. See Seng Tan and Amitav Acharya, (Singapore: National University of Singapore Press, 2008), 132–35.

75. George Kennan to James Byrnes, 22 February 1946, 9, Harry S. Truman Administration File, Elsey Papers, Harry S. Truman Library digital collection, http://www.trumanlibrary .org/whistlestop/study_collections/coldwar/documents/index.php?documentdate=1946-02 -22&documentid=6-6&studycollectionid=&pagenumber=9 (accessed 21 November 2011).

76. Arthur Dean, "United States Foreign Policy and Formosa," *Foreign Affairs* 33, no. 3 (1955): 360–75.

77. "Speech of Senator William F. Knowland, 64th Continental Congress of the Daughters of the American Revolution, Constitution Hall, Washington, D.C., 21 April 1955," WFK Papers, Carton 299.

78. William F. Knowland, statement before Subcommittee on UN Charter Revision (SF), 9 April 1955.

79. 84 Cong. Rec. 4434–35 (1955).

80. 83 Cong. Rec. 9426 (1954); and Goldman, *Crucial Decade*, 285.

81. "An Interview with Senator Knowland," *American Mercury* (September 1957), WFK Papers, Carton 299.

82. "The Behind the Scenes Struggle Over the Yalta Papers," *Newsweek*, 1 November 1954, 42–43.

83. William Henry Chamberlin, "From Yalta to Formosa," *Human Events*, 12 February 1955 (reprint), WFK Papers, State Department Files, Carton 285, "Human Events: From Yalta to Formosa."

84. John E. Grady, "Schlesinger Attacks Dulles for Yalta Papers Release, *Harvard Crimson*, 21 March 1955, http://www.thecrimson.com/article/1955/3/21/schlesinger-attacks-dulles-for -yalta-papers/ (accessed 31 May 2012); and Raymond J. Sontag, "Reflections on the Yalta Papers," *Foreign Affairs* 33, no. 4 (1955): 615.

85. Sen. Styles Bridges, 22 March 1955 press release, WFK Papers, State Department Files, Carton 285, "Yalta—State Department (II)."

86. "Text of General MacArthur's Statement," *New York Times*, 4 April 1955.

87. Staff of the Senate Republican Policy Committee, "Highlights of the Yalta Papers and Related Data" (March 1955), WFK Papers, State Department Files, Carton 285, "Yalta—State Department (I)."

88. Tucker, *China Threat*, 27–28.

89. Dept. of State Press Release No. 376, "Chinese Representation in the United Nations," 8 July 1954, WFK Papers, Carton 285, "Secretary of State, 1955–1956 (II)."

90. Quoted in Joshua Botts, Office of the Historian, US Department of State, "'Out of the Frying Pan Into the Fire': The Politics of the Yalta *FRUS*," paper prepared for delivery at the SHAFR Annual Conference in Alexandria, http://history.state.gov/frus150/research/politics-of -the-yalta-frus (accessed 31 May 2012).

91. Dulles to Knowland, 7 August 1956, WFK Papers, Carton 247, "Corr.—Dulles, John Foster (I)"; John Foster Dulles, advance copy (25 June 1957) of speech to be delivered before Lions International in San Francisco, 28 June 1957, WFK Papers, State Department Files, Carton 284, "Secretary of State Files, 1956–1958 (II)"; and Knowland to Dulles, 27 June 1957, WFK Papers, State Department Files, Carton 284, "Secretary of State Files, 1956–1958 (II)."

92. Emelyn Knowland Jewett, "My Father's Political Philosophy and Colleagues" (interview by Ruth Teiser), in *Remembering William F. Knowland* (1981), 2.

93. Buckley, *Up from Liberalism*, 27–28; Montgomery and Johnson, *One Step from the White House*, 248–49; Jewett, "My Father's Political Philosophy and Colleagues," 7; and Kurt Schuparra, *Triumph of the Right: The Rise of the California Conservative Movement, 1945–1966* (Armonk: M. E. Sharpe, 1998), 27–41.

94. Schuparra, *Triumph of the Right*, 39.

95. "The Knowland Story," 37.

96. Kohlberg to Knowland, 11 June 1956, WFK Papers, Carton 273. See also Montgomery and Johnson, *One Step from the White House*, 213–19; and Dudziak, "Brown as a Cold War Case," 20, 23.

Chapter 4

1. 81 Cong. Rec. 14204–6 (1950). See also 81 Cong. Rec. 14878–81 (1950).

2. Knowland to Thomas K. Finletter, 5 January 1951, William F. Knowland Papers, Bancroft Library, UC Berkeley, BANC MSS 75/97 c (hereafter cited as WFK Papers), Box 241.

3. Knowland to Harold E. Talbott, 9 July 1953, WFK Papers, Box 241; and T. A. Young (special asst. to secretary of the Army) to Knowland, 27 May 1954, WFK Papers, Box 241.

4. Welch to Knowland, 23 August 1953, WFK Papers, Box 241; Welch to James Gleason, 16 December 1953, WFK Papers, Box 241; Knowland to Harold E. Talbott (Sec. of Air Force), 31 December 1953, WFK Papers, Box 241; Elizabeth Foreman Lewis to Knowland, 16 July 1956, WFK Papers, Box 241; and Knowland, 30 July 1956 memo re: John Birch file, WFK Papers, Box 241. See also G. Edward Griffin, *The Life and Words of Robert Welch* (Thousand Oaks: American Media, 1975), 189.

5. Griffin, *Life and Words of Robert Welch*, 108.

6. Ibid., 159.

7. Kohlberg to Welch, 8 April 1952, Alfred Kohlberg Papers, Hoover Institution Archives, Stanford University (hereafter cited as Kohlberg Papers), Box 200.

8. Robert Welch, *May God Forgive Us* (Chicago: Henry Regnery, 1952), 61.

9. Ibid., 47.

10. Ibid., 97–98.

11. Ibid., 76.

12. Henry Regnery, advance pamphlet for Robert H. W. Welch Jr., *May God Forgive Us*, 1952, 3.

13. Henry Regnery to Alfred Kohlberg, 19 May 1952, Kohlberg Papers, Box 147.

14. Griffin, *Life and Words of Robert Welch*, 164–65.

15. Robert Welch, "If You Want It Straight . . . ," *American Opinion* 2, no. 11 (1959): 24–26, Gordon Hall and Grace Hoag Collection of Dissenting and Extremist Printed Propaganda, John Hay Library, Brown University, MS 76.23 (hereafter cited as Hall-Hoag Coll.), "John Birch Society: Robert Welch, Inc.," Box 10B.

16. Robert Welch to William F. Buckley Jr., 24 November 1958, William F. Buckley Papers, Yale University Manuscripts and Archives, MS 576 (hereafter cited as Buckley Papers), Part I, Box 6.

17. Robert Welch, *The Politician* (Belmont: Belmont Publishing, 1963), 6.

18. Welch, *May God Forgive Us!*, 45.

19. Welch, *May God Forgive Us!*, v, 97; and Robert Welch, "A Report to Friends Concerning *May God Forgive Us*," 15 November 1952, 2, Kohlberg Papers, Box 200.

20. Robert H. W. Welch Jr., *The Life of John Birch* (Chicago: Henry Regnery, 1954), 8–13.

21. Letters from John Birch, 21 September 1943 and 13 August 1945, WFK Papers, Box 241.

22. Letter from John Birch, 15 May 1943, WFK Papers, Box 241.

23. Letter from John Birch, March 1944, WFK Papers, Box 241.

24. Welch to Mr. and Mrs. George S. Birch, 20 July 1953, WFK Papers, Box 241.

25. Welch to William F. Knowland, 25 October 1953, WFK Papers, Box 241. For Welch's receipt of the Birch file, see Welch to William F. Knowland, 20 July 1953, WFK Papers, Box 241.

26. Welch, *Life of John Birch*, 56–65.

27. Copy of 18 June 1947, verbal report by Col. J. Wilfred Smith, 7, WFK Papers, Box 241.

28. Welch, *Life of John Birch*, 8, 40.

29. Government officials and bodies like HUAC stridently emphasized how communist atheism threatened an individual's freedom to worship, but even the most virulent among them did not proselytize to convert more souls to a specific religion. For example, see Committee on Un-American Activities, US House of Representatives, "100 Things You Know About Communism and Religion" (Washington, DC), Kohlberg Papers, Box 121.

30. Quoted in Welch, *Life of John Birch*, 21.

31. Welch, *Life of John Birch*, 15–16.

32. John S. Service, John Paton Davies, and John Carter Vincent were all sons of missionaries

sent to China. For an insightful account of interwar missionary life, see Grace Service, *Golden Inches: The China Memoir of Grace Service* (Berkeley: University of California Press, 1989).

33. Welch to Alfred Kohlberg, 7 June 1954, Kohlberg Papers, Box 200.

34. Welch, *Life of John Birch*, 4.

35. Welch, *Again, May God Forgive Us* (Belmont: Belmont Publishing, 1960), 125. In his essays and editorial pieces, Welch had the curious habit of referring to himself in the third person.

36. Chiang Kai-shek, "Letter to the Editor," 22 June 1956, *One Man's Opinion* 1, no. 4 (1956): 11, Hall-Hoag Coll. 1595, "John Birch Society: One Man's Opinion."

37. *One Man's Opinion* 2, no. 7 (1957).

38. Welch, *Again, May God Forgive Us*, 112–13.

39. Welch, *Again, May God Forgive Us*, 123, 175; and Cohen, *America's Response to China*, 118–19.

40. T. Christopher Jespersen, *American Images of China, 1931–1949* (Stanford: Stanford University Press, 1999); 24–44; and Robert E. Herzstein, *Henry R. Luce, Time, and the American Crusade in Asia* (New York: Cambridge University Press, 2005), 32–75.

41. Chiang famously converted to Methodism as a requirement for marriage to Soong Mei-ling. Her father had been baptized in 1880 in Wilmington, Delaware, while he was serving as the mess boy on a US Treasury Department patrol cutter. Emily Hahn, *The Soong Sisters* (New York: Doubleday, Doran & Co., 1941), 4–12; and Hannah Pakula, *The Last Empress: Madame Chiang Kai-shek and the Birth of Modern China* (New York: Simon & Schuster, 2009), 6.

42. Welch, *Again, May God Forgive Us*, 140, 151.

43. Ibid., 126.

44. Ibid., 172.

45. Ibid., 151.

46. Robert Welch to Alfred Kohlberg, 24 May 1957, Kohlberg Papers, Box 200.

47. Kohlberg to Welch, 20 May 1957, Kohlberg Papers, Box 200.

48. Welch wrote his own poetry and was an avid student of American verse. His biographer has suggested that had his life followed a different course, Welch might have been a professor of English literature at some quiet but 'honest' ivy-covered college." Griffin, *Life and Words of Robert Welch*, 117.

49. Robert Welch, "A Report to Friends," 1.

50. Robert Welch, "Dear Reader . . . ," *One Man's Opinion* 1, no. 1 (1956), quoted in Griffin, *Life and Words of Robert Welch*, 193.

51. *One Man's Opinion* 1, no. 5 (1956): 8–11, Hall-Hoag Coll. 1595, "John Birch Society: One Man's Opinion"; Robert Welch to Alfred Kohlberg 24 May 1957, Kohlberg Papers, Box 200; and Alfred Kohlberg to Robert Welch, 31 May 1957, Kohlberg Papers, Box 200.

52. Robert Welch, *The New Americanism: And Other Speeches and Essays* (Boston: Western Islands Publishers, 1966), 5.

53. Ibid., 7.

54. Ibid., 9 (original emphasis).

55. Ibid., 11.

56. Ibid., 4–6, 11, 13.

57. Ibid.,12.

58. Welch to William Schlamm, 30 June 1955, Buckley Papers, Part I, Box 4; Schlamm to Welch, 4 July 1955, Buckley Papers, Part I, Box 4; and Welch to William F. Buckley Jr., 6 June 1957, Buckley Papers, Part I, Box 4.

59. For a recent, laudatory assessment focusing only on Buckley's criticism of the John Birch

Society, see David Welch, "Where Have You Gone, Bill Buckley?," *New York Times*, 4 December 2012.

60. Robert Welch, "Why People Become Communists," *American Opinion* 1, no. 1 (1958): 15–27, Hall-Hoag Coll., "John Birch Society: Robert Welch, Inc.," Box 9B.

61. Lee Edwards, "Highlight of the Month In Washington," *American Opinion* 1, no. 4 (1958): 36–38, Hall-Hoag Coll., "John Birch Society: Robert Welch, Inc.," Box 9B.

62. Robert Welch, *The Blue Book of the John Birch Society* (Appleton: Western Islands, 28th printing, 2000), 66. See also Welch to William F. Buckley Jr., 28 April 1958, Buckley Papers, Part I, Box 6.

63. *American Opinion* 2, no. 1 (1959), Hall-Hoag Coll., "John Birch Society: Robert Welch, Inc.," Box 10B.

64. Griffin, *Life and Words of Robert Welch*, 251.

65. Welch to Alfred Kohlberg, 13 March 1959, Kohlberg Papers, Box 200.

66. Welch, *Blue Book*, 1.

67. Ibid., 3.

68. William E. Dunham (Home Office of John Birch Society) to Mrs. C. G. Vogt, 28 June 1963, Buckley Papers, Part I, Box 26, Fol. "John Birch Society, 1963."

69. The first volume of *The Decline of the West* was published in 1918, and the second in 1922. Oswald Spengler, *The Decline of the West*, trans. Charles Francis Atkinson (New York: A. A. Knopf, 1926–28).

70. Adam Paulsen, "Reconstruction or Decline? The Concept of Europe and Its Political Implications in the Works of Ernst Troeltsch and Oswald Spengler," in *European Self-Reflection Between Politics and Religion: The Crisis of Europe in the Twentieth Century*, ed. Lars. K. Bruun, Karl Christian Lammers, and Gert Sørensen, (New York: Palgrave Macmillan, 2013), 68–69.

71. John Farrenkopf, *Prophet of Decline: Spengler on World History and Politics* (Baton Rouge: Louisiana State Press, 2001), 55.

72. Welch, *Blue Book*, 37.

73. Ibid., 36.

74. H. Stuart Hughes, *Oswald Spengler: A Critical Estimate* (New York: Charles Scribner's Sons, 1952), 153.

75. P. Geyl, "Toynbee's System of Civilizations," review of *A Study of History* by Arnold Toynbee, *Journal of the History of Ideas* 9, no. 1 (1948): 93; and Edward Fiess, "Toynbee as Poet," review of *A Study of History* by Arnold Toynbee, *Journal of the History of Ideas* 16, no. 2 (1955): 275.

76. Welch, *Blue Book*, 34.

77. Revilo P. Oliver, "Arnold Toynbee," *American Opinion* 6, no. 6 (1963): 27–36, Hall-Hoag Coll., "John Birch Society: Robert Welch, Inc.," Box 9B; and Robert H. Montgomery, "Arthur Schlesinger, Jr.," *American Opinion* 5, no. 9 (1962): 7–18, Hall-Hoag Coll., "John Birch Society: Robert Welch, Inc.," Box 9B.

78. Farrenkopf, *Prophet of Decline*, 236–37; and Paulsen, "Reconstruction or Decline?," 76.

79. Robert Welch, "The Man the Communists Fear Most: Chiang Kai-shek," *One Man's Opinion* 2, no. 7 (1957), Hall-Hoag Coll. 1595, "John Birch Society: One Man's Opinion."

80. Welch, *Blue Book*, 146.

81. Kohlberg to Welch, 8 July 1957, Kohlberg Papers, Box 200; and Welch to Kohlberg, 24 January 1958, Kohlberg Papers, Box 200.

82. Welch, *Blue Book*, 61.

83. Ibid., 93.

84. Ibid., 63.

85. William J. Lederer and Eugene Burdick, *The Ugly American*, 3rd ed. (New York: W. W. Norton, 1999), 43–65.

86. George Orwell, *1984* (London: Harcourt, Brace, Jovanovich, Inc., 1949), 48.

87. Griffin, *Life and Words of Robert Welch*, 124.

88. Kevin P. Phillips, *The Emerging Republican Majority* (New Rochelle: Arlington House, 1969), 444, 450; and Douglas T. Miller and Marion Nowak, *The Fifties: The Way We Really Were* (New York: Doubleday, 1977), 99.

89. Examples include Alan Brinkley, "The Problem of American Conservatism," *American Historical Review* 99, no. 2 (1994): 418–19; Linda Kintz, *Between Jesus and the Market: The Emotions that Matter in Right-Wing America* (Durham: Duke University Press, 1997), 20–23; Kurt Schuparra, *Triumph of the Right: The Rise of the California Conservative Movement, 1945–1966* (Armonk: M. E. Sharpe, 1998), 42–58; Rick Perlstein, *Before the Storm: Barry Goldwater and the Unmaking of the American Consensus* (New York: Hill and Wang, 2001), 120–40; and Michelle M. Nickerson, *Mothers of Conservatism: Women and the Postwar Right* (Princeton: Princeton University Press, 2012).

90. McGirr, *Suburban Warriors*, 21.

91. Griffin, *Life and Words of Robert Welch*, 131–32.

92. John H. Rousselot, *Viewpoints From the John Birch Society*, Los Angeles: Pacifica Tape Library, 1961; 1 sound reel: analog, 3¾ ips, 2 track, 5 in., BANC Phonotape 3011c, Bancroft Library, UC Berkeley. See also Schuparra, *Triumph of the Right*, 53, 57.

93. Welch, *Blue Book*, 47.

94. Ibid., 48.

95. Ibid., 135.

96. Ibid., 50–51.

97. Darren Dochuck, *From Bible Belt to Sunbelt: Plain-Folk Religion, Grassroots Politics, and the Rise of Evangelical Conservatism* (New York: W. W. Norton, 2011), xi–xv, 141–43. See also Miller and Nowak, *The Fifties*, 98–99.

98. Charles E. Harvey, "Dr. Fifield of Los Angeles' First Congregational Church Against the Ecumenical Movement," *Southern California Quarterly* 53, no. 1 (1971): 67.

99. Eckard V. Toy Jr., "Spiritual Mobilization: The Failure of an Ultraconservative Ideal in the 1950's," *Pacific Northwest Quarterly* 61, no. 2 (1970): 77–78; and Alfred Kohlberg to Directors of the Committee, 30 August 1957, Buckley Papers, Part I, Box 3.

100. Lisa McGirr, *Suburban Warriors: The Origins of the New American Right* (Princeton: Princeton University Press, 2001), 172–73.

101. Harold R. Isaacs, *Scratches on Our Minds: American Images of China and India* (Armonk: M. E. Sharpe, 1980), 124–32.

102. Donald T. Critchlow, *Phyllis Schlafly and Grassroots Conservatism: A Woman's Crusade* (Princeton: Princeton University Press, 2005), 80–81.

103. "The John Birch Society (an outline of basic principles and beliefs)," "Additional Beliefs of Members of the John Birch Society," Political Ephemera Collection, Huntington Library, San Marino, Fol. 5, Box F44.

104. Welch, *Blue Book*, 153.

105. Ibid., 65.

106. Miller and Nowak, *The Fifties*, 248, 251–52.

107. Welch, *Blue Book*, 68–69, 92–93. See also "Audiotapes," Boxes 23–25, John Birch Society Records, John Hay Library, Brown University.

108. Respective authors: William Guy Carr, Robert H. Williams, Anthony Kubek, and

Paul C. Niepp. All titles from the Papers of Florence Ranuzzi, 1919–2001, Huntington Library, San Marino. Ranuzzi, along with her husband, ran Poor Richard's bookstore in Los Angeles, one of the major distributors of literature and right-wing paraphernalia approved by the John Birch Society.

109. Henry Regnery remained the preeminent name in conservative publishing, but it had competition from the newer presses like Pere Marquette, Liberty Bell, and Arlington House. Similar firms such as Devin-Adair and Caxton also throve during the 1960s.

110. Gerald Schomp, *Birchism Was My Business* (New York: Macmillan, 1970).

111. Ibid., 67–71.

112. Quoted in Schomp, *Birchism*, 74.

113. Alfred Kohlberg to Robert Welch, 30 November 1959, Kohlberg Papers, Box 17.

114. Schomp, *Birchism*, 73.

115. "John Birch Society: Impeach Earl Warren Committee," Hall-Hoag Coll. 3015; Hall-Hoag Coll. 0062, "John Birch Society: Committee to Warn of the Arrival of Communist Merchandise," Box 3B.

116. "Please, President Eisenhower, Don't!," enclosed in Robert Welch to Alfred Kohlberg, 29 June 1959, Kohlberg Papers, Box 200.

117. Charles Edison and Estelle Nash, "Committee for the Monroe Doctrine" (1965), Hall-Hoag Coll. 1144.

118. John Birch Society, Public Relations Department, *The Heartbeat of the Americanist Cause* [pamphlet] (Belmont, 1976).

119. Rosalie Gordon, "Nine Men Against America: The Supreme Court and Its Attack on American Liberties," *American Opinion* 4, no. 3 (1961), Hall-Hoag Coll., "John Birch Society: Robert Welch, Inc.," Box 10B; Revilo P. Oliver, "An Introduction to the Contemporary History of Latin America," *American Opinion* 4, no. 5 (1961), Hall-Hoag Coll., "John Birch Society: Robert Welch, Inc.," Box 10B; and Russell Kirk, "The Intemperate Educator," *American Opinion* 4, no. 10 (1961): 13–20, Hall-Hoag Coll., "John Birch Society: Robert Welch, Inc.," Box 10B.

120. Welch, *Blue Book*, 149.

121. William F. Buckley Jr., "The Uproar," *National Review*, 22 April 1961, 241.

122. "The John Birch Society" (1976 diagram), Hall-Hoag Coll.

123. John Birch Society, *Heartbeat*.

124. Welch, *Blue Book*, xix–xx

125. WOR-TV, transcript of "Ladies of the Press Meet Mr. Robert Welch, Founder of the John Birch Society. Moderator: Clifford Evans" (program air date: 24 October 1963), released 26 October 1963, 7, Buckley Papers, Part I, Box 26, Fol. "John Birch Society, 1963."

126. McGirr, *Suburban Warriors*, 20–110, 147–216; and Schuparra, *Triumph of the Right*, 3–41.

127. "Look at the Score," *One Man's Opinion* 2, no. 10 (1957): 1–10.

128. "*American Opinion* Scoreboard," *American Opinion* 1, no. 6 (1958): 23, Hall-Hoag Coll., "John Birch Society: Robert Welch, Inc.," Box 9B.

129. "A World Gone Crazy: A Panoramic Survey of the Degree of Communist Influence in Each of 107 Countries," *American Opinion* 3, no. 7 (1960), Hall-Hoag Coll., "John Birch Society: Robert Welch, Inc.," Box 9B: *American Opinion* 4, no. 7 (1961), Hall-Hoag Coll., "John Birch Society: Robert Welch, Inc.," Box 10B; *American Opinion* 5, no. 7 (1962), Hall-Hoag Coll., "John Birch Society: Robert Welch, Inc.," Box 9B; and *American Opinion* 9, no. 7 (1966), Hall-Hoag Coll., "John Birch Society: Robert Welch, Inc.," Box 10B.

130. Robert Welch, "The Truth About Vietnam" (1967), Hall-Hoag Coll. 0002, "John Birch Society: American Opinion," Box 1B.

131. Medford Evers, "Foreign Policy: Being Mao-Maoed by Big Brother," *American Opinion* 15, no. 3 (1972): 45, Hall-Hoag Coll., "John Birch Society: Robert Welch, Inc.," Box 9B.

132. G. Edward Griffin, *This is the John Birch Society: An Invitation to Membership* (Thousand Oaks: American Media, 1970), 6.

133. William F. Buckley to Robert Welch, 21 October 1960, Buckley Papers, Part I, Box 12; Buckley to Cap Beezley, 7 November 1960, Buckley Papers, Part I, Box 12; and memo to Buckley, re: John Birch Society, 26 March 1961 (for editorial conference of 28 March 1961), Buckley Papers, Part I, Box 14.

134. Goldwater to Buckley, 14 January 1962, Buckley Papers, Part I, Box 20.

135. Welch to Romney, 1 September 1962, Buckley Papers, Part I, Box 20.

136. John H. Rousselot, "Beliefs and Principles of the John Birch Society," extension of remarks, 12 June 1962, *Congressional Record*, Buckley Papers, Part I, Box 20.

137. *Village Voice*, 16 May 1963, 6.

138. Griffin, *Life and Words of Robert Welch*, 7. In his novel *Libra*, Don DeLillo dramatized the extremist reputation of the JBS through the character of right-wing General Ted Walker, whom DeLillo painted as the real target of Lee Harvey Oswald's actions in Dallas. Don DeLillo, *Libra* (New York: Viking, 1988).

139. Bob Dylan, "Talkin' John Birch Paranoid Blues," http://www.bobdylan.com/us/songs /talkin-john-birch-paranoid-blues (accessed 16 September 2012). See also Robert Welch, *The Politician*.

Chapter 5

1. Pres. John F. Kennedy, News Conference 59, 1 August 1963, Washington, DC, John F. Kennedy Presidential Library and Museum, http://www.jfklibrary.org/Research/Research-Aids /Ready-Reference/Press-Conferences/News-Conference-59.aspx (accessed 25 August 2014). Regarding Kennedy's attitude toward the Chinese, see Roderick MacFarquhar, ed., *Sino-American Relations, 1949–1971* (New York: Praeger Publishers, 1972), 182, 185–86.

2. Barry Goldwater, "The Best Way to Avoid War," statement to the American Society of Newspaper Editors, 18 April 1964, Washington, DC, reprinted in James M. Perry, *Barry Goldwater: A New Look at a Presidential Candidate* (Silver Spring: National Observer, 1964), 157.

3. James Burnham, "Some Proposals to a Goldwater Administration Concerning Foreign Affairs," *National Review*, 14 July 1964, 589.

4. William F. Buckley Jr. to Robert Welch, 21 October 1960, William F. Buckley Papers, Yale University Manuscripts and Archives, MS 576 (hereafter cited as Buckley Papers), Part I, Box 12.

5. Rick Perlstein, *Before the Storm: Barry Goldwater and the Unmaking of the American Consensus* (New York: Hill and Wang, 2001), 471–516; Lisa McGirr, *Suburban Warriors: The Origins of the New American Right* (Princeton: Princeton University Press, 2001), 143–46; and Kurt Schuparra, *Triumph of the Right: The Rise of the California Conservative Movement, 1945–1966* (Armonk: M. E. Sharpe, 1998), 101–2.

6. Barry M. Goldwater, *With No Apologies: The Personal and Political Memoirs of United States Senator Barry M. Goldwater* (New York: William Morrow, 1979), 34–36.

7. Goldwater, *With No Apologies*, 46.

8. Dean Smith, "Goldwater Assesses His Eight Presidents," *Platte Valley Review* 10, no. 1 (1982): 8, Arizona Historical Foundation, FE EPH GF-22.

9. Goldwater, *With No Apologies*, 49.

10. Bruce Schulman, *From Cotton Belt to Sunbelt: Federal Policy, Economic Development, and*

the *Transformation of the South, 1938-1980* (New York: Oxford University Press, 1991), 124-26; and Alfred de Grazia, *The Western Public: 1952 and Beyond* (Stanford: Stanford University Press, 1954), 7-59.

11. Stephen C. Shadegg, *Arizona Politics: The Struggle to End One-Party Rule* (Tempe: Arizona State University Press, 1986), 50-56.

12. Goldwater, *With No Apologies*, 59.

13. Campaign brochure from 1952, p. 63, William E. Saufley Collection, Arizona Historical Foundation, Tempe, MS FM MSS 63 (hereafter cited as Saufley Coll.), Subgroup I, SSGI, S. 1, Box 1, Fol. 1.

14. Shadegg, *Arizona Politics*, 61; William T. Hull, "Candidates, Parties, and Political Change: 1952 and the Beginning of a New Political Era in Arizona," 14, Arizona Historical Foundation, Tempe, FM MSM-63; and Lee Edwards, *Goldwater: The Man Who Made a Revolution* (Washington, DC: Regnery Books, 1995), 48.

15. Joe Puchendeux to Barry Goldwater, 17 July 1954, Saufley Coll., Subgroup 1, SSGII, S. 1, Box 3, Fol. 1.

16. Barry Goldwater to William Saufley, 18 February 1955, Saufley Coll., Subgroup I, SSGII, Box 3, Fol. 1.

17. Rob Wood and Dean Smith, *Barry Goldwater: The Biography of a Conservative* (New York: Avon Books Division, 1961), 15; Perry, *Barry Goldwater*, 62; and Goldwater, *With No Apologies*, 52, 68.

18. Shadegg, *Arizona Politics*, 62.

19. Goldwater, *With No Apologies*, 68, 175.

20. Ibid., 95-96.

21. F. B. Hubachek to Orme Lewis, 13 November 1958, Orme Lewis Collection, 1930s-80s, Arizona Historical Foundation, Tempe, MS FM MSS 27 (hereafter cited as Lewis Coll.), Box 6, Fol. 12.

22. Goldwater, *With No Apologies*, 99.

23. Barry M. Goldwater, *The Conscience of a Conservative* (Shepherdsville: Victor Publishing, 1960), book jacket.

24. Goldwater, *With No Apologies*, 100.

25. Perlstein, *Before the Storm*, 61; and Donald T. Critchlow, *Phyllis Schlafly and Grassroots Conservatism: A Woman's Crusade* (Princeton: Princeton University Press, 2005), 111.

26. Theodore H. White, *The Making of the President 1964: A Narrative History of American Politics in Action* (New York: Atheneum Publishers, 1965), 88.

27. Barry Goldwater, *Conscience of a Conservative*, rev. ed. (Princeton: Princeton University Press, 2007), 6 (original emphasis).

28. Ibid., 79.

29. Ibid., 82.

30. Goldwater, "The Best Way to Avoid War," 159.

31. Goldwater, *Conscience*, 89.

32. Ibid., 115.

33. Ibid.,107.

34. Ibid., 111-12, 114.

35. Ibid., 111-12, 114-15.

36. Ibid., 99.

37. Ibid., 22.

38. Ibid., 89, 91.

39. Mike Newberry, "The Trail of Goldwater's Youth Corps Leads to the Chiang Kai-shek Lobby," *The Worker*, 28 March 1961, 5.

40. Barry M. Goldwater, *Why Not Victory?* (New York: McGraw-Hill, 1962), 113-15, 117.

41. Ibid., 69-98.

42. Goldwater, *Conscience*, 108.

43. Goldwater, *Why Not Victory?*, 141-42.

44. Secret Memorandum: On the Question of the Chinese Representation in the United Nations at the Twenty-First Regular Session of the General Assembly, 1 August 1966, T'ang Wu Papers, Box 5, Fol. "Papers on the China Representation Issue at the UN (1958, 1966-1969)"; and Goldwater, *Why Not Victory?*, 144.

45. Goldwater, *Why Not Victory?*, 145.

46. Ibid., 149.

47. Ibid., 144-45.

48. Critchlow, *Phyllis Schlafly*, 112.

49. Wood and Smith, *Barry Goldwater*, 17, 102.

50. Barry M. Goldwater (with Jack Casserly), *Goldwater* (New York: Doubleday, 1988), 109-11; Geoffrey Kabaservice, *Rule and Ruin: The Downfall of Moderation and the Destruction of the Republican Party* (New York: Oxford University Press, 2012), 72-122; and Perlstein, *Before the Storm*, 356-70.

51. Quoted in Wood and Smith, *Barry Goldwater*, 150-52.

52. Barry Goldwater, "Conservatives Should Support Nixon," *Human Events*, 4 August 1960, 333-34. See also Critchlow, *Phyllis Schlafly*, 112-15.

53. Tony Smith to Theodore Humes, 3 July 1962, Theodore Humes Collection, Arizona Historical Foundation, Tempe, MS FM MSS 65 (hereafter cited as Humes Coll.), Box 1, Series 1, Fol. 1.

54. John M. Lupton to Goldwater, 12 November 1962, Humes Coll., Box 1, Series 1, Fol. 1.

55. Perlstein, *Before the Storm*, 171-200; McGirr, *Suburban Warriors*, 111-46; and Schuparra, *Triumph of the Right*, 83-84.

56. "Ben" to Theodore Humes, 19 December 1963, Humes Coll., Box 1, Series 1, Fol. 1; Thomas L. Phillips to Humes, 1 October 1963, Humes Coll., Box 1, Series 1, Fol. 1; and Humes to Russell Kirk, 24 January 1963, Humes Coll., Box 1, Series 1, Fol. 1.

57. "Let's Try Goldwater" (undated), 7, Arizona Historical Foundation MSM 1-600, Box 28, Fol. 7.

58. Phyllis Schlafly, *A Choice Not an Echo* (Alton: Pere Marquette Press, 1964), 78.

59. George Sokolsky, "These Days, " 2 August 1960, Saufley Coll., Subgroup 1, SSGI, S. 3, Box 1, Fol. 2.

60. "Ten Reasons Why We Should Select Goldwater for President," Humes Coll., Box 1, Series 2, Fol. 1.

61. Schlafly, *A Choice*, 115. See also Critchlow, *Phyllis Schlafly*, 121.

62. Critchlow, *Phyllis Schlafly*, 121.

63. Schlafly, *A Choice*, 4; and William Stueck, *The Wedemeyer Mission: American Politics and Foreign Policy During the Cold War* (Athens: University of Georgia Press, 192), 101-24.

64. CBS Television, Transcript: *60 Minutes*, Vol. XVIII, No. 35 (11 May 1986), 11, Barry M. Goldwater Papers, Personal and Political Series I, Arizona Historical Foundation, Tempe (hereafter cited as BG PP I), Box 9: Fol. 7.

65. Theodore Humes to J. W. Brandt, 20 August 1963, Humes Coll., Box 1, Series 1, Fol. 1; Wood and Smith, *Barry Goldwater*, 107; Goldwater, *With No Apologies*, 119; Critchlow, *Phyllis Schlafly*, 127; and McGirr, *Suburban Warriors*, 112-13.

66. Clare Boothe Luce, "The Crisis in Soviet-Chinese Relations: Commencement Address Delivered by the Hon. Clare Boothe Luce at St. John's University's 94th Annual Commencement, Jamaica, New York, Sunday, June 14, 1964" (press release), 1-2, Buckley Papers, Series 1, Box 31.

67. Ibid., 5-7.

68. Ibid., 10.

69. Goldwater, *Goldwater*, 127-28. See also Goldwater, *With No Apologies*, 72.

70. *Barry Goldwater Speaks Out on the Issues* (Washington, DC: Citizens for Goldwater-Miller Committee, 1964), 3-4, Arizona Historical Foundation, Tempe, FE-EPH-GP-31. See also Goldwater, *With No Apologies*, 152.

71. Barry Goldwater to William Saufley, 27 September, 1963, Saufley Coll., Subgroup 1, SSGII, S. 1, Box 1, Fol. 2.

72. Goldwater, *Where I Stand*, 59-65; and Edwards, *Goldwater*, 210. See also undated brochure, Saufley Coll., Subgroup I, SSGI, S. 1, Box 1, Fol. 1; and *Barry Goldwater Speaks Out on the Issues*, 5.

73. *Barry Goldwater Speaks Out on the Issues*, 11.

74. Goldwater, *Where I Stand*, 49.

75. Goldwater, *Where I Stand*, 23-24, 49, 50, 53, 90-91; and Barry Goldwater (speech delivered in California, 1964), Barry M. Goldwater Papers, Presidential Campaign—"W" Series, Arizona Historical Foundation, Tempe, Box 12, Fol. 12.

76. Goldwater (speech delivered in California, 1964); and Goldwater, *Where I Stand*, 71.

77. Press release, 23 March 1964, Humes Coll., Series 3, Fol. 2.

78. White, *Making of the President*, 297-300.

79. Ibid., 315.

80. Barry Goldwater, acceptance speech at 1964 GOP National Convention, reprinted in Goldwater, *Where I Stand*, 13.

81. Goldwater, *Where I Stand*, 13, 28-29; and *Barry Goldwater Speaks Out on the Issues*, 11 (original emphasis).

82. Frank R. Donovan, *The Americanism of Barry Goldwater* (New York: Macfadden-Bartell, 1964), 176. See also "Let's Try Goldwater," 7, Arizona Historical Foundation MSM-327.

83. *Barry Goldwater Speaks Out on the Issues*, 11.

84. Gordon H. Chang, "Asian Americans and Politics: Some Perspectives from History," in *Asian Americans and Politics: Perspectives, Experiences, Prospects*, ed. Gordon H. Chang (Stanford: Stanford University Press, 2001), 21-28.

85. For a synopsis of the Chinese Consolidated Benevolent Association's antileftist activity during the 1950s and 1960s, see Mae M. Ngai, "Legacies of Exclusion: Illegal Chinese Immigration During the Cold War Years," *Journal of American Ethnic History* 18, no. 1 (1998): 15-16, 27.

86. Goldwater, *Where I Stand*, 52-53; and Goldwater with Casserly, *Goldwater*, 224.

87. Clare Boothe Luce quoted in the *Arizona Republic*, 12 July 1964.

88. Jackie Robinson quoted in Morrie Ryskind, "Calling the Turn" (syndicated newspaper column), Saufley Coll., Subgroup 1, SSGI, S. 3, Box 1, Fol. 2. See also "The New Men," *New Republic*, 25 July 1964, 40-42.

89. Goldwater with Casserly, *Goldwater*, 154.

90. Barry Goldwater, "Remarks Made by Senator Barry Goldwater before the Platform

Committee of the Republican National Convention, July 10, 1964," reprinted in Goldwater, *Where I Stand*, 119–26; White, *Making of the President*, 198; Victory Lasky, "Say It Straight," *Arizona Republic*, 12 July 1964, Saufley Coll., Subgroup 1, SSGI, S. 3, Box 1, Fol. 2; and Stephen C. Shadegg, *Winning's A Lot More Fun* (London: MacMillan 1969), 12.

91. Firing Line Collection, Hoover Institution Archives, Stanford University, Episode 013 Transcript: "The Future of the Republican Party (taped 26 May 1966), 11–16, 25–26.

92. Goldwater with Casserly, *Goldwater*, 197–214; Perlstein, *Before the Storm*, 413–15; and Kabaservice, *Rule and Ruin*, 115–22.

93. Goldwater, *With No Apologies*, 179.

94. Campaign organizer Theodore Humes wrote after the election, "Our biggest need is a salesmen for conservatism, and Barry was just our only focal point, he happened along when the movement ripened, and he was charismatic but not anywhere near profound enough to carry a campaign; he was trite, banal, etc." Theodore Humes to Bill Gill, 1 August 1965, Humes Coll., Box 1, Series 1, Fol. 2.

95. Hon. John M. Ashbrook, "The Red China Lobby" (reprint of speech delivered 28 June 1966), *Congressional Record*, 1, Right Wing Pamphlet Collection, Yale Manuscripts and Archives, MS 775, Box 10, Fol. "China Lobby."

96. Miriam and Walter Judd, Christmas letter, December 1967, Buckley Papers, Series 1, Box 51, Fol. "Judd, Walter."

97. Firing Line Collection, Hoover Institution Archives, Episode 029 Transcript: "Communist China and the United Nations: a debate with Max Lerner and William F. Buckley, Jr. on Firing Line with William F. Buckley" (taped 19 September 1966), 18, 29–30; and John B. Judis, *William F. Buckley, Jr.: Patron Saint of Conservatives* (New York: Simon & Schuster, 1988), 265–66.

98. Firing Line Collection, Hoover Institution Archives, Episode 068 Transcript: "Firing Line: Senator Charles Percy—'A Foreign Policy for the GOP'" (taped 11 September 1967), 11.

99. Transcript: "Meet the Press," 13 June 1965, 2–3, Buckley Papers, Part I, Box 35, Fol. "Goldwater, Barry."

100. Goldwater to Albert Wedemeyer, 21 October 1966, Barry M. Goldwater Papers, Personal and Political Series II, Arizona Historical Foundation, Tempe (hereafter cited as BG PP II), Box 1P, Fol. 46.

101. Statement by Secretary of State Dean Rusk before Senate Preparedness Subcommittee on 25 August 1966, Dept. of State Publication 8139, General Foreign Policy Series 215 (Washington, DC: Office of Media Services, Bureau of Public Affairs, September 1966), 3–4.

102. "American Investment Climate in Taiwan," 16 November 1966, pp. 1–3, BG PP I, Box 1, Fol. 14; and *A Story of Economic Success* (Taipei: China Publishing, 1966), BG PP I, Box 1, Fol. 14.

103. Goldwater to Brig. Gen. William F. Pitts, 2 February 1967, BG PP II, Box 1P, Fol. 46; and Albert Wedemeyer to Goldwater, 16 November 1966, BG PP II, Box 1P, Fol. 46.

104. Itinerary for 6–8 January 1967, BG PP I, Box 1, Fol. 14; and Barry M. Goldwater Photographs, Arizona Historical Foundation, Tempe, Fol. GP-437 to Fol. GP-474 (Taipei, January 1967), Box: GP-300 to GP-617 (Political).

105. Moyca Manoil to Frances Kerr (USIS), undated report, BG PP II, Box 1P, Fol. 46.

106. Goldwater to President and Mme Chiang Kai-shek, 17 January 1967, BG PP II, Box 1P, Fol. 46.

107. Goldwater to President and Mme Chiang Kai-shek, 17 January 1967, BG PP II, Box 1P, Fol. 46; Mme Chiang Kai-shek to Goldwater, undated, BG PP I Box 1, Fol. 14; Ambassador Chow Shu-kai to Goldwater, 25 November 1967, BG PP II, Box 1P, Fol. 46; and Goldwater to President and Mme Chiang, 13 June 1968, BG PP II, Box 1P, Fol. 46.

108. Chu Ching-tong to Goldwater, 29 April 1967, BG PP II, Box 1P, Fol. 46. See also Tsuh-ming Lee Chen to Goldwater, 10 January 1967, BG PP II, Box 1P, Fol. 46.

109. Robert Welch, *The Truth About Vietnam* (Belmont: American Opinion, 1967), 4.

110. Ibid., 3.

111. Ibid.,19.

112. American Experience (PBS), *Timeline: Nixon's China Game*, http://www.pbs.org/wgbh /amex/china/timeline/timeline5.html#1968 (accessed 2 January 2013).

113. Rockefeller quoted in James Mann, *About Face: A History of America's Curious Relation-ship with China, from Nixon to Clinton* (New York: Alfred A. Knopf, 1999), 18.

114. Michael Schaller, *The United States and China: Into the Twenty-First Century* (New York: Oxford University Press, 2002), 173; Nancy Bernkopf Tucker, *Strait Talk: United States Taiwan Relations and the Crisis with China* (Cambridge, MA: Harvard University Press, 2009), 28; and William Burr, ed., *The Kissinger Transcripts: The Top Secret Talk with Beijing and Moscow* (New York: New Press, 1998), 9–11.

115. Richard M. Nixon, "Asia After Viet Nam," *Foreign Affairs* 46, no. 1 (1967): 111; Richard Nixon, *RN: The Memoirs of Richard Nixon* (New York: Grosset & Dunlap, 1978), 282; Patrick Tyler, *A Great Wall: Six Presidents and China* (New York: Public Affairs, 1999), 41; and Nancy Bernkopf Tucker, "Taiwan Expendable? Nixon and Kissinger Go to China," *Journal of American History* 92, no. 1 (2005): 116–17.

116. Tucker, *Strait Talk*, 46–48.

117. William F. Buckley Jr. to Marvin Liebman, 28 July 1961, pp. 2–3, Buckley Papers, Part I, Box 15, Fol. "Liebman, Marvin (1961)."

118. Tanzania was pointed to as an example of the latter. Its delegates had openly celebrated after the General Assembly voted to admit the PRC into the UN. Firing Line Collection, Hoover Institution Archives, Episode S0028 Transcript: "Firing Line: The American Conservatives and Mr. Nixon" (taped 29 October 1971), 1, 2.

119. Firing Line Collection, Hoover Institution Archives, Episode S0023 Transcript: "Firing Line: The Meaning of the China Vote" (taped 29 October 1971), 3–5.

120. Walter H. Judd to William F. Buckley Jr., 22 November 1972, Buckley Papers, Part II, Series I, Box 172, Fol. "Judd, Walter"; and Walter H. Judd to William F. Buckley Jr., 5 January 1972, 2, Buckley Papers, Part II, Series I, Box 172, Fol. "Judd, Walter."

121. Firing Line Collection, Episode S0028 Transcript, 2–3.

122. Firing Line Collection, Hoover Institution Archives, Episode 000a Transcript: "Firing Line: American Conservatives Confront 1972" (taped 5 January 1972), 1–6, 21.

123. "An Address by Senator Barry Goldwater of Arizona. 'Salute to the President's Dinner,' Atlanta, Georgia, November 9, 1971" (press release, 10 November 1971), pp. 2–3, Buckley Papers, Series I, Box 147, Fol. "Goldwater, Barry."

124. James N. Werring to the editor, *Arizona Republic*, 23 January 1972, 7, Saufley Coll., Sub-group 1, SSGI, Box 1, Fol. 3.

125. Goldwater, *With No Apologies*, 233–34, 239; and Tucker, *Strait Talk*, 75.

126. Firing Line Collection, Episode 000a Transcript, 21.

127. Ibid., 6.

128. "Joint Statement Following Discussions With Leaders of the People's Republic of China" (Shanghai: 27 February 1972) in US Department of State, *Foreign Relations of the United States, 1969–1976, Vol. XVII, China, 1969–72* (Washington, DC: US Government Printing Office, 2006), document 203, 812–16.

129. Firing Line Collection, Hoover Institution Archives, Episode S0039 Transcript: "Firing Line: The Meaning of China" (taped 29 February 1972), 13.

130. Firing Line Collection, Hoover Institution Archives, Episode S0047 Transcript: "Firing Line: The Implications of the China Trip" (taped 5 May 1972), 3–5.

131. Goldwater, *With No Apologies*, 240, 242; William F. Buckley Jr. to Barry Goldwater, 24 March 1972, Buckley Papers, Series I, Box 147, Fol. "Goldwater"; and Barry Goldwater to William F. Buckley Jr., 28 March 1972, Buckley Papers, Series I, Box 147, Fol. "Goldwater."

132. Barry Goldwater to William F. Buckley Jr., 27 July 1973, Buckley Papers, Part II, Series I, Box 147, "Fol. "Goldwater, Barry (1972–1975)."

133. Nixon, *RN*, 1068.

134. Greg Mitchell, *Tricky Dick and the Pink Lady: Richard Nixon vs. Helen Gahagan Douglas—Sexual Politics and the Red Scare, 1950* (New York: Random House, 1998); and Herbert S. Parmet, *Richard Nixon and His America* (Boston: Little, Brown, 1990), 151–251.

135. Schuparra, *Triumph of the Right*, 66–68; and Perlstein, *Before the Storm*, 165–67.

136. Buckley to Barry Goldwater, 3 July 1974, Buckley Papers, Part II, Series I, Box 147, "Fol. "Goldwater, Barry (1972–1975)."

137. Iwan Morgan, "Richard Nixon, Reputation, and Watergate," in Michael A. Genovese and Iwan W. Morgan, *Watergate Remembered: The Legacy for American Politics* (New York: Palgrave MacMillan, 2012), 110.

138. Arthur M. Schlesinger Jr., *The Imperial Presidency* (Boston: Houghton Mifflin, 1973), 269–73. See also Mark J. Rozell, "Executive Privilege: Secrecy vs. Accountability," in *Watergate and the Resignation of Richard Nixon: Impact of a Constitutional Crisis*, ed. Harry P. Jeffrey and Thomas Maxwell-Long (Washington, DC: CQ Press, 2004), 63, 67–68; and Stanley I. Kutler, *The Wars of Watergate: The Last Crisis of Richard Nixon* (New York: Alfred A. Knopf, 1990), 126–27, 130–60.

139. Barry Goldwater, "Conscience of the Right," interview with Harry Riesener, 9 March 1980, Arizona State University, Hayden Library Microforms, REC S6 Mar. 1980, No. 1; and Smith, "Goldwater Assesses His Eight Presidents," 14.

140. Nancy Bernkopf Tucker, *Taiwan, Hong Kong, and the United States, 1945–1992: Uncertain Friendships* (New York: Twayne Publishers, 1994), 126.

141. Goldwater to William Steiger, 29 January 1975, Buckley Papers, Series II, Part I, Box 147, Fol. "Goldwater, Barry (1972–1975)."

142. Mann, *About Face*, 66.

143. "Goldwater Upholds Strong Delegation," *China Post*, 14 April 1954, BG PP II, Box 4P, Fol. 28; and Tucker, *Strait Talk*, 73.

144. Harry Harding, *A Fragile Relationship: The United States and China since 1972* (Washington, DC: Brookings Institution, 1992), 47; and Burr, *Kissinger Transcripts*, 371.

145. Sister Agnes U. Higgins to Goldwater, 16 April 1975, BG PP II, Box 4P, Fol. 28; and Shu Wan Shen to Goldwater, 24 April 1975, BG PP II, Box 4P, Fol. 28.

146. Long to Goldwater, 16 April 1975, BG PP II, Box 4P, Fol. 28.

147. Quoted in Burr, *Kissinger Transcripts*, 372.

148. Dana and Phyllis Craig to Goldwater, 15 April, 1975, BG PP II, Box 4P, Fol. 28; and Nancy Atland Teng to Goldwater, 15 April 1975, BG PP II, Box 4P, Fol. 28.

149. Firing Line Collection, Hoover Institution Archives, Episode S0255 Transcript: "Firing Line: 'What's Going on in China?'" (taped 4 November 1979), 4.

150. Mann, *About Face*, 72–73.

151. *New York Times*, "US and China Opening Full Relations; Teng Will Visit Washington on Jan. 29," 16 December 1978.

152. Sen. Bob Dole to members of Congress, 15 January 1979, Barry M. Goldwater Papers, Personal and Political Series III, Arizona Historical Foundation, Tempe, Box 14, Fol. 3; Firing Line Collection, Hoover Institution Archives, Episode S0354 Transcript: "Firing Line: 'The Recognition of China'" (taped 18 January 1979), 12; George F. Will, "A Price for Taiwan," *Washington Post*, 21 December 1978; and Patrick J. Buchanan, "Throwing Taiwan to the Wolves," *New York Daily News*, 24 December 1978.

153. Barry M. Goldwater, "Another View on China" [sound recording of speech delivered in Phoenix on 22 December 1978], (Encyclopedia Americana/CBS News Audio Resource Library, 1978).

154. Barry M. Goldwater, "We Are the Last Hope for Sound Free Government" [sound recording of speech delivered at Republican National Convention, 16 August 1976] (Encyclopedia Americana/CBS News Audio Resource Library, 1976).

155. David F. Schmitz and Vanessa Walker, "Jimmy Carter and the Policy of Human Rights: The Development of a Post-Cold War Foreign Policy," *Diplomatic History* 28, no. 1 (2004): 113–43; and Douglas Brinkley, "Bernath Lecture: The Rising Stock of Jimmy Carter: The 'Hands on' Legacy of Our Thirty-Ninth President," *Diplomatic History* 20, no. 4 (1996): 518–29.

156. Brinkley, "Bernath Lecture," 522.

157. Li Jie, "China's Domestic Politics and the Normalization of Sino-U.S. Relations, 1969–1979," in *Normalization of U.S.-China Relations: An International History*, ed. William C. Kirby, Robert S. Ross, and Gong Li (Cambridge, MA: Harvard University Asia Center, 2005), 82–83.

158. Warren I. Cohen, *America's Response to China: A History of Sino-American Relations* (New York: Columbia University Press, 2010), 223.

159. Mann, *About Face*, 75–89, 94.

160. "Excerpts from Speeches by Vance and Brzezinski on America's China Policy," *New York Times*, 16 January 1979; and Harding, *A Fragile Relationship*, 77–81.

161. Department of State, "Diplomatic Relations with the People's Republic of China and Future Relations with Taiwan," December 1978 news release, reproduced in *Normalization of U.S.-China Relations: A Collection of Documents and Press Coverage* (New York: China Council of the Asia Society, January 1979), 28–30.

162. Harding, *A Fragile Relationship*, 84–85.

163. Goldwater to US Senators, 6 June 1979, Barry Goldwater Bills Sponsored Series, Barry M. Goldwater Papers, Arizona Historical Foundation, Tempe (hereafter cited as BG BSS), Box 14, Fol. 45.

164. Quoted in Alona E. Evans, "Goldwater v. Carter," *American Journal of International Law* 74, no. 2 (1980): 442.

165. Evans, "Goldwater v. Carter," 446.

166. *Barry Goldwater et al. v. James Earl Carter, President of the United States, et al.*, no. 79–856, 444 US 996 (1979), http://caselaw.lp.findlaw.com/cgi-bin/getcase.pl?court=US&vol=444&invol=996 (accessed 31 May 2011); and Barry M. Goldwater, *China and the Abrogation of Treaties* (Washington, DC: Heritage Foundation, 1978), BG BSS, Box 14, Fol. 45.

167. Goldwater to Jimmy Carter, 18 October 1979, BG BSS, Box 14, Fol. 76.

168. Goldwater, "Another View on China."

169. Statement of J. Terry Emerson before the Heritage Foundation Editorial Seminar on China Relations, 4 December 1978, BG BSS, Box 14, Fol. 45.

170. *Goldwater v. Carter*. Justice Rehnquist provided a more specific opinion, calling the

issue a political question inappropriate for judicial resolution. On the other hand, Justice Brennan did consider decision-making authority as a matter of constitutional law and under the court's jurisdiction. His opinion was in the minority, however.

171. "Taiwan Relations Act, 1979," http://china.usc.edu/ShowArticle.aspx?articleID=393&A spxAutoDetectCookieSupport= (accessed 31 May 2011). See also Tucker, *Taiwan, Hong Kong, and the United States*, 134, and *Strait Talk*, 116–26; and Robert G. Sutter, *U.S.-Chinese Relations: Perilous Past, Pragmatic Present* (New York: Rowman & Littlefield, 2010), 80.

172. Tucker, *Strait Talk*, 121.

173. Schaller, *United States and China*, 190; and Tucker, *Taiwan, Hong Kong, and the United States*, 134.

174. Harding, *A Fragile Relationship*, 86–87.

175. Taylor Jones, op-ed cartoon, BG BSS, Box 14, Fol. 45.

176. Barry Goldwater, speech of 31 January 1991, pp. 1–2, BG PP II, Box 14P, Fol. 16P.

177. Barry Goldwater, quoted in Kathryn M. Olson, "From There to Eternity: Reagan's Rhetorical Attempts to Transform Collective Memory of Goldwater's 1964 Campaign to Secure Conservatism's Continued Ascent" (University of Wisconsin, Department of Communication, 1994), 6, Arizona Historical Foundation, Tempe, MSM-305.

Conclusion

1. Seweryn Bialer and Joan Afferica, "Reagan and Russia," *Foreign Affairs* 61, no. 2 (1982): 249–71; Norman Podhoretz, "The Reagan Road to Détente," *Foreign Affairs* 63, no. 3, America and the World 1984 (1984): 447–64; and Nancy Bernkopf Tucker, *Strait Talk: United States Taiwan Relations and the Crisis with China* (Cambridge, MA: Harvard University Press, 2009), 127.

2. Harry Harding, *A Fragile Relationship: The United States and China since 1972* (Washington, DC: Brookings Institution, 1992), 109; and Tucker, *Strait Talk*, 130–32.

3. Michael Schaller, *The United States and China: Into the Twenty-First Century* (New York: Oxford University Press, 2002), 193–96; James Mann, *About Face: A History of America's Curious Relationship with China, from Nixon to Clinton* (New York: Alfred A. Knopf, 1999), 116–19; Robert G. Sutter, *U.S.-Chinese Relations: Perilous Past, Pragmatic Present* (New York: Rowman & Littlefield, 2010); and Nancy Bernkopf Tucker, *Taiwan, Hong Kong, and the United States: Uncertain Friendships* (New York: Twayne Publishers, 1994), 149.

4. Robert S. Ross, *Negotiating Cooperation: The United States and China, 1969–1989* (Stanford: Stanford University Press, 1995), 163, 169; Tucker, *Strait Talk*, 136; and Mann, *About Face*, 119.

5. Mann, *About Face*, 128–29.

6. Harding, *A Fragile Relationship*, 107–8.

7. "Text of U.S. China Communiqué on Taiwan," *New York Times*, 18 August 1982; and Mann, *About Face*, 126–27.

8. Tucker, *Strait Talk*, 148

9. Warren I. Cohen, *America's Response to China: A History of Sino-American Relations* (New York: Columbia University Press, 2010), 228.

10. Mann, *About Face*, 129–32.

11. Tucker, *Strait Talk*, 153–55; and Sutter, *U.S.-Chinese Relations*, 82–84, 93–94.

12. Tucker, *Strait Talk*, 129.

13. Mann, *About Face*, 134–35; Cohen, *America's Response to China*, 229; and Harding, *A Fragile Relationship*, 147–49.

14. Ross, *Negotiating Cooperation*, 202, 206–14; and Sutter, *US-Chinese Relations*, 89.

15. Mann, *About Face*, 136–139; and Schaller, *United States and China*, 196.

16. Ross, *Negotiating Cooperation*, 240.

17. Kim Phillips-Fein, *Invisible Hands: The Making of the Conservative Movement From the New Deal to Reagan* (New York: Norton, 2009), 236–62.

18. Andrew Ross, *Fast Boat to China: High-Tech Outsourcing and the Consequences of Free Trade—Lessons from Shanghai* (New York: Vintage Books, 2006), 240.

19. Firing Line Collection, Hoover Institution Archives, Stanford University, Episode S0524 Transcript: "Is There a New China?" (taped 24 September 1982), 17.

20. Ronald Reagan, *An American Life: The Autobiography* (New York: Simon & Schuster, 1990), 368–69; Tucker, *Strait Talk*, 161; and Mann, *About Face*, 145.

21. Barry Goldwater, address delivered at American Graduate School of International Management, 31 January 1991, Barry M. Goldwater Papers, Personal and Political Series II, Arizona Historical Foundation, Tempe, Box 16P, Fol. 16.

22. H. Bradford Westerfield, *Foreign Policy and Party Politics: Pearl Harbor to Korea* (New Haven: Yale University Press, 1955), 245.

23. NHLiberty4Paul, "John Huntsman's Values," http://www.youtube.com/watch?v=tZeVqj-t1Uo (accessed 6 January 2013).

24. Commission on Presidential Debates, Transcript: "President Barack Obama and Former Gov. Mitt Romney Participate in a Candidates Debate, Hofstra University, Hempstead, NY," 16 October 2012, http://www.debates.org/index.php?page=october-1–2012-the-second-obama-romney-presidential-debate (accessed 6 January 2013).

25. Commission on Presidential Debates, Transcript: "President Barack Obama and Former Gov. Mitt Romney Participate in a Candidates Debate, Lynn University, Boca Raton, FL," 22 October 2012, http://www.debates.org/index.php?page=october-22–2012-the-third-obama-romney-presidential-debate (accessed 6 January 2012).

26. Irving Kristol, "The Neoconservative Persuasion," *Weekly Standard*, 23 August 2003, 23–25.

Index